Marriage and Death Notices

from Upper S.C. Newspapers
1843-1865

Abstracts from Newspapers in Laurens, Spartanburg, Newberry and Lexington Districts

Abstracted By:

Brent Holcomb, C.R.S., C.G

Please Direct All Correspondence and Book Orders to:

Southern Historical Press, Inc.
PO Box 1267
375 West Broad Street
Greenville, SC 29602-1267
or
southernhistoricalpress@gmail.com

----

southernhistoricalpress.com

ISBN #0-89308-043-8

Printed in the United States of America

INTRODUCTION

These abstracts are from all of the newspapers which could be located from the districts of Spartanburg, Laurens, Newberry, and Lexington, South Carolina, issues before 1866. Of course, in any state marriage notices and obituaries are important. Marriage records in South Carolina are especially important, because with few exceptions there are no official marriage records before the year 1911. These marriage notices and obituaries are not only from all over the state of South Carolina (nearly every district being represented by at least one time), but from the adjoining states of North Carolina and Georgia, and notices of persons who had left the state and gone to Alabama, Mississippi, Texas, California, etc.

Because these notices are so valuable, the location of each issue is given in brackets. If no location is given, the issue can be seen (either the original or a microfilm copy) at the South Caroliniana Library, University of South Carolina, Columbia, S. C. The abbreviations used are Duke--Perkins Library, Duke University, Durham, N. C.; UNC--Wilson Library, University of North Carolina, Chapel Hill, N. C.; Library of Congress, Washington, D. C.; Laurens--Laurens County Library, Laurens, S. C.

Brent Holcomb, G. R. S.
Clinton, S. C.
July 16, 1976

CONTENTS

Issue of November 26, 1845 [Duke]
Departed this life on the 15th inst., at the residence of her father near this village, Catherine, 2nd daughter of John G. and Sarah Klinch.

From the Greenville Mountaineer
Died at the residence of her husband at Laurens C. H., S. C. on the 7th inst, Mrs. Ann
H. Bailey, wife of Dr. N. V. Bailey, formerly of Charleston, in the 19th year of her
age.
Died at Laurens C. H., S. C. on Thursday the 18th inst., Mrs. F. E. Wright, wife of
Major J. D. Wright in the 20th year of her age.

Issue of December 3, 1845 [Duke]
Married on the 25th inst. by the Rev. Henry Reid, Mr. William Lindsay to Miss Mary
E. Gill, all of this district.

Issue of December 10, 1845 [Duke]
Married on the evening of the 3rd inst., by Rev. J. L. Young, Young T. S. Willson
of Newberry District, to Miss M. A. Caroline, eldest daughter of William Dean, Esq. of
this District.
ANTOHER REVOLUTIONARY PATRIOT GONE!
Died at his residence in this District, on the 30th ult., Samuel Fraser[?] Senr...
born 4 May 1763, served in the latter part of the Revolution under Pickens, also at
Ninety Six...John M'Hay was killed by the Tories somewhere on Little River...Mr. Franks
received two hacks from Tory Holmes.

Issue of June 16, 1848 [USC]
Died on 4th May, at his residence in Newberry District, Robert Maxwell, Esq.

Issue of July 7, 1848 [USC]
Married on the 29th ult by Rev. T. Robinson, Mr. Thos L. Badget to Miss Susan Kenn-
ady.
Died in this District on the 8th ult., in the 34th year of her age, Mrs. Elizabeth
Coleman, wife of William B. Coleman and daughter of Abram and Nancy Thompson...member
of the Associate Reformed Church.

Issue of September 8, 1848 [USC]
Married on the 5th instant by Rev. S. B. Lewers, Maj. S. A. Goodman to Miss Margaret
E. Watts of Laurens District.
On the 28th ult, by Rev. J. L. Anderson, Mr. Draton Kernals to Miss Roda Wakefield,
all of Laurens.

Issue of September 15, 1848 [USC]
Married on the 7th inst, by Rev. Silas Knight, Mr. Joshua Cook to Miss Margaret E.
Blakely, both of Greenville District.
Married on the 10th inst by Rev. T. Robinson, Mr. John A. Glenn to Miss Ann J.
McAfee, both of Laurens District.
Departed this life at his residence in Union Village, on the 20th August 1848, after
a long protracted illness, Col. Richard S. Wright, in the 31st year of his age...brought
up in Laurens District, settled in Union C. H. in 1842...commenced a practice of law...
at the threshold of his fame, the pride of his aged parents has been taken away...leaves
a broken hearted wife.

Issue of September 29, 1848 [USC]
Died in Chickasaw County, Mississippi of Congestive Fever, on the 24th day of August,
Mrs. Tabitha Bowen, wife of Capt. George Bowen of this District, and for several years
a resident of our village. At the organization of the Presbyterian Church at Laurens
C. H. on 1 Apr 1832, she professed her faith...leaves husband and children.
Died on the 10th inst, at the residence of his son, near Centreville, Richard Jones,
aged 85 years.

Issue of October 13, 1848 [USC]
Married on the 26th September by the Rev. J. C. Vaughan, Mr. John G. Turner to Miss
Savannah A. Boazman, all of Laurens District.

Issue of October 20, 1848 [USC]
Died at his residence at Laurens C. H., Andrew Adamson...leaves a wife.

Issue of November 17, 1848 [USC]
Married on the 14th inst, by Rev. S. Knight, Mr. James Bruce to Miss Emily Brown,
all of this District.

Married on Tuesday evening the 24th ult, by Rev. S. B. Lewers, Mr. John McClellan of Newberry, to Miss Mary Thompson of Laurens District.

Married on the 7th inst at Abbeville C. H. by the Rev. D. M. Turner, James A. Allen, Esq. to Miss Frances E. Dendy, daughter of Charles Dendy, Esq.

Died in Abbeville District, on the 6th inst, Mrs. Mary Crawford, aged 71 years.

Issue of December 1, 1848 [USC]

Married on the 21st inst by Rev. Silas Knight, Mr. Samuel Power to Miss Mary Pool, all of this District.

Married on the 23rd inst, by the Rev. D. F. Hadden, Mr. A. Thompson to Miss Jane E. Coleman, all of this District.

Issue of December 8, 1848 [USC]

Married on the 30th ult, by the Rev. J. L. Young, Mr. E. C. Simpson to Miss Nancy Abel, all of this District.

Married in Anderson District, on the 30th ult by the Rev. B. F. Mauldin, Mr. Samuel Garrett of this District to Miss Amaline Ford.

Issue of December 15, 1848 [USC]

Married on the 7th inst by the Rev. J. C. Vaughan, Mr. Alexander Austin to Miss Mary Nelson, all of this District.

Married on the 7th inst, by Rev. S. Knight, Mr. James H. Martin to Miss Mary Watkins, all of this District.

Died of Colic, at his residence on the 3d instant, Captain John H. Park, in the 25th year of his age.

Died on the 17th ult, near the village of Greenville, Mrs. Sarah Gantt, consort of the Hon. Richard Gantt, whose faithful partner she had been for 55 years. She has left numerous descendants.

Issue of December 22, 1848 [USC]

Married on the 14th inst by the Rev. A. Ray, Mr. George Farrow of Spartanburg, to Miss Matilda Couch of this District.

Married on the 14th inst by the Rev. Silas Knight, Mr. Robert Reynolds to Miss Amanda Moats, all of this District.

Married on the 19th inst by Rev. S. B. Lewers, Dr. M. M. Hunter of Laurens to Miss H. Kilgore of Greenville.

Married on the 12th inst, by the Rev. Thomas L. McBryde, Mr. William W. Logan of Greenwood to Miss Louisa R., only daughter of Mr. Henry Power, all of Abbeville District.

Died on the 22d ult at his residence in Houston, MIss, D. Griffin Esq. formerly a citizen of this Distrct.

[Death notice of Capt. John H. Park repeated with a long eulogy.]

Issue of January 12, 1849 [USC]

Married on the 25th ult. by Rev. J. C. Vaughan, Mr. William Word to Miss Nancy Sadler, all of this district.

Married on the 2nd inst. by Rev. J. C. Vaughan, Mr. John J. Hill of Newberry, to Mrs. Martha Owens of Laurens District.

Married on the 4th inst., by Rev. J. C. Vaughan, Mr. E. Weels to Miss A. G. White, all of Newberry District.

Married on the 7th inst. by Elihu Madden, Esq. Mr. Henry Sims to Miss Martha Nelson, all of this District.

Married on the 4th inst. by Elihu Watson, ESq., Mr. Elijah Teague of Anderson Dist., to Mrs. Nancy Dalrymple of Newberry District.

Married on the 9th inst. by Rev. Rilas [Silas] Knight, Mr. John G. Mackay to Miss Larissa Ann Hale, all of this Distrct.

Married on the 2nd inst. by Rev. W. Gaillard, Mr. J. L. Glasgow of Newberry, to Miss Sarah E. Owens, of Laurens District.

Issue of January 19, 1849 [USC]

Married in this district on Sunday the 14th instant, at Chestnut Ridge Church by Rev. Toliver Robinson, Mr. Melmouth Atwood to Miss Susan Crisp.

Death of John Y. Barksdale, formerly of Laurens District, S. C....died 19 December in Oxford, being about 24 years of age...left Laurens District in fall of 1846...took up a school in Lafayette Co...[long eulogy]...Oxford, Miss. Dec. 28, 1848.

Issue of February 2, 1849 [USC]

Married on the 28th ult., by Henry Oneall, Esq., T. Y. Neely to Miss Louisa Willard, all of Laurens District.

Died on the 23d ult., at his residence in this District, Dr. William Leake, aged 43 years, 3 months, 19 days...[long eulogy].

Issue of March 23, 1849 [USC]
Married in this District, on the 11th inst. by Rev. Mr. Hill, Mr. M. Elmore to Miss S. Knight.
Married in Abbeville District, on the 13th inst., by Rev. Wm. H. Davis, Mr. A. H. McAlister, to Miss L. J. Coon.
Married in Union District, on the 13th inst., by Rev. E. Ray,   Mr. John Harris of this district, to Miss Sarah Harlan.
Married in this district, on the 14th inst, by Rev. E. Lindsay, Dr. Geo. Young of Newberry District, to Miss A. Ferguson.

Issue of April 6, 1849 [USC]
Married in Monroe Co., Ark., on Sunday morning March 4th at the residence of Mrs. Mahala Wiles, by the Rev. R. S. Bell, Dr. A. L. Wilson, formerly of this District, to Miss M. Ann Madden, formerly of Harris Co., Ga.
Married in DeSoto, Miss., on the 8th ult., by the Rev. Mr. Burns, Mr. James L. Dubuy of Marshall Co., Miss to Miss Ophelia A. Rodgers, formerly of this District.
Married in Pickens District on the 18th ult., by Rev. Mr. Frances, Mr. Andrew Harris Sen of Anderson Dist. to Widow Edgar.
Married in Greenville District, on the 22d ult., by Rev. B. F. Mauldin, Mr. William R. Berry to Miss Elizabeth Lenhardt.

Issue of April 27, 1849 [USC]
Married on the 12th inst. by Rev. W. R. Hemphill, Rev. D. G. Phillips of Jefferson County, Ga., to Miss Mary J. Hearst. Also by the same at the same time, Rev. John W. McCane of Stewart County, Ga., to Miss Sarah A., Hearst, both daughters of John Hearst, deceased of White Hall, Abbeville District.
Departed this life at his residence in Newberry District on the 7th inst., in the 33d year of his age, Mr. Mason Young, leaving an only child, a son about 3 years of age.

Issue of May 4, 1849 [USC]
Married in Anderson District, on the 15th ult., by William S. Shaw, Esq., Mr. James S. Russell of Chambers County, Ala., to Miss Eliza Stuart.
Married at Newberry C. H. on the 25th ult., by the Rev. John G. Bowman, Mr. A. H. Farrow, formerly of this District, to Miss Eliza B. Lorick.
Married in this district, on the 24th ult., by the Rev. E. F. Hyde, Robert C. Brown of Columbia to Miss Elizabeth Watts.
Died in Anderson District, at her residence near Slab Town, Mrs. Sarah Smith.
Died in Anderson District, on the 8th ult., Mrs. Elizabeth Richards in the 90th year of her age.
Died in Navasso County, Texas, at the residence of Wm Richies, of Winter Fever, Capt. A. H. Hanna, late of Spartanburg District.
Died in Edgefield District, on the 5th ult., Mrs. Sarah Watson Moss in the 45th year of her age.
Died in Edgefield District, on the 21st ult., John W. Thomas, in the 24th year of his age.
Died in Spartanburg District, on the 9th ult., Mrs. Martha Woodruff, aged 64 years.
Died in Pontotoc County, Mississippi, in the 77th year of his age, Mr. John Stephens, who spent the greater part of his life in Laurens District, having been a citizen of the above named county for five or six years.

Issue of May 11, 1849 [USC]
Married in Newberry District, on the 1st inst. by Rev. J. L. Young, A. Wideman, Esq., of Abbeville District, to Miss Eliza Renwick.
Died in Abbeville District, on the 27th ult., Annette, eldest daughter of Col. J. C. Martin, in the 12th year of her age.
Died in Anderson District, on the 13th ult., Mrs. Margaret A. Wilkes, wife of Thomas C. Wilks and [cut off].

Issue of May 18, 1849 [USC]
Died in this District in the 15th inst., Mr. Chaney Stone, aged about 70 years.
Died in this District, on the 8th inst., Mr. Hampton Finley.
Died in Edgefield District, on the 6th inst., Mr. Hezekiah Strom, in the 38th year of his age.
Died at Due West, Abbeville District, on the 23d ult., Mrs. Sarah Jane Allen, in the 24th year of her age.
Died at Calhoun's Mills, in Abbeville District, on the 23d ult., Mrs. Rebecca Darri-oott, in the 85th year of her age.
Died in Greenville District, on the 27th ult., James M. Cely in the 10th year of his age.
Died in Greenville District, on the 5th inst., Mrs. Susan C. Earle, in the 31st year

4

her age.
    Died in Spartanburg District, on the 17th ult., Joseph J. Gaseon in the 22nd year of
his age.
    Married in this District on the 10th inst., by Rev. W. B. Boyd, Mr. J. H. Helums to
Miss Narcissa South.
    Married in this District on the 13th inst., by J. A. Arnold, Esq., Mr. Allen Watson
to Miss Elizabeth Scott.
    Married in Anderson District, on the 3d inst., by Rev. W. G. Mullinax, Mr. James
Johnston to Miss Sarah Newton.
    Married in Anderson District, on the 26th ult., by A. D. Gray, Esq., Mr. Robert Todd
to Miss Malinda Garle.
    Married in Pickens District, on the 29th of March by Rev. M. Chastian[sic], Mr. Fran-
cis W. Dryman to Miss Elizabeth Bryson.
    Married in Edgefield District on the 26th ult., Dr. WM. S. Dozier to Miss Henrietta
F. Sheppard.

Issue of May 25, 1849 [USC]
    Married at Cokesbury, Abbeville District, on the 15th inst., by Rev. J. W. McCall,
Mr. S. E. Graydon of Laurens District, to Miss Susan Dunwoody.
    Married in Abbeville District, on the 15th inst., by Rev. John McLeese, Mr. Robert
P. Buchanan, to Frances, eldest daughter of William Buchanan.
    Married in Abbeville District on the 17th inst by Rev. Mr. Cauley, Mr. Wm. D.
Calhoun to Miss Ellen Jones.
    Married in Abbeville District, on the 10th inst. by Rev. McNeill Turner, Mr. Daniel
Jordan of Rockingham, N. C. to Miss N. A. Ritchie.
    Married at Greenville C. H., on the 15th inst., by Rev. Mr. Hopkins, Mr. Thomas S.
Crayton of Anderson to Miss Mary Long.
    Married at Pickens C. H. on the 26th ult., by Rev. J. L. Kennedy, Dr. J. W. Earle to
Miss Eliza Keith.
    Married in Pickens on the 7th inst., by A. Alexander Esq., Mr. G. W. A. Smith, to
Miss Martha Jane Mauldin.
    Married in Pickens on the 15th inst., by Rev. J. B. Hillhouse, Mr. H. R. Hughes, to
Miss E. F. Dendy.
    Died at his residence in Pickens District, on the 17th inst., Mr. Elisha Lee, aged
about 83 years.
    Died in Stokes County, N. C., on the 17th ult., John Lowry, aged 100 years.
    Died in Abbeville District, on the 6th inst., Mr. Alexander Hamilton, in the 26th
year of his age.
    Died in Anderson District, on the 1st inst., Albert T. Carpenter, Esq.
    Died in Anderson District, on the 16th inst., Mr. Edward H. Earle in the 28th year
of his age.
    Died in Anderson District on the 13th inst., Miss Nancy T. Lewis, in the 24th year
of her age.
    Died in Laurens District, on the 23d inst., Mr. William Moore, aged about 70.

Issue of June 29, 1849 [USC & Laurens]
    Died in the town of New Albany, Pontotoc County, Mississippi, on the evening of 14
June, Mr. William Brewster, formerly of Laurens District, aged 52 years.

Issue of July 6, 1849 [USC]
    Married on the evening of 22d June by Rev. E. F. Hyde, Mr. James A. Jones to Miss
Ann, daughter of Mrs. Elizabeth Leman, all of Laurens District.
    Married on Thursday 28th June, by Rev. S. B. Lewers, Mr. George L. Crisp to Miss
Elizabeth Austin, all of this District.
    Died of dropsy in Laurens District, on the 29th ult., John Hitch, Esq., in the 77th
year of his age. Since 4 Feb last, member of the Methodist Episcopal Church, South
    Died at his plantation in Chickesaw County, Mississippi, on the 3d inst., Mr.
Samuel H. Irby, aged 53 years, a native of Laurens District, for the last five years
a resident of Miss.
    Obed Wait Graves, born Laurens District, Oct 4th, 1822, died Due West, Abbeville
District, July 5th, 1849, held a prominent position in the sophomore class of Erskine
College. [long eulogy.]

Issue of July 13, 1849 [USC & Laurens]
    Married by Rev. T. Ray, on the 25th ult., Dr. W. T. Harris, to Miss Martha Grier, all
of Union District.
    Married on the 5th by Rev. B. M. Palmer, John J. Brown of Laurens, to Mrs. Matilda
C. Brown, daughter of the late Henry P. Taylor, of Columbia.

Issue of July 27, 1849 [USC]
    Married on Tuesday morning the 3d of July, at Woodland, near Pendleton, S. C., by
the Rev. A. Cornish, Dr. John C. Calhoun, Junr., son of Hon. J. C. Calhoun, to Miss
Annie R., daughter of the Rev. Jasper Adams, all of Pickens District.
    Died on the 14th June last, after a long & painful illness John J. Mays, in the
29th year of his age...member of Masonic Lodge and Odd Fellows. Edgefield Advertiser.

Issue of August 3, 1849 [USC & Laurens]
    An aged woman. Mrs. Lourania Knower, died on 29 March last at her residence in
Scriven Co., Ga., whose age is set down as not less than 130 years. Some place it is
as high as 137 years.
    Died in the Village of Spartanburg, Dr. Samuel Farrow in the 63d year of his age.

Issue of August 17, 1849 [USC & Laurens]
    Married in Caddo Parish, La., on the 12 of July by Elder John Bryce, Mr. John W.
Smith of Shreveport, La., formerly of Kentucky to Miss Harriet Jane Elizabeth Gary,
formerly of this District.
    Departed this life in Laurens District, on the 7th inst., of Bilious Fever, Miss
Emily Francis, second daughter of M. D. Pinson, Esq., in the 13th year of her age.

Issue of August 24, 1849 [USC]
    Died in Laurens District, at the house of Mr. J. B. Pitts, his brother-in-law, on the
20th inst., of typhoid fever, Abram Bolt jr., in the 37th year of his age...on 18 Feb
1840, under Rev. William P. Martin, joined the Baptist Church at Friendship.
    Died on the 18th inst., Daniel Felder, aged 3 year, 5 months, 9 days, son of J. W.
and Louisa Wallace of this District.

Issue of September 14, 1849 [USC & Laurens]
    Married on the 30th ultimo, by Rev. Moses Hill, Dr. Thomas Davenport to Miss
Louisa Fuller, daughter of Jesse Fuller.
    Married on the 9th inst., by M. P. Evans, Esq., Mr. Robert Hand and Miss Ennice
Smith, all of this District.

Issue of October 5, 1849 [USC]
    Married on Thursday the 27th ult., by the Rev. Moses Hill, Mr. George West to Miss
Jane Chandler, all of this District.
    Departed this life on the 27th of September at his residence in this District,
Jonathan Wallace, aged 73 years, 7 months, 7 days.

Issue of October 19, 1849 [USC]
    Married in Pontotoc Co., Miss on the 16th inst., by   Rev. James Wear, Mr. Shadrach
Jamison, formerly of Laurens District, to Miss Sarah, daughter of Dr. Fugua.

Issue of November 2, 1849 [USC]
    Married on the 24th inst., by Rev. E. Lindsay, Major O. A. Watson to Miss C. C. East,
all of Laurens.
    Married on the 30th ult., by Rev   James L. Young, Dr. Thomas S. Jacks to Miss Sarah
Raiford, all of this District.
    Died of measles, near Cambridge, Abbeville District, Sunday evehing the 7th inst.,
Mrs. Elizabeth Smith, consort of Mr. John W. Smith, aged 23 years...member of the Baptist
Church.
    Death of Mr. Joseph Sullivan of this District occured on the 20th inst., in the city
of Charleston...in the 54th year of his age...visited the city on business.
    Died in the 37th year of his age, Mr. Meredith Fowler...died near Scuffletown, Laurens
District, 16th Oct 1849, of typhoid fever...leaves a wife, a mother, and 5 children.

Issue of November 9, 1849 [USC & Laurens]
    Married on the 1st inst., by Rev. C. A. Crowell, Mr. Gowan Zeigler of Barnwell Dis-
trict, and Miss Lavinia A. F., youngest daughter of Rev. Samuel Dunwoody of Cokesbury,
S. C.
    Married on the 1st inst., by Rev. C. B. Stewart, Mr. W. Lewers and Miss Mary Blakely,
all of Laurens.
    Married on the 1st inst., by Rev. J. L. Young, Mr. Samuel C. Todd and Miss Letitia
Henry, all of this District.
    Married on the 31st October, by Rev. M. Hill, Mr. E. G. Nelson and Miss Margaret
McPherson, all of this District.
    Died in the 43rd year of his age, Mr. Drayton Cheek, near Mountain Shoals, Laurens
District, 15 Oct 1849...left a wife and 8 children.

6

Issue of November 16, 1849 [USC]
Died at his residence in Union District, on the 7th inst., in the 29th year of his age, G. W. Wesson.
Died at his residence in the upper part of Edgefield District, near the Island Ford, on the 22nd ult., Capt. John Foy.
Died on the 5th inst., at his residence in Abbeville District, in the 70th year of his age, William Chiles, Esq.

Issue of November 23, 1849 [USC]
Married on the 6th inst., by Rev. E. Lindsey, Mr. James Rook to Miss Mary Spake of Newberry.
Married on the 15th inst., by Mr. Housell [sic], Mr. James Denson to Miss Elizabeth Mathus of Newberry.
Married on the 15th inst., by Rev. S. Leland Kennedy, Mr. W. A. Templeton of Pickens Dist., to Miss M. A. M., youngest daughter of Dr. Wm K. Hamilton of Cobb Co., Ga.
Married on the 8th inst., by Rev. Joel Anderson, Mr. Thomas Wakefield and Miss Sarah Bonds, all of this District.

Issue of November 30, 1849 [USC]
Married on the 22d inst., by the Rev. Z. W. Barnes, Mr. John Dial to Miss Louricey Gary, all of Laurens District.
Married on the 1st inst., by Rev. Z. W. Barnes, Mr. Henry Johnson to Miss Clarisa Abercrombie, all of this District.

Issue of December 7, 1849 [USC]
Married on the 29th ult. by Rev. Toliver Robinson, Mr. Asa Forgy to Miss Ethalinda Barksdale, all of this District.
Married on the same evening by the same, Mr. John Shockley to Miss Emily Martin, all of Laurens District.
Married on the 25th ult., by the Rev. B. F. Corley, Mr. Alfred Cheatham, to Miss Emily, second daughter of Mr. Simeon Chaney, all of Abbeville District.
Married on the 20th ult., by Rev. Mr. Williams, R. L. Tinsley of Laurens to Miss S. E. Verden, of Greenville District.
Died on Thursday, the 29th ult., of Typhoid fever, Miss Laura W., eldest daughter of Dr. John W. Simpson of this village.
Died on the 16th ult., of Bilious Fever, at his residence at Double Springs, Oktibbeha Co., Mississippi, Mr. George Vaughan Sen'r...member of Warrior Creek Baptist Church 20 years...removed at the end of 1844 to Mississippi and attached himself to Bethlehem Baptist Church...leaves a wife and children.
Died at the residence of her father in Newberry District on Monday night, the 26th November, Miss Frances Young Griffin, second daughter of Col. Bluford F. and Agnes Griffin, in the 20th year of her age.

Issue of December 14, 1849 [USC & Laurens]
Married on the 6th inst., by Rev. Tolaver Robinson, Mr. Thomas Mosely to Miss Tarissa Toland, all of this District.

Issue of December 21, 1849 [USC]
Married on the 13th inst., by Rev. Tolaver Robinson, Mr. Wesley Duval, to Miss Rody Couch, all of Laurens District.
Died on the 11th inst., of Typhoid fever, Mrs. Elizabeth P. Connors, wife of Maj. G. W. Connors of Laurens District, in the 26th year of her age...leaves a husband and 3 children, father and mother...member of the Baptist Church.

Issue of December 28, 1849 [USC]
Married on the 24th inst., by W. H. Langston, Esq., Mr. Richard Huckaby of Union, to Miss Sarah Robinson, of Laurens District.
Married on the 25th inst., in this District by W. H. Langston, Esq., Mr. Andy Junior, of Georgia, to Miss Elizabeth Nix, of Union District.
Married on the 21st ult., by Rev. Mr. Meitrick, DR. M. A. Hunter to Miss Nancy Gilbert, both of Laurens District.
Died on Sunday evening, the 15th inst., at the residence of James Bailey, near Stoney Point, Abbeville District, Isaiah, son of James & Bieth Caldwell, in the 12th year of his age.

Issue of January 4, 1850 [USC]

Married on the 20th ult., by Rev. Wm P. Hill, Mr. Thomas Chatham of Greenwood, Abbeville District, to Mrs. E. Anderson of Edgefield District.

Died near Spring Grove, on the 22d ult., Miss Cornelia Jones, daughter of Gen. T. F. and Emily Jones, aged 17 years.

Issue of January 11, 1850 [USC]

Married on the 20th ult., by the Rev. Elbert Lindsay, Mr. D. H. A. Mason to Miss M. E. Copeland, all of this District.

Issue of January 18, 1850 [USC]

Married on Thursday, the 27th ult., by Rev. C. B. Stewart, Mr. R. L. Waters to Miss Louisa Fowler, of Spartanburg District.

Married on the 24th ult., by Jefferson Arnold, Edq., Mr. Christopher Spence to Miss Martha Boling, all of this District.

Married on the 10th inst., by Rev. J. C. Vaughan, Mr. William Lindsay to Miss Carry Nance, all of Newberry District.

Married on the 8th instrant by Rev. J. C. Vaughan, Mr. J. R. Scurry of Edgefield District, to Miss E. W. Vall of Laurens District.

Married on the 28th ult., by Rev. J. C. Vaughan, Mr. Henry Fooshee to Miss Elizabeth R. Dlehubor[sic], all of this District.

Married on the 25th ult., by Rev. J. W. McCall, Mr. Thomas Anderson to Miss Caroline Gray, all of this District.

Married on the 27th of December 1849, by the Rev. Mr. Searsey, Maj. William M. Cargill to Miss Elizabeth L. Tolbert, both of Mayfield, Graves Co., Ky.

Died near Tylersville, on the 10th inst., Charles Butler, only son of A. H. and Nancy Smith, aged 2 years, 5 months, 10 days.

Died in DeKalb County, Georgia, on the 24th ult., Mr. Solomon Goodwin, Sr., formerly of this District, in the 86th year of his age.

Issue of January 25, 1850 [USC]

Married on the 16th ult by Elihu Watson, Esq., Mr. John Jason to Miss Martha Jean Neill, both of Newberry District.

Married on the 10th inst., by Rev. Tolaver Robertson, Mr. Graydon Riddle to Miss Gillee Fowler, both of Laurens District.

Married on the 17th inst., by the same, Mr. Newton Babb of Laurens, to Miss Ann Pinson of Greenville.

Married on Sunday, the 20th inst., by the same at New Hope Church, Mr. Ewel Teague of Laurens to Miss Caroline Miles of Spartanburg.

Married on Tuesday, the 22nd, by the same, Mr. James Shell to Miss Mary Chalmers, both of Laurens District.

Died on the 26th of December last, at the residence of his father, in the city of Memphis, Tenn., Hayne J. Klinck, eldest son of John G. Klinck, Esq., formerly of this place...in his 16th year.

Issue of February 1, 1850 [USC]

Married on the 24th inst., by Rev. p. L. Young, Dr. W. W. Leake of Cass County, Ga., to Miss Rachel Leake of this District.

Married on the 17th inst., at the house of Z. P. Hudson, by the Rev. W. Drummond, Thomas Woodruff, Esq., of Spartanburg District, to Mrs. Polly Hawkins, daughter of the late Rev. Lewis Rector of Greenville District.

Married on Sunday evening, the 13th inst., by the Rev. Simpson, Drummond, Mr. William A. Todd of Laurens, to Miss Mary Ann Bobo, of Spartanburg District.

Issue of February 8, 1850 [USC]

Married on the 29th ult., by Rev. J. Holmes, Mr. W. A. French to Miss A. J. Raiford, all of Laurens District.

Married on the 29th ult., by Rev. James Smith, Mr. James Smith to Miss F. E. Clanahan, all of Abbeville District.

Married on the 15th ult., by Rev. D. Humphries, Mr. T. G. Trimmier, to Miss M. L. Thomson, all of Anderson District.

Issue of February 15, 1850 [USC]

Married on the 24th ult., by Rev. William T. Farrow, Mr. Clement P. Thomson to Miss Nancy E. Lindsay, all of Union District.

Married on the 5th inst., by M. P. Evins, Esq., Mr. Miles R. Garrett to Miss Nancy Studdard, all of Laurens District.

Married on the 22d ult., by Rev. William H. Turnley, D. S. Calhoun, M. D., to Miss Ellen D. Neely, all of Catahoula Parish, La.

Died on the 5th inst., at the residence of Mr. Shubel Starnes, near Fishdam Ford, Laurens District., Col. Ebenezer Starnes, in the 80th year of his age...as a soldier he was the bravest.

Died in Green County, Alabama, on the 26th of December last, Mr. Thomas Nickles, a native of this District, and a resident for many years on Little River, 4 miles below this village...left a large family.

Issue of February 22, 1850 [USC]
Married on the 12th inst., by Rev. Tolaver Robertson, Mr. Richard Henderson to Miss Barbary Simpson, all of Laurens District.

Married in Sumter District, on the 14th inst., by Rev. M. W. Brunson, Mr. A. A. Gilbert of Walterboro' to Miss Ellen Sarah, daughter of T. E. Flowers, of Sumter.

Issue of March 1, 1850 [U S C]
Married on the 21st inst by Rev. J. H. Zimmerman, Mr. Joseph S. McMorris, to Miss Angeline Pratt, all of Newberry village.

Married on the 12th ult., by the Rev. D. Humphreys, V. W. Barns, Esq., to Miss A. E. Dorsey of Columbia County, Ga.

At the same time and place, Dr. J. L. Wilkes of Lincoln County, to Miss M. J. Dorsey.

Issue of March 8, 1850 [USC]
Died on Sabbath morning, the 3rd inst., of consumption, Henry Laurens, son of Dr. A. F. Golding, Laurens District, S. C., aged 23 years.

Died on Saturday the 9th ult., at the residence of DR. A. F. Golding, Christiana Neely, daughter of Maj. Calvin Foster, of Spartanburg District, S. C., aged 6 years.

Issue of March 15, 1850 [USC]
Married on the 7th inst., by Rev. Samuel Townsend, Mr. John W. Arnold to Miss Mary Frances, daughter of Oswalt and Margaret Richardson, all of this village.

Married on the 21st ultimo, by Rev. W. D. Boyd, Mr. S. F. Moore to Miss R. C. Deal, all of Laurens District.

Married on the 7th instant, by Rev. J. L. Young, Mr. Mathew Benjamin to Miss Martha J. Martin, all of Laurens District.

Died on Thursday, the 7th inst., Stella Margaret, infant daughter of S. A. and Margaret E. Godman, aged 4 months and 6 days.

Died on the 3rd inst., at the res. of Mr. David Bell, 8 miles West of this village, Mr. Abner H. Cureton.

Issue of March 22, 1850 [USC]
Married on the 7th inst., Pacolett [sic] Bend, by Rev. William T. Farrow, Dr. John R. Lyons to Miss Nancy R. Thompson, all of Union District.

Died on the 12th inst., at his residence in Laurens District of apoplexy, Mr. Newman Gary, in the 68th year of his age.

Issue of March 29, 1850 [USC]
Married on the 19th instant by Rev. C. B. Stewart, Mr. John Templeton to Miss Martha Spear, all of this District.

Died on the 7th inst., in the 33d year of her age, Mrs. Frances Mitchell, wife of William Mitchell, of Laurens District...member of the Baptist Church at Poplar Springs. She left a kind husband, five children, only only 10 days old.

Died on the 8th inst., in the 62d year of her age, Mrs. Huldah Cunningham, consort of Mr. James Cunningham of Laurens District...member of the Baptist Church at Friendship...baptized by Elder Henry Hill in 1815...left a husband, and an only daughter and son-in-law.

Died on the 26th inst. at his residence in Laurens District, Mr. Whited Wilkes, aged about 63 years.

Issue of April 12, 1850 [USC]
Married on Tuesday evening, the 2d inst., by Rev. Moses HIll, Mr. John T. Wait to Miss Ruth Watson, all of Laurens District.

Issue of April 19, 1850 [USC]
Died in Anderson village, on Tuesday the 19th ult., Mrs. Martha Jane Towers, wife of Alexander B. Towers, youngest daughter of Rev. D. Humphreys, within 1 day of attaining 19 years...member of the Presbyterian Church...left an infant son aged 14 months.

Issue of April 26, 1850 [USC]
Another Revolutionary Soldier Gone!
Died at the residence of William Easton, in the lower part of this District, on Wednesday, 3rd inst., Joseph Griffin, aged 88 years...soldier under Col. James Williams...in Mus-

grove's Mill...under Col. Hays...present at Hammond's Store..at Cow Pens, Guilford C. H., Long Cane, Siege of Ninety Six, etc..."he would Kill Joe Griffin and Yancey Saxon if they were the last men between Heaven and Hell."

Issue of May 4, 1850 [USC & Laurens]
Died on the 20th inst., in Laurens District, at the house of Mr. N. Day, his brother-in-law, Mr. John Simmons, Teacher in the 45th year of his age.

Issue of May 17, 1850 [USC & Laurens]
Married on the 9th inst., by Rev. Clark B. Stewart, Capt. F. S. Ferguson of Spartanburg to Miss Cinthia A. Parks of Laurens.
Married on the same evening, be Rev. Clark B. Stewart, Mr. James Bell to Miss Martha Bell, all of Laurens.
Married on the 13th by Rev. S. Townsend, Rev. Dr. Joel Anderson, to Miss Margaret Burnside, all of this District.

Issue of May 10, 1850 [USC]
Married on the 2nd inst., by Rev. W. P. Martin, Mr. William Mitchell to Miss Nancy E. Putman, all of this District.
Married at Abbeville C. H. on Wednesday, the 1st inst., by Rev. A. H. Cornish, of Pendleton, H. C. Ca--- [torn] of Richmond, Va., to Miss Jane C. Alston of Abbeville.
Married on Tuesday evening, the 20th ult., at the same village, by Rev. Mr. Reid, John C. SImkins, Esq., of Edgefield to Miss Rosalie, daughter of Judge Wardlaw.

Issue of May 24, 1850 [USC & Laurens]
Died on the 3rd inst., at the residence of his father, the infant son of Travis Davenport, aged 6 years, 5 months, 6 days.

Issue of May 31, 1850 [USC]
Married on the 14th inst., near Lodi, by the Rev. B. F. Corley, Mr. Medy Mays, to Mrs. Nancy Calhoun, all of Abbeville District.
Married on the 21st inst., near Cartersville, Cass county, by Rev. C. A. Crowell, Mr. M. A. Leak, of Cass County, Ga. to Miss Sarah A. Leak, of Edgefield, S. C.
Died at his residence in Laurens District, on the 23rd inst., Hastin Dial, Senr, in the 74th year of his age.

Issue of June 7, 1850 [USC & Laurens]
Married on the 30th ultimo, at Scuffletown, by Rev. C. B. Stewart, Rev. E. F. Hyde, to Miss N. A. Hunter, all of this District.
Died in Laurens Dist., on the 26th ult., Mrs. Martha Glen, wife of Jeremiah Glenn, Esq., aged 25 years, 4 months, 18 days.
Died on the 31st ult., in the upper part of Laurens District, Mrs. Amy Jones, in the 75th year of her age...member of the M. E. Church.

Issue of June 14, 1850 [USC]
Married in Chickasaw Co., Mississippi, on Thursday, may 9th, by the Rev. J. N. Caruthers, Mr. Warren Davis Lawrence, of Pickens District, S. C. to Miss Martha, dau. of Col. Anderson Bean, of said county.

Issue of June 21, 1850 [USC]
Married on the 18th inst., by Rev. C. B. Stewart, Mr. Samuel Franks, to Miss E. J. Templeton, all of this District.
Died on the 12th inst., at the house of Capt. James M. Latimer, her son-in-law near her own residence in Greenville District, Mary Sullivan, widow of Hewlett Sullivan, Sen. ...born 17 Feb 1772, in the Four Holes, brought up in St. George Dorchester, her native Parish of this State. Her parents were Joseph Dunklin, an emigrant from Ireland and her mother, Mary Warthen of England, both of whom sailed from London and after their arrival in Charleston, married. Mary was the fourth child, her two oldest brothers, Joseph and John served with Marion and Horry through the greater part of the Revolution. Her father died about the close of the war and her mother two years after. The balance of her family moved in 1785 to Greenville on the Reedy River, where Mary married Hewlett Sullivan, a native of Virginia 19 Dec 1787. Twelve children, 8 sons and 4 daughters were the fruits of her marriage. Her husband died 11 July 1830 and she thereafter joined the Methodist Church.

Issue of June 28, 1850 [USC]
Married on the 13th inst., by Rev. J. C. Vaughan, Mr. Thomas Taylor of Newberry Dist., to Mrs. Susan Cook of Laurens District.

Issue of July 12, 1850 [USC]

Died on the 7th inst. of Congestive fever, at Woodville, Abbeville District, Sarah, daughter of John and Nancy Hefferman, aged 17 years and 5 days...member of the M. E. Church.

Downs Calhoun, Esq., died on Saturday evening, the 29th ult., at his residence in Abbeville District, near Puckett's Ferry...age 54 years, 2 months, 9 days--..leaves a large number of relatives and friends.

Issue of July 19, 1850 [USC]

Married on Sunday, 7th of July, by the Rev. L. Dean, Mr. Thomas C. Johnson, to Miss Caroline, daughter of A. H. Cureton, of Greenville District.

Married by Rev. Jas. Cheek, July the 14th, Mr. Rogers of Spartanburg District, to Miss V. Dunn of Laurens District.

Issue of July 26, 1850 [USC]

Married on the 23rd inst by the Rev. Mr. Seay, Mr. B. Richards of Newberry, to Miss Elizabeth Kitchens of Unionville.

Died at his residence in Laurens District, on 25 June, William Ligon, in the 78th year of his age...born in Virginia in 1772. In 1800, emigrated to Laurens District... a husband and a father [long eulogy]...Cross Hill, July 1, 1850.

Died on the 18th inst., Oscar Green, infant son of Samuel and Mary Franks, aged 3 years and 2 months.

Issue of August 2, 1850 [USC & Laurens]

Died on the evening of the 15th ult., at the residence of his father in Laurens District, James Henry, son of Lewis J. and Isabella Duvall, aged 1 year, 11 months, and 3 days.

Died on the 23d at his residence in Laurens District, William Rook, Senr. A native of Northampton Co., N. C., born 3 Feb 1772. Left a wife, 8 children, grandchildren, and great grandchildren.

Married on the 21st ult., by Rev. J. H. Humbert, Mr. William Riley of Laurens Dist., to Miss Frances C. Gaines of Greenville District.

Married on the 25th ult., by Rev. Wm. B. Byrd, Mr. Allen Poole to Miss Rebecca Langston, all of this District.

Married on the same day, by Rev. E. Lindsey, Mr. Benjamin James of Newberry village, to Miss L. F. Martin, of this District.

Issue of August 9, 1850 [USC]

Died in Ludlow, Scott County, Mississippi, on the 17th of June, Mr. James Little, formerly of this District...leaves w wife and several children.

Married on the 4th inst., by Rev. W. B. Boyd, Mr. A. Townsend to Miss Elizabeth Hardy, all of this District.

Issue of August 16, 1850 [USC]

Died near Woodruff's, on the 30th July last, William Jefferson, eldest son of Mrs. Catherine Brady, in the 10th year of his age.

Died in Tippa County, Mississippi, on the 7th of July last, Mr. Stephen Braddock, in the 68th year of his age, a native of Laurens District.

Died on Thursday, the 8th inst., Alice Adelia, youngest daughter of Mary A. and S. Franks, aged 12 months.

Married on Thursday, the 1st inst., by Rev. Dr. Henry Pasly, Dr. F. G. Fuller of Laurens District, to Miss Amelia Watson, of Abbeville District.

Issue of August 23, 1850 [USC]

Married on the 18th inst., by Rev. J. C. Vaughan, Mr. William White of Newberry District, to Miss Amanda Cheatham, of Abbeville District.

Married on Wednesday evening, the 14th inst., by   Rev. D. F. Haddon, Mr. James Lee of Spartanburg District, to Miss Margaret M. Sloan of Laurens District.

Issue of September 6, 1850 [Laurens]

Married on the 6th ult., by Rev. Dr. Scruggs, Dr. J.M. Boyce to Miss Lizzie Patterson, all of Marshall County, Mississippi.

Married at the residence of Mr. R. S. Finny, Laurens District, on the 28th of August, by the Rev. S. B. Lewers, Mr. C. H. Finny to Miss F. A. Griffin, youngest daughter of Capt. A. Griffin, all of Laurens District. [N. B. This may be actually PHINNEY--BHH]

Departed this life on the 13th July last, Mrs. Elizabeth Campbell, wife of Dr. Robert Campbell, Senr., in the 67th year of her age...member of the Presbyterian Church over 40 years.

Issue of September 27, 1850 [USC]
    Mrs. Barbara Milam, wife of Mr. Turner Milam, was murdered two miles below this
village, on Wendesday, the 25th inst., by a negro woman...a daughter of Alexander Kir-
patrick, decd, aged 27 years.

Issue of October 4, 1850 [USC & Laurens]
    Married in Greenville village, on the 29th ult., by the Rev. R. S. Turner, Mr. Lewis
S. Thruston to Miss Henrietta F. D'Oyley, all of the former place.
    Died at his residence in Eutaw, Alabama, on the 11th September, Robert Creswell, Esq.,
in the 78th year of his age. A native of Laurens District, about 1816, he was elected
Comptroller General and later Lt. Gov.
    Died on the 24th ult., in Newberry District, in the 70th year of her age, Mrs.
Nancy Bonds, widow of John Bonds, decd...reared 7 children..member of the Baptist Church.

Issue of October 11, 1850 [USC]
    Died in Laurens District, on the 20th of September, Mrs. Charity Stark, about 73
years of age.
    Married on Thursday the 3d inst., by the Rev. W. B. Boyd, Mr. Hastings Dial to Miss
Ophelia Little, all of Laurens District.
    Married on Sunday, the 22d ult., by the Rev. J. H. Humbert, Mr. Benjamin Gains of
Greenville District, to Mrs. Nancy Jones, of Laurens District.
    Married on the 29th ult., by the Rev. Tolaver Robertson, Mr. Robertson Owins to Miss
Charity Garret, all of Laurens District.
    Married on Sunday, the 29th ult., by the Rev. J. G. Humbert, Mr. Joel Ellison to Miss
Jane E. Carter, all of Laurens District.
    Married on the 24th ult., by the Rev. Tolaver Robertson, Mr Melmoth Willis to Miss
Armstrong, all of Laurens District.
    Married on Thursday, the 10th inst., by the Rev. J. W. McCall, Maj. Calvin Foster to
Miss N. C. Wright, eldest daughter of General Thomas Wright, of Laurens District.

Issue of October 18, 1850 [USC and Laurens]
    Married on the 6th of October, by Rev. J. C. Vaughan, Mr. Joseph Kennedy of Fairfield
Dist., to Mrs. Nancy Maxwell of Newberry District.
    By the same on 8 Oct., Mr. Benjamin Fooshe to Mrs. Sarah Grant, all of Laurens Dist.
    By the same on 9 Oct, Wm. R. Smith of Laurens Dist., to Miss Ursula Burnham of
Newberry Dist.
    By the same on 10 Oct., Mr. J. C. Hill of Newberry Dist., to Miss E. C. Smith of
Laurens District.
    Married on the 8th inst., by Mathew P. Evans, Esq., Mr. James Q. Robertson to Miss
Elizabeth Patton, all of Laurens District.
    Married on the 8th inst., by Rev. Moses Hill, Mr. Pleasant Watson to Miss Thursday
Reddin, all of Laurens Dist.
    Married on the 15th inst., by the same, John Anderson to Miss Sarah Henderson, all
of Laurens District.
    Married on the 15th ult., by the Rev. Z. L. Holmes, at Liberty Spring Church [Presby-
terian, Cross Hill, S. C.], Mr. Richard F. Goulding of Mississippi to Miss Ellen McGowan
of Laurens Dist.
    Died in this District, on 20 September, Andrew T. Adams, aged 11 years and 6 months,
youngest son of William & Polly Adams.

Issue of October 25, 1850 [USC & Laurens]
    Died at the residence of Mr. Jesse Teague in Laurens District, on Tuesday, the 1st
inst., Mrs. Martha Bailey, consort of Zachariah Bailey, decd, aged 66 years. A native
of North Carolina, removed to Laurens District, in 1805. Shortly after her removal here
she married Martin Miller. She was raised 12 children, ten of whom are sons. She was
a member of the Baptist Church.

Issue of November 8, 1850 [USC]
    Married on the 31st ult., by M. P. Evins, Esq., Mr. O. P. Moore to Miss Nancy Owings,
all of this District.

Issue of November 15, 1850 [USC]
    Married on the 5th inst., at Greenwood, Abbeville District, by Rev. C. H. Raymond,
Mr. E. P. Vaughan of Newberry District to Miss Fannie Byrd, daughter of Capt. Thomas
Byrd, of the former place.

Issue of Novebmer 25, 1850 [USC]
    Married on the 4th inst., by the Rev. Moses Hill, Mr. John Lipford to Miss Elizabeth
King, all of this District.

12

Issue of November 29, 1850 [USC & Laurens]
    Married on the 24th inst., by Rev. J. J. O'Connell, Mr. Coleman B. Walker of Laurens
to Miss Elizabeth Alice McKenny of Columbia.
    Married on the 19th inst., by Rev. J. C. Vaughan, Mr. T. L. Turner to Miss Jane
Todd, all of this District.
    Died at his residence, eight miles above Laurens C. H., Mr. Marmaduke Pinson, in the
51st year of his age, leaving a widow and eight children....Mr. Pinson was born in
Laurens District, and on 2 Dec 1832 married Elizabeth Sullivan. About 2 years after her
death, on 18 Dec 1849, married to Elizabeth Finley...member of the Baptist Church.
    Died on the 10th inst., at his residence near Scuffletown, Mr. Jonathan Blakely, in
the 58th year of his age. He has left a wife and five children.

Issue of December 27, 1850 [USC]
    Married on the 12th inst., by Rev. Tolaver Robertson, Mr. James Rose to Miss Eliza-
beth Mosely, both of Laurens District.
    Married on the 19th inst. by the same, Mr. Edward Garrett, to Miss Sarah Durham,
both of Laurens.
    Married on the 24th inst., by the same, Mr. John Edwards, to Miss Semantha Brown,
both of Laurens.

Issue of January 3, 1851 [USC]
    Married on Thursday, the 12th inst., by Rev. T. S. Arthur, W. H. Campbell Esq. (of
the Greenville Mountaineer) to Miss Caroline Matilda Lewis, all of Greenville.
    Married on Tuesday, the 31st ult., by the Rev. J. W. McCall, Maj. T. F. Anderson to
Miss Nancy Jane, daughter of A. Williams, Esq. , of Greenville.
    Married on Thursday, the 19th ult., at Thomas Crumley's, by the Rev. Elbert Lindsey,
Dr. James Tinsly to Miss Martha Stapleton, all of Laurens.
    Died on 11 Dec 1850, Sarah Elizabeth Williams, only daughter of the late Dr. James
T. and Mrs. Anna S. Williams, aged 7 years and 3 months.

Issue of January 10, 1851 [USC]
    Died on the 30th ultimo of Typhoid Fever, after a protracted illness of 18 days,
Mr. Gideon Owens, in the 53d year of his age...leaves a wife and 6 children.
    Died on Saturday morning, 4 January, of Consumption, Mr. Anthony G. Cook, in the
43d year of his age...leaves a wife and 5 small children.
    Died on Thursday, the 2nd inst., at his father's residence, of Typhoid Fever, Mr.
Andrew J. Putnam, in the 24th year of his age...leaving a father, brothers and sisters.

Issue of January 17, 1851 [USC]
    Died at his residence in Laurens District, on the 4th inst. of Pulmonary Consumption,
William A. Waldrop, in the 44th year of his age...leaving a large interesting family.

Issue of January 24, 1851 [USC & Laurens]
    Died near Greenwood in Abbeville District, on the night of the 7th inst., while
seated in a chair by the fire, Mrs. Mary Weir, consort of Mr. Thomas Wier, aged about
80 years. She was a native of Ireland and emigrated to this country with her husband
sometime after their marriage...member of the Presbyterian Church for many years.
    Married on the 16th inst., by Rev. Samuel Townsend, Mr. Ludy[?] P. Davenport
to Miss Susan E. Shaw, all of Laurens District.
    Married on Thursday evening, the 9th inst., by Rev. J. W. McCall, Dr. W. Agnew of
Due West, Abbeville, to Miss Lizzie T., daughter of Dr. John Sullivan, of Greenville
District.
    Married on Thursday evening, the 16th inst., by Rev. J. W. McCall, Mr. M. A. Hardin
of Cass Co., Ga., to Miss Emma A., daughter of Dr. John C. Sullivan of Greenville Dist.
    Married on the 16th inst., by Rev. Tolaver Robertson, Mr. Joseph Burdett to Miss
Amanda Putman, both of Laurens District.
    Married on the 22nd inst., by Rev. Tolaver Robertson, Rev. James Woodruff of Spartan-
burg, to Miss Adaline Lockhart of Laurens District.
    Married on the 23d inst., by Rev. Tolaver Robertson, Mr. John Mills and Miss Nancy
Mary Patterson, both of Laurens District.

Issue of January 31, 1851 [USC]
    Married on the 30th inst., Mr. Wm PHilson to Miss Jane E. Wright, all of this Dist.

Issue of February 7, 1851 [USC]
    Married on the 30th ult., by Rev. W. B. Boyd, Capt. H. H. Watkins, to Miss Hannah,
daughter of Capt. John Culbertson, all of Laurens District.
    Married on the 1st inst., at the residence of Dr. James Tinsly, by Rev. E. Lindsay,
Mr. James Williams, to Miss Mary T. Johnson, all of Laurens District.
    Married on 21 January last, by Rev. Joshua Gilbert, Mr. T. B. Nelson to Miss Elizabeth
Massey, all of Greenville District.

Issue of February 7, 1851 (contd.)
Married on the 31st January, by the same, Mr. T. P. Massey, to Miss Elizabeth Nelson, all of Greenville District.

Issue of February 14, 1851 [USC]

Died at Tylersville, Laurens, S. C. on the 5th inst., Mrs. Elizabeth Craig, wife of Thomas Craig, Esq., in the 56th year of her age...member of the Presbyterian Church more than 30 years.
Died on the 12th inst., at the residence of her father, Miss Nancy N. Calhoun, daughter of Col. P. L. and Mrs. Martha Calhoun, in the 14th year of her age.

Issue of February 21, 1851 [USC]

Died on Sunday, the 9th inst., at the residence of her father, in Laurens District, Miss Lavinia, youngest daughter of Elijah Teague, in the 16th year of her age, and on Wednesday the 12th inst., the father, Elijah Teague, in the 60th year of his age, both of Typhoid Pneumonia.

Issue of February 28, 1851 [USC]

Married on the 23rd inst., by Rev. Abrnette Smith, Maj. G. W. Connor of Laurens,to Miss Mary Jane, daughter of Dr. W. L. M. Austin of Greenville.
Died at the residence of his mother, near Laurensville, James P. Kennedy, in the 34th year of his age.

Issue of March 7, 1851 [USC]

Died on the 23rd ult. at his residence, after a severe illness, Mr. Elihu Nelson, in the 45th year of his age...left a widow and 10 children.
Died at the residence of her father in Laurens District, on the 21st ult., Mary Elizabeth, 2nd daughter of Albert and Margaret Miller, in the 17th year of her age... member of the M. E. Church.
Died on the 1st inst., at the residence of her uncle, Dr. Watts, in Laurens District, Anna Watts Ball, daughter of Narcissa and John Ball, aged 18 years and 4 months.

Issue of March 14, 1851 [USC]

Married on the 20th ult.,by M. P. Evins, Esq., Mr. A. F. Moore to Miss Amanda Gillespie, all of Laurens District.
Died at the residence of her brother, on the 1st inst., Miss Sarah G. Pinson, in the 20th year of her age...member of the Baptist Church.

Issue of March 21, 1851 [USC]

Married in Desoto County, Mississippi, on the 16th January last, by the Rev. S. B. Lewers, Mr. James M. Love, to Miss Nancy Ligon, all of the county and state aforesaid.

Issue of March 28, 1851 [USC]

Married on the morning of the 18th inst., Mr. John Hill to Miss Lucinda Adair, all of this district.

Issue of April 11, 1851 [USC]

Married by the Rev. J. L. Young, on the 3rd [torn], J. L. Williams to Miss Sarah Ann Finney...Laurens District.

Issue of April 25, 1851 [USC]

Married at the residence of John Johnson, Esq., on the 10th inst., by J. Johnson, Esq., Mr. Isaac Jacks, son of Wm & Polly Jacks, to Miss Sarah Dillard, daughter of James and Elizabeth Dillard, all of Laurens District.
Died at the residence of her father, in Laurens District, on the 27th of March last, Sabra, second daughter of John W. and Elizabeth Coleman, in the 27th year of her age... member of the Baptist Church.
Died on Wednesday, the 9th inst.,at his residence in Laurens District, Samuel Gary in the 69th year of his age...Deacon in the Baptist Church.
Died on the morning of the 28th ult., at the residence of Dr. E. G. Simpson, Abbeville Dist., Mrs. Sarah Cunningham, relict of Robert Cunningham, decd.,aged about 73 years...a member of Liberty Spring [Presbyterian] Church about 6 years. She was a sister of Dr. R. Campbell, Sen., an elder of Liberty Spring Church, who is now the only surviving member of his father's family.

Issue of May 9, 1851 [USC]

Married on the 4th inst.,by Rev. D. F. Hadden, Mr. O. Burgess to Miss Rebecca Johnson, both of this village.
Died at the residence of her father in this District, on the 27th of March, Sally Elizabeth second daughter of James C. and Sally P. Young, aged 1 year and 11 months.

14

Also on the 8th of April, Nancy Washington, [died], eldest daughter of the same parents, aged 3 years and 6 months.

Issue of May 16, 1851 [USC]
    Married on the 13th inst., by Rev. Mr. Townsend, Mr. Joseph J. Lyons, of Abbeville, to Miss Sarah S. Godfrey, of Laurens.
    Married on the 6th inst., by the Rev. Wm. B. Boyd, Mr. Masten Henderson to Miss Lucinda Pinson, all of Laurens District.
    Married on the 6th inst., by the Rev. Tolaver Robertson, Mr. Melmoth Woods to Miss Emily Dial, all of this District.
    Married on the 29th ult., by Rev. C. B. Stewart, Mr. J. F. Saxon to Miss M. E. Pitts, all of this District.
    Married on the 1st inst., by the same, Mr. Samuel J. Craig of Tylersville, to Miss Sarah Saxon, daughter of Joshua and E. Saxon, all of this District.
    Died on the 13th inst., Mrs. Susan Allen, wife of Charles Allen, Esq., at the residence of her husband in Laurens District. She had reached the 87th year of her age... member of the M. E. Church...an aged husband, whose youth was actively spent in the scenes of the revolution, and with whom she has lived for 68 years, still lingers totteringly.

Issue of May 30, 1851 [USC]
    Married in Perry County, Alabama, on the 6th inst., by Rev. D. D. Sanderson, Dr. George W. Brownder to Miss Rebecca, eldest daughter of John Cunningham, Esq., formerly of Laurens District, S. C.
    Died on the 1st inst., in Abbeville District, Sarah Frances, wife of Dr. Enoch Agnew, and daughter of John C. Sullivan of Greenville District, in the 27th year of her age...member of the M. E. Church...leaves husband and two infant daughters.

Issue of June 6, 1851 [USC]
    Died on the 28th ult., in this village, Mrs. Elizabeth, consort of Capt. James Word, aged 73 years. Mother Word came to this District in early life...joined the M. E. Church in 1831...she has left children and grandchildren in this and other states.

Issue of June 13, 1851 [USC]
    Died at her fathers residence near Huntington, Laurens District, Miss Eunicy Templeton, in the 37th year of her age...member of the Presbyterian Church.
    Died of cholera Infantum, on the 30th ult., at the residence of his father in Laurens District, George Stennis, son of Samuel & Mary A. McKittrick, aged 1 year, 9 months, 26 days.
    [The notice of the death of Solomon Bobo appears in this issue with a notation from Carolina Spartan. See issue of June 5, 1851 of Spartan.]

Issue of June 30, 1851 [USC]
    Died in Pontotoc County, Miss., on the 22d May last, of Ulcer of the Stomach, Mr. John F. Houlditch, son of George and Jane Houlditch, aged 31 years, 1 month, and 5 days, leaving a wife and two small sons by a former marriage...born in Laurens District, 17 April 1820, where he lived until the winter of 1841, when he removed to Pontotoc County, Miss.... joined the Baptist Church at a Protracted Meeting in July 1847.... at Cherry Creek.

Issue of July 4, 1851 [USC]
    Married on the 22d ult., by Rev. Christopher Sewel, Augustus A. Coleman, formerly of this District, to Miss Ann Smith of Jackson County, Ga.
    Married on 20 May last at W. McGowan's by the Rev. James C. Vaughan, Mr. W. B. Coleman to Miss Martha McWilliams.

Issue of July 11, 1851 [USC]
    Mrs. Caroline Shell, wife of Henry R. Shell, died near Laurensivlle, on the 28th June last, aged 42 years and 19 days. On the 4th instant, her infant daughter followed...a good mistress to her servants, a fond and devoted mother...member of the Baptist Church for 15 years.

Issue of July 18, 1851 [USC]
    Married on the 8th inst., Mr. Brooks of Newberry, to Mrs. M. Goodman of Laurens.
    Married on the 13th inst., Mr. Aaron Pitts to Miss M. Catharine Sadler, all of Newberry.
    Died in Floyd County, Ga., on the 13th June ult., Elizabeth Harden, daughter of Eli and Jane Harden, age unknown to the writer. She was the granddaughter of John and Nancy Ball of this District.
    Died of Pneumonia, at his residence in Sumter County, Alabama, on the 29th of May, Mr. Willis Ball...born and raised in Laurens District, emigrated to Alabama in 1828...member of the Baptist Church...leaves wife and three small children, brothers and sisters, and an aged father.

Issue of July 18, 1851 (Contd.)
    Died at Summerville, S. C. on the 4th inst. of Apoplexy, Mr. Daniel Cook, formerly of
this District, and for several years a resident of Charleston...an affectionate husband,
a kind father.

Issue of August 1, 1851 [USC]
    Married on the 15th inst., by Rev. C. C. Wightman, Thomas Jones to Miss Jane Cromwell
of Abbeville.
    Married on the 17th inst., by Rev. D. W. Bartow, J. J. W. Whitmore to Miss Emma Crom-
well, all of Abbeville.
    Died at her residence in this District, of Dropsy of the Chest, produced from Rheu-
matism, Catharine Hitch, consort of John Hitch, decd, aged 67 years, 9 months, 19 days.
She leaves friends, 4 children, and a number of grandchildren...member of the Presbyterian
Church.
    On the 14th ult., departed this life, Dr. C. F. Gary, aged about 52 years, leaving a
wife and 6 children...born and raised in Laurens District...spent the summer at Chick's
Springs, near Greenville for his health, but grew worse...member of the Baptist Church.
    On the 17th ult., of Chronic Diarrhea, died at the residence of her parents in Miss.,
Ann Elizabeth, daughter of M. D. and J. P. Martin, aged 17 months.

Issue of August 15, 1851 [USC]
    Married on the 24th ult., by Rev. Tolaver Robertson, Mr. P. Garrett and Miss Susan
Durham.
    Married on the 31st ult., by Rev. Tolaver Roberson, Mr. Washington Shell and Miss Mary
Dial.
    Married on Thurs a. m., the 17th ult., in Monroe County, Arkansas, by Rev. J. B. Lam-
bert, Dr. Thos. G. Wilkes, formerly of this District, to Mrs. S. A. E. Hall, late of Tenn.

Issue of August 22, 1851 [USC]
    Died in DeSoto County, Mississippi, on Monday night, 14th July last, Mr. Thomas A.
Brownlee, long a citizen of Laurens District, S. C., in the 62d year of his age...removed
from Laurens District in 1849 and spent the last year in Tennessee...in January moved to
DeSoto County, Miss. He has left a large family...two daughters still in the land of
their nativity.

Issue of September 12, 1851 [USC]
    Married on the 31st of August, by the Rev. J. Cheek, Mr. D. Neely to Miss E. Mitchell,
all of Laurens.
    On the 28th ult., by Rev. Tolaver Robertson, Mr. Wilson Kellar to Miss Sarah Lamb,
both of Spartanburg District.
    Married on the 21st ult., by Rev. J. L. Young, Mr. Isaac Adair to Miss Eliza A.
Dillard, all of Laurens.
    Married on the 7th ult., by Rev. W. B. Boyd, Mr. James F. Henderson, to Miss Melinda
Clardy, all of Laurens District.
    Died of Typhoid Fever in Pontotoc County, Miss., on the 4th of August, Mrs. Mary S.
Bailey, consort of Samuel R. Bailey, and daughter of Isaac and Martha Mitchell, formerly
of Laurens District, aged 27 years, 7 months, and 1 day....born in Laurens District, 3
Jan 1824, m. to Samuel Bailey in Dec. 1842, and removed with her husband to this county
in the fall of 1848. In August 1843, joined the Baptist Church at Bethabara, Laurens
District. She has left 4 small children, all sons...the two youngest, twins about 13
months old.

Issue of September 19, 1851 [USC]
    Married on the 11th inst., by Rev. Mr. D. Humphries, Mr. Thomas Wilkes of Anderson
District, to Miss Martha Hix, of this Village.

Issue of September 26, 1851 [USC]
    Married on the 25th inst., by Rev. T. J. Pearce, Mr. Samual Vance, Sr. to Miss
Clarissa D. Simmons, all of this District.

Issue of October 3, 1851 [USC]
    Died at her residence in Laurens District, on the 8th ult., Mrs. Henrietta Cook, relict
of Abram Cook, Esq., formerly of Georgia. She was a daughter of the late Capt. William
Irby of Laurensville, S. C....born in the year 1796 and died of Consumption...leaves three
daughters and a son.
    Died on the 16th ult., at his residence in Laurens District, Mr. Robert Taylor Sen'r,
in the 77th year of his age.
    Died on the 4th ult., at her residence in Pickens District, Mrs. Elizabeth Williamson,
daughter of Rev. Hendrick T. and Mary Arnold, in the 31st year of her age...member of the
Methodist Protestant Church for 8 or 10 years before her death.

16

Issue of October 17, 1851 [USC]
    Died of croup, Joseph J. Sullivan, child of J. H. and M. D. Sullivan, aged 3 years and 6 months.
    Died on the 6th inst., Mary M., daughter of Thomas and Sophronia Darnall, aged 1 year and 29 days.
    Died on the 13th inst., at the residence of his father, near Spring Grove, Laurens District, William Thomas, oldest son of Thos. A. and Eliza Rudd, aged 2 years and 6 months and 12 days.

Issue of October 24, 1851 [USC]
    Married on Thursday, the 16th inst., at Lexington C. H., Maj. J. C. Eichelberger of Newberry, to Miss Lizzie Addison of Lexington.
    Married on the 30th ult., by Rev. Tolaver Robertson, Mr. Wm Blakely to Miss Melinda Mahaffy, both of Greenville.
    Married on the 24th ult., by the same, Mr. A. Alexander to Miss Mary Willis, both of Spartanburg.
    Married on the 25th ult by the same, Mr. Franklin Blakely to MIss Susan Moore, both of Spartanburg.
    Married on the 25th ult., by the same, Mr. Samuel Simpson, to Miss Lucy Millener, both of Laurens.
    Married on the 21st inst., by the same, Capt. Wm Leek to Miss M. M. Willis, both of Laurens.
    Died in Pickens District, on the 10th inst., of congestion of the brain, William Leland, infant son and only child of William A. and M. A. M. Templeton, aged 1 year, 1 month and 20 days.

Issue of October 31, 1851 [USC]
    Married on the 2d inst., by Rev. W. B. Boyd, Mr. John Knight to MissNancy Caroline Bolt., both of Laurens.
    Married on the 24th inst., by the same, Mr. Chesley Devaule, to Miss R. E. Blakely, of Laurens.

Issue of November 7, 1851 [USC]
    Died on the 13th ult., of Bilious Fever, George W. Bailey, son of W. & L. F. Bailey, in his ninth year.
    Died on the 31st ult., Thos S. Bonds, in the 47th year of his age...leaves a widow, three children, three brothers, and three sisters.
    Died on the 6th inst., ----son Henry, son of Albert and Martha---- [torn], aged 2 years 11 months, and 4 days.

Issue of November 14, 1851 [USC]
    Married on the 13th inst., by Rev. S. Townsend, Mr. WM. M. Badgett to Miss Clarissa D., daughter of John Simmons, all of this village.
    Married on the 6th inst., by Rev. Samuel Townsend, Capt. B. L. Potter to Miss Martha Hewet, all of this village.

Issue of November 28, 1851 [USC]
    Married on the 6th inst., by Rev. Jas. Cheek, G. W. Neely to Miss Parmelia Ann Melloy, both of this district.
    Married by Rev. C. B. Stewart, Mr. Andrew Tod to Miss Sarah McKitrick, all of Laurens, [no date given].
    Married on the 4th inst., in Laurenceville, Geo., by Rev. J. C. Patterson, Mr. John S. Porter of Richmond, to Miss Mary M. Mills of Gwinnett Co., Geo.
    Married on the 20th inst., in Newberry Dist., by the Rev. J. F. Peterson, Dr. J. Y. Henderson, of Edgefield District, to Miss Elizabeth A. Huggins.
    Married on the 19th inst., by Rev. J. C. Vaughan, Mr. David Boazman, to Miss N. E. Griffin, all of this District.
    Died on the 24th inst., Martha Caroline, daughter of William and Matilda Richardson, aged 7 months and 26 days.
    Died of typhoid fever, on the 23rd inst., Mr. William B. Sheldon, in the 58th year of his age...member of the Presbyterian Church.

Issue of December 12, 1851 [USC]
    Murder on Monday last [8 Dec.?], of W. A. Pitts, by negro George.

Issue of December 19, 1851 [USC]
    Married in Tippah Co., Miss., on the 18th of September, by Rev. A. Slaver, C. M. Hewet, to Miss Ann Hughy, all formerly of this District.
    Married on the 25th of Nov., by Rev. James Dennis, Mr. J. Tharra of Desoto to Miss Caroline S. Pasley (formerly of this district) of Panola, all of Miss.

Married on the 11th inst., by R. J. Sullivan, Esq., Mr. Wesley Morrison, to Miss Rhoda Baldwin, both of Laurens District.

Died on the 20th ult., of croup, Rebecca Jane, eldest daughter of Kennedy S. and Margaret A. Taylor, aged 3 years, 9 months, 19 days.

Died in Cusseta, Ala., on the 21st ult., of croup, William James, son of Burris and Martha A. Johnson, aged 4 years, 6 months, and 6 days.

Issue of January 23, 1852 [USC]

Married on the 8th inst., by Rev. Miles Puckett, Maj. C. H. Dillard to Mrs. D. E. Tarrant, all of Union District.

Married on the 11th ult., by Rev. James C. Patterson, Mr. John W. N. Williams to Miss Louisa R. A., daughter of Robert Craig of Gwinnet Co., Georgia.

Married on the 1st inst., by Rev. S. L. Knight, Mr. J. W. Simpson of Greenville, to Miss Pyrenia Holcombe, of Laurens District.

Issue of August 20, 1852 [USC]

Died on the 20th ult., in Shreveport, La., Sarah Lucy, daughter of J. W. and H. J. E. Smith, and granddaughter of the late Samuel and Lucy Gary of this District, aged 1 year, 10 months, and 2 days.

Departed this life in Pickens District, S. C., William Andrew Templeton, in the 25th year of his age...leaves a wife and infant sons, a widowed mother, brothers and sisters... member of the Presbyterian Church.

Departed this life on the 3rd of July in Victoria, Texas, of Cholera, Dr. William S. Leeke, formerly of Laurens District, in the 29th year of his age...leaves a large circle of relatives and friends.

Issue of August 27, 1852 [USC]

Departed this life on Tuesday, the 28th of July last, Mrs. Phoebe C. Williams, wife of Col. John Williams, in the 43rd year of her age...2nd daughter of James and Rhoda Young, born in Laurens District at Mountville, 10 March 1810...member of the Presbyterian Church.

Died on the 17th inst., Mr. James Bramblet, in the 41st year of his age...leaving a wife and 3 small children.

Issue of September 17, 1852 [USC]

Married on Tuesday, the 14th inst., by Rev. Mr. Archer, Mr. W. C. McCullough of Alabama, to Miss Harriet A. Donaldson, of Greenville District.

Married on the 6th inst., by G. W. Jaratt, Esq., Mr. H. C. Elliott of this place to Miss Altha S. Duckworth of Morganton, N. C.

Issue of October 15, 1852 [USC]

Departed this life in the 60th year of his age, on 28 August last, of typhoid fever, at his own residence in DeSoto County, Miss., Rev. Samuel B. Lewers, after an illness of 26 days...a native of Laurensville, S. C....received his education, literary and Theological in his native state...a graduate of South Carolina College...member of the Laurensville Bar and practiced law...he volunteered services in Creek Indian War of 1813...elected Colonel of the Regiment of Cavalry in his own District...the only son of a pious mother... presented himself to Friendship [Presbyterian] Church...commenced laboring at a church, which is now Bethany, before an edifice was there...sleeps in burial ground of Fredonia Church, DeSoto Co....funeral services conducted by Rev. L. B. Gaston from Oxford, formerly from Pendleton, S. C....leaves a wife and children....Rock Mills, Sept. 30, 1852. [this obituary over one column long.]

Issue of October 22, 1852 [USC]

Married by Rev. William B. Boyd, Mr. Harrison Fuller to Miss Elizabeth, daughter of Rev. William Hitt, all of this District.

Died at his residence in Laurens District, on the 11th inst., Charles Fowler in the 68th year of his age...member of the Presbyterian Church.

Issue of January 7, 1853 [USC]

Married on the 23d ult., by Rev. Tolaver Robertson, Mr. James Coleman, to Miss Levinia Teague.

Married on the 16th ult., by Rev. Tolaver Robertson, Mr. Patillo Moore to Miss Martha Todd.

Married on the 21st ult., by Rev. Tolaver Robertson, Mr. Moses Madden to Miss Martha Tinsley, all of this District.

Married on the 16th ult., by Rev. S. Spruell, Mr. James E. Watson of Laurens, to Miss Lury B. Reeder, of Newberry.

Married on the 21st ult., by Rev. C. B. Stewart, Mr. G. L. Martindale to Miss Martha Minerva, daughter of Isabella and A. S. Hutchinson, Esq., all of Laurens District.

Issue of March 4, 1853 [USC]
    Married on Thursday, the 24th of February, by Rev. D. F. Hadden, Mr. David Stoddard to Miss Jane Sloan, both of Laurens.

Issue of March 11, 1853 [USC]
    Died in Mud Springs, Eldorado County, California, in the 23d year of his age, on the 17th inst., Mr. Elihu McPherson, a native of Laurens District, S. C., whence he emigrated to this state 10 months since, engaged in mining...attached himself to the Baptist Church in 1848.   Mud Springs, Calif.   24 Dec 1853 [sic].

Issue of March 18, 1853 [USC]
    Married on the 8th inst., by M. P. Evins, Esq., Arthur Rogers to Miss Celista Curry, all of this District.
    Died at his residence in Laurens District, on the 16th February, Abram Thompson, in the 65th year of his age...member of Associate Reformed Church at Head Springs.

Issue of March 25, 1853 [USC]
    Died at his residence in Laurens District, 27th February 1853, Mr. Jeremiah Leak, in the 70th year of his age...member of the Methodist Episcopal Church, South, for 45 years.
    Departed this life at her residence near Mountville, on the 5th inst., Mrs. Sarah Motes, in the 76th year of her age...leaving a large family of children, some of whom reside in the west...she was never a member of any church, but lived an exemplary life.
    Died at his residence on Wednesday, the 16th inst., Mr. Riley Milam, in the 75th year of his age...member of the Baptist Church.

Issue of April 1, 1853 [USC]
    Married in Camden, on the 22d ult., by Rev. S. W. Capers, Mr. Albert H. Farrow of Newberry to Miss Margaret Ann, eldest daughter of John R. and Sarah A. Joy, of Camden.
    Died on the 28th inst., at the residence of her mother in this District, Miss Mary Cheek, in the 21st year of her age...leaves a mother, brothers and sisters.

Issue of April 8, 1853 [USC]
    Died on the 1st of March 1853, in Newton County, Ga., at the residence of Abraham Riley, Patrick Riley, in the 69th year of his age, a native of Laurens District.

Issue of June 10, 1853 [USC]
    Married on the 2d inst., at Thomas Dendy's, by W. D. Watts, Esq., Mr. A. S. Taylor to Miss Urilla[sic] Milam, daughter of the late Col. R. Milam, of this District.

Issue of June 24, 1853 [USC]
    Mr. Robert Thompson died yesterday morning at the residence in this town [Newberry].
                                                            Newberry Sentinel.
Issue of July 22, 1853 [USC]
    Married on the 12th inst., by Rev. D. F. Hadden, Mr. Timothy Sloan to Miss Sophia Power, all of this District.
    Died of Paralysis, on the 10th of July, Sunday, Mrs. Martha Roberts,   consort of Goerge Roberts, aged 67 years...born in Laurens District, emigrated to Meriwether Co., Ga., in 1846 where she died.

Issue of October 7, 1853 [USC]
    Died at the residence of William Studdard, in the upper part of Laurens District, 15th September last, James Dunlap, in the 79th year of his age...son of Samuel and Nancy Dunlap, who emigrated from Ireland a short time before the Revolution, and settled in Laurens District, where James was born...member of the Methodist Episcopal Church.
    Died on the 25th ult., at the residence of their father in this District, Dr. Henry Martin Meredith and Rebecca Priscilla Meredith, eldest son and daughter of Samuel and Lucinda Meredith...the former born Feb. 19, 1829 and the latter Oct. 31, 1830...only 6 hours intervened between their deaths, Rebecca died at noon and Henry died at 6 P. M....Dr. Henry recently graduated from the Medical College at Charleston...leaves parents and a brother and sister..
    Died at his residence in this District, on the 27th ult., Mr. Jesse Garrett, aged 87 years and 20 days...leaving a large family and many friends.

Issue of December 23, 1853 [USC]
    Married on Sunday morning, the 11th inst., by Rev. A. Acker, George M. McDavid to Miss Maria L. Shumate, all of Greenville District.
    Married on the 15th inst., by Rev. D. F. Hadden, Capt. R. H. Williams, of Martin's Depot, to Miss Jane A. Read, of Newberry District.
    Married on the 1st inst., by Rev. R. F. Babb, Mr. Martin Woods to Miss Emily Mahaffy, all of this District.

Issue of December 23, 1853 [contd.]

Married on the 15th inst., by Rev. R. F. Babb, William P. Traynham to Miss Sarah J. Avery, all of this District.

Married on the 1st inst., by Rev. Silas Knight, Mr. W. M. J. Boyd, eldest son of Rev. W. B. Boyd to Miss Agnes Lowe, eldest daughter of Capt. James Lowe, decd, all of Laurens District.

[Copies of the following issues of the LAURENSVILLE HERALD have been recently discovered and made available just in time for inclusion here..Film copies are in the Laurens County Library.]

Issue of January 5, 1846

Departed this life near Laurensville, on the 30th ult., Mrs. Sarah Sullivan, consort of C. P. Sullivan, Esq....body found in Little River...[apparently a suicide]...leaves mother, husband, and four small children. [a long obituary].

Issue of January 12, 1846

Married on the 23d ult., by Rev. C. B. Stewart, Mr. Archibald Smith to Miss Nancy Templeton.

Married on the 4th ult., by Rev. J. Young, Mr. Henry Davis to Miss Jane Todd.

Married on the 1st inst., by Reuben Thomas, Esq., Mr. George W. Leak to Miss Mahala Thomason, all of this District.

Issue of March 2, 1846

Married on the 26th ult., by Rev. Mr. J. McCall, Reb. Judge Glenn to Miss Jane, eldest daughter of Squire Calhoun.

Issue of March 9, 1846

Married on the 3d inst., by Rev. Edwin Cater, Mr. Jesse S. HIx to Miss Mary H. Young, both of this District.

Married on the 3rd inst. by Rev. Samuel B. Lewers, Thos. R. Gerguson of Spartanburgh, to Miss Martha E., daughter of Mr. Noah Smith of this District.

Married on the 3d inst., by Rev. Samuel B. Lewers, Alexander W. Glenn to Miss Lucinda M., daughter of Mr. Noah Smith, all of this District.

Married in Spartanburg District, on the 26th ult., by Rev. J. L. Young, Mr. Albert Copeland to Miss Charlotte A. C. Ferguson.

Issue of April 6, 1846

Married at Union Court House, on the 24th ult., by S. T. Crenshaw, Esq., Mr. W. A. Hoard to Miss Almira Clark.

Died on the 10th[?] Feb last, Mrs. Margaret G. Nance, wife of Mr. F. Nance, in the 30th year of her age...member of the Presbyterian Church...leaves a husband and five children.

Issue of April 20, 1846

Married on the 16th inst., by Rev. Mr. Haltum, Mr. John N. Golding, to Miss Martha Ann, youngest daughter of James and Frances Anderson, all of this District.

Departed this life, March 25, 1846, aged 24 years and 13 days, Mrs. Matilda Elizabeth, wife of Cornelius T. Tribble...member of the Associate Reformed Church at Providence, Laurens District....left husband and four children. [Providence A. R. P. Church is now located in Clinton, S. C.--BHH]

Issue of May 4, 1846

Married on Thursday the 23d ult., by Rev. J. W. McCall, Capt. Wm. L. Gunnels to Miss Sarah Imogene Pinson, both of Greenville District.

Married on the same evening, by Rev. William P. Martin, Mr. Elisha Williamson of Laurens District ot Miss Elmira Mattison of Anderson District.

Issue of May 18, 1846

Died in Laurensville this morning, Eliza Ann Henry, daughter of N. V. Bailey, in the 7th month of her age.

Died of Bronchitis, in Chickasaw Co., Miss, about 7 o'clock PM, 31st March last, Mrs. Arianna Gates, aged about 20 years, wife of George E. Gates, and daughter of Capt. George Bowen of Waterloo, Laurens District, S. C. She and a younger sister were married at the last mentioned place Sept. 5, 1844 and left shortly for Mississippi...member of the Presbyterian Church.

Issue of June 8, 1846

Married on Thursday evening, the 28th ult., by Rev. Dr. Pasley, Mr. J. C. Babb to Miss Emily N., daughter of James S. and Emily R. Rodgers, all of Laurens District.

[additional issues of the Laurensville Herald are found beginning p. 122]

Issue of January 6, 1854 [Duke]
    Married in Columbia, S. C., on the 25th inst., by the Rev. J. J. O'Connell, Mr. Madison Farrow of Laurensville, to Miss Mary Ann Brady of the former place.

Issue of January 13, 1854 [Duke]
    Married on Tuesday evening the 3rd inst., by Rev. S. Knight, Joseph Atwood, Esq., to Miss Elizabeth, daughter of Salathiel Shockley, all of Laurens District.
    Married on the 12th inst., by Rev. D. Wills, Col. W.C. Harris to Miss Corrinna M. Pressley, all of this village.

Issue of January 20, 1854 [Duke]
    Married on the 20th o December last, by Rev. R. F. Babb, Mr. Martin Mahaffy to Miss Clarinda Armstrong.
    Married on the 22nd of December, by Rev. R. F. Babb, Mr. Martin Bolt to Miss Lawrissa Bolt, daughter of Edmond Bolt.
    Married on the 12th inst., by Rev. R. F. Babb, Capt. Dempsey Armstrong, to Miss Lucinda Bolt., all of Laurens District.
    Died on the 12th inst. at his residence near Dunlapsville, Mr. Allen Walker, aged 63 years...left a devoted wife and 6 children, never attached himself to any denomination.
    Died at her residence in Laurens District, on Sunday evening, the 1st inst., Mrs. E. J. Todd, relict of the late Dr. John Todd, in the 69th year of her age...emigrated from Virginia (her native state) to Georgia in 1799 and remained about 8 years, removed to Laurens District and settled near the Mountain Shoals, at which place she lived until her death...member of Associate Reformed Church. She was particularly attached to her children.

Issue of January 27, 1854 [Duke]
    Married on the 24th inst. by Rev. E. Lindsay, Col. J. W. Simmons, to Miss Elizabeth Hunter, all of Laurens District.

Issue of February 10, 1854 [Duke]
    Departed this life on the 1 January last in Greenville District, S. C., Mrs. Eleanor Narcissa, youngest daughter of Mr. James and Mrs. Agnes Woodside, and consort of Mr. Robert Martin...joined Presbyterian Church of Friendship, after which she attached herself to Fairview Church...Shortly after marriage, she and her husband removed to Georgia... helped organize church at Frostown...after remaining there about 10 years, removed to Greenville District.

Issue of February 24, 1854 [Duke]
    Married on the 2d inst., by Rev. John Norman, Mr. B. F. Jones of Union District to Miss Catharine Blakely of Laurens.
    Married on Thursday, the 2nd inst., by Elihu Watson, Esq., Mr. William Leavell to Miss Margaret McCoy, all of Laurens District.
    Married in Cassville, on the evening of the 14th inst., by Rev. C. A. Crowell, Mr. Henry Z. Clardy to Miss Louisa Chapman, all of that place.
    Died at his residence in Laurens District, on the 21st inst., Mr. Robert Allison in the 77th year of his age...left a large family of children and grandchildren.
    Departed this life on the 11th inst. at the residence of her brother in Laurens District, Miss Mary Wallice, only daughter of the late Jonathan and Elizabeth Wallice, aged 46 years...member of the Methodist E. Church at Bramlets for 20 years.
    Died at Cross Hill, on the 3d inst., Helen Gray Lindsay, only daughter of William and Mary Lindsay, aged 4 years.

Issue of March 3, 1854 [Duke & USC]
    Died on the morning of the 22d ult., James Edwin, infant son of Benjamin and Mary Johnson, aged 3 months.

Issue of March 10, 1854 [Duke]
    Married at Bivingsville, on the 22d February, by H. White, Esq., Mr. R. S. Briggs of Laurens to Miss Sarah D. LOckman, of Spartanburg.
    Departed this life in this place on the 8th ult., Mrs. Elizabeth Saxon, consort of J. F. W. Saxon, in the 33d year of her age...left a husband and six interesting children ...member of the Presbyterian Church.

Issue of March 17, 1854 [Duke]
    The Chester (SC) Standard announces the death of John Rosborough on the 2d inst., Clerk of Common Pleas for that District since 1800.

Issue of March 31, 1854 [Duke & USC]
    Died of pneumonia in this District, on the 25th inst., Pierce Butler, son of Wm T. and Adelia D. Chappel, aged 2 years, 5 months, 6 days.

Issue of April 7, 1854 [Duke & USC]
Married on the 23d ult., by Rev. E. Lindsay, Mr. Robert Waldrop to Miss Susan C. Vance of Laurens.
Married on the 23d ult., by Rev. R. F. Babb, Mr. Robert Wham to Miss Elizabeth Owens.
Married on Thursday evening, the 3oth inst., by Rev. J. C. Vaughan, Mr. S. A. Dunn, formerly of Laurens D. H., to Miss Matilda Gates, of the neighborhood of Vaughanville.
Married on the 30th ult., by Rev. T. Robertson, Mr. Jeremiah Glenn to Miss Elizabeth Barksdale, all of Laurens.

Issue of April 28, 1854 [Duke]
Married on the 18th inst., by Rev. Z. L. Holmes, Mr. R. S. Owens to Miss Nancy Blakely, all of Laurens.
Married on the 20th inst., by Rev. D. .F Haddon, Mr. Joseph F. Ramage to Miss Mary Bell, all of Laurens.
Died near Looxahoma,Desoto County, Miss., on the 5th inst., Simeon Liles, in the 50th year of his age...removed from Laurens District in winter of 1850...leaves wife and children...member of the Presbyterian Church.
Died in Newberry District, on the 15th inst. of Typhoid pneumonia, James T. Martin, in the 37th year of hi age...born and raised near Laurens C. H....member of Cross Road Baptist Church.

Issue of May 5, 1854 [Duke & USC]
Died on Monday morning, the 10th ult., Mrs. Nancy M. Watt, wife of Rev. J. B. Watt, of Mecklenburg, N. C., in the 34th year of her age...leaves a husband and 3 children.

Issue of May 12, 1854 [Duke & USC]
Married by Rev. J. J. Brantly in the Baptist Church at Newberry, on Tuesday evening, the 2d inst., Col. S. L. Rook of Laurens, to Miss Charlotte E., daughter of the Hon. T. B. Higgins of Newberry.
Departed this life on the 21st ult., in the lower part of this District., Mrs. Eliza Rudd, consort of Mr. T. A. Rudd, aged 24 years...leaves a husband and three small children.
Died near Adairsville, Gordon County, Georgia, on the 2d inst., with cholera infantum, Georgia Caroline, youngest child of R. C. and M. E. G. Saxon, aged 10 months.

Issue of May 19, 1854 [Duke & USC]
Died at Centreville in this District of paralysis, on the 12th of November 1853, Abner Jones Sr., in the 67th year of his age...leaves wife and 9 children.
Died at her residence near Tylersville in Laurens District, on Tuesday the 16th inst., of Dysentery, Mrs. Sarah Langston, in the 85th year of her age...native of Ireland, came to America when ten years of age...married in Laurens District to the late Henry Langston ...mother of a large family.

Issue of May 26, 1854 [Duke & USC]
Married on the 9th inst., by Rev. E. Lindsay, Mr. James. E. Young of Laurens, to Miss E. Dalrymple of Newberry.
Died at her residence in Newberry on Monday, 8 May 1854, Mrs. Elliott Dandridge Read, consort of the late Wm Read, aged 85...member of the Presbyterian Church.

Issue of June 2, 1854 [Duke & USC]
Married on the 16th ult. by Rev. Mr. Wills, Thomas Stobo Farrow of Laurensville, to Miss Laura A., daughter of the late Maj. James Edward Henry, of Spartanburg.
Departed this life in Laurens District, Mrs. Sophia Martin, wife of Lewis Martin in the 33d year of her age...in early life attached herself to the M. E. Church...died 1 May 1854...left a husband and four little children.
Died at her residence in Pontotoc County, Miss, on the 12th ult., Mrs. Nancy Funk in the 68th year of her age.
Died on the 20th ult., in this district of dropsy, Mr. Simeon Putman, in the 37th [87th?] year of his age...leaving a wife and five small children...member of the Baptist Church.

Issue of June 9, 1854 [Duke]
Died at her residence on Raiborns'[sic] Creek in Laurens District, May the 26th, Mrs. Sarah McNese, in the 86th year of her age...Her first husband, Capt. Lewis Saxon, an officer in the Revolution, died leaving her and 12 children. She then married Robert McNese, a soldier of the Revolution, whom she survived...member of th Baptist Church.
Departed this life on the 25th ult., Mrs. Mary Ann Elizabeth Hunter, wife of Henry M. Hunter and the last survivng child of Elihu Payne...Two years ago she was surrounded by a family of brothers and sisters.

Issue of June 16, 1854 [Duke & USC]
     Died on the 6th inst., at his residence in this district, Dr. Thomas Teague in the
65th year of his age...engaged in his profession about 30 years...[long eulogy].
     Died on the 8th inst., in this district, James, infant son of Tucker and Lucinda
Chandler, aged 19 months, 7 days.

Issue of June 23, 1854 [Duke & USC]
     Departed this life on the 18th inst, after an illnes of 16 days, James Laws Milles,
M. D. aged 80 years.

Issue of June 30, 1854 [Duke & USC]
     Died at the residence of her uncle, J. M. Sullivan in Greenville District, on the 13
of June 1854, Sarah Josephine, eldest daughter of George W. and Jane Sullivan, of Laurens
District, aged 15 years and 7 days.
     Died at his residence in this District, on Saturday morning, the 17th instant, of
typhoid dysentery, Mr. Thomas Hood, aged 82 years...born in the lower part of Laurens
District, soon after his parents emigrated from Ireland...later settled on Reedy River...
never married.
     Died in Laurensville, on the 11th inst., James H. Wright of typhoid fever...a young
man, just entering the arena of life's drama.

Issue of July 7, 1854[Duke & USC]
     Died suddenly at the residence in Pickens District, William D. Arnold, in the 70th
year of his age on 23 June...a native of Abbeville.
     Died on the 15th June at the residence of her son, Dr. Watts, in this District, Mrs.
Margaret Pollard Watts, relict of the late John Watts, aged 86 years...Capt. James
Pollard, the father of Mrs. Watts, moved to S. C. from Culpeper County, Va., and settled
on Saluda River, Laurens District, in 1772, where Richard Watts now resides.

Issue of July 21, 1854 [Duke]
     Died in this place on Thursday, the 13th inst., Mr. W. M. Crowder, aged 25 years...
born in Chester District, but principally raised in Lancaster.
     Died at the residence of her father, in this District, on the 15th inst., of Diarrhea
Miss Amanda Malvina, only daughter of John and Rachel Duvall, aged 19 years, 9 months,
10 days.
     Died at his residence, 5 miles west of Laurens C. H. on the 8th inst., of typhoid
fever, William Parker, in the 26th year of his age.

Issue of July 28, 1854 [Duke & USC]
     Married on the 23rd of July by Rev. E. Lindsey, Mr. John B. Parson of Pickens, to
Miss Margaret Ann Cook of Laurens District.
     Married on the 20th inst., by Rev. R. F. Babb, Mr. Turner R. Putman, to Miss Irena
Thomas, all of this district.
     Mrs. Margaret Dunlap, a native of this District, member of the Presbyterian Church,
died at her own residence near the place of her nativity, on Saturday morning, the
22nd inst., aged about 78 years...daughter of Judge John Hunter, who first represented
Ninety Six in the Congress of the U. S., widow of Maj. William Dunlap, who distinguished
himself as a Whig at Hayes' Station.
          [Her residence was about 3 miles south of Clinton, S. C. on Highway 72.
          She is buried in the family cemetery there.]

Issue of August 4, 1854 [Duke & USC]
     Married on the 27th of July, by the Rev. Mr. Telford, Mr. W. H. Manly to Miss E. M.
Murrey, all of Newberry,
     Died on the 25th ult., Colista, wife of Washington Curry, and daughter of Thomas and
Nancy Babb of Greenville, in the 30th year of her age...member of the Methodist Church.
     Died at his residence in this place, on the 22d ult., of bilious cholia, W. M.
Badgett, in the 35th year of his age...for many years a citizen of Laurens...member of
the Presbyterian Church.

Issue of August 11, 1854 [Duke]
     Departed this life on the 18th May near Euharley, Cass County, Ga., Ida, infant
daughter of Mardison and Mrs. D. A. Milam, aged 2 years, 26 days.
     Died on the 26th May, at the same place, Mrs. Dorrathea A., wife of Madison Milam,
aged 36 years, 1 month, 29 days.
     Died also on 23 June, Miss Frances E., eldest daughter of M & D. A. Milam, aged 14
years, 1 month and 9 days.
     Mr. M. and family moved to Cass County from Laurens District some years since. Mrs.
M. was a member of the Methodist E. Church.

Dr. J. W. Hitch, together with William Wilson and Isaac M. Christian, were on the 2nd ult., about 2 3/4 o'clock P. M., while sitting and conversing on the piazza of James M. Swann in Newton County, Ga., instantly killed by a stroke of lightning. Dr. Hitch was the second son of W. W. Hitch of Laurens District, S. C., aged 28 years, 1 month, and 15 days. In 1849 and 1850 he taught school in the neighborhood of Kings Chappel M. E. Church in his native District. He was awakened by a sermon of Rev. Henry Bass...He joined the Masonic order in 1851.

Issue of August 18, 1854 [Duke & USC]
    Died on the 3d inst., near Cherry Creek, Pontotoc, Mississippi, Sarah Ann, only child of J. N. and J. M. Jones, formerly of Laurens District, S. C., aged 1 year and 4 months.

Issue of August 25, 1854 [Duke & USC]
    Married on the 17th inst., by Rev. D. F. Hadden, Mr. Nathan C. Todd to Miss Margaret Todd, all of Laurens.
    Married on the 22d inst., by David Keller, Esq., Mr. John M. Clark of Laurensville, to Miss Nancy E. Dansby of Abbeville District.
    Died August 10, 1854, at his residence in Laurens District, Mr. Jeremiah Glenn, of dysentery, aged 40 years...left a wife, 2 children, and an aged mother.

Issue of September 1, 1854 [Duke & USC]
    Died on 9 July last, John Samuel, youngest son of Nathaniel and Martha Barksdale, aged 4 years and 3 months.

Issue of September 8, 1854 [Duke & USC]
    Married on the night of the 30th ult., by Rev. Jas. F. Smith, of Abbeville, Mr. William Scott to Miss Permelia Arnold, both of Laurens District.
    Married on the 30th ult., on Saluda, by Rev. A. Machan, Mr. J. J. Ritchey of Abbeville to Miss Polly Whitley of Laurens.

Issue of September 15, 1854 [Duke & USC]
    Married on the 12th inst., at the residence of James Bell, by Rev. E. Lindsey, Mr. R. J. Bell of Miss. to Miss Ruth Ann Bell of this District.

Issue of September 22, 1854 [Duke]
    Died near this place, on the 26th ult., in the 24th year of her age, Mrs. Elizabeth Rose, consort of James M. Rose...leaving a husband, two children & numerous relatives and friends.
    Died on the 7th inst., Harriet Susan, infant daughter of James M. and Elizabeth Rose, aged 5 months.
    William Fleming died on the 11th inst at Mount Bethel Camp-meeting...member of the Presbyterian Church at Friendship.

Issue of September 29, 1854 [Duke & USC]
    Married on the 26th inst., by Rev. R. F. Babb, Roland Jones to Mehali Coats, all of this District.
    Died on Wednesday, the 9th inst., at the residence of her mother, Mrs. Dr. Earle of Greenville, in the 27th year of her age, Emily, the wife of David J. Williams, Esq., of Laurens District...member of the Baptist Church...leaves a husband and 4 children, brothers and sisters, an aged mother.
    Died at this place, Monday, the 25th inst., John Wesley Saxon, in the 17th year of his age...orphan of Pleasant and _____ Saxon, who emigrated from this District to Miss. and died there leaving five boys and two girs. John became an apprentice in the Laurensville Herald office.
    Died near this place, on the 9th inst., Mrs. James Williams, in the 61st year of her age...member of the Presbyterian Church.
    Died on the 19th inst., Elmire, daughter of Mark and Mary Cooley, in the 13th year of her age.

Issue of October 6, 1854 [Duke & USC]
    Married on the 1st inst., by Rev. James M. Smith, Mr. John H. Spoon to Miss Elizabeth Graves, all of Laurens District.
    Departed this life on the 22d September last, at his residence in this District, Mr. John Bolt, in the 66th year of his age.
    Died on the 21st ult., Mrs. Mary Louisa Styles, consort of Dr. S. Farrow Styles of this District...daughter of Richard Ferguson, Esq., of Duncan's Creek, graduated two years ago from Limestone Springs.
    Died at his residence in this District, on the 7th ult., Rev. Miles Franks, in the 30th year of his age...preacher of the M. E. Church.

Issue of October 13, 1854 [Duke & USC]

Married in Cass County, Ga., September 27th, by Rev. Richard Milner, Mr. George W. Carey to Miss Otheley M. Speer, of Cass Co.

Married on the 25th September, by Rev. Richard Milner, Mr. McMoody to Miss Emily Sprowl, of Cass. Co.

Departed this life on the 19th ult., Mrs. Martha Barksdale, wife of Nathaniel Barksdale, in the 47th year of her age, leaving a husband and children...member of the Baptist Church over 20 years.

Issue of October 20, 1854 [Duke & USC]

Died on the 9th inst. of dysentery, Miss Nancy Jane Parks, in the 23d year of her age.

Died at his residence in Laurens District, on Friday the 4th August last, Wm Dial, in the 55th year of his age...leaving a wife and three children...member of the Methodist Church.

Issue of October 27, 1854 [Duke & USC]

Married on the 15th inst., by Rev. D. F. Hadden, Mr. Henry Bailey of Pontotoc Co., Mississippi to Miss Elizabeth Nugen of Laurens.

Married on Thursday, the 19th inst., by Rev. W. B. Boyd, Dr. Robert McDaniel to Miss Margaret Moore, all of this District.

Issue of November 3, 1854 [Duke]

Married on the 25th ult., by Rev. C. B. Stewart, Capt. M. J. Jenkins of Newberry District to Miss Eliza L. Jones of Laurens District.

Died at the residence of George Wolk on the 20th inst., Mr. Franklin Hellams, in the 27th year of his age.

Issue of November 10, 1854 [Duke & USC]

Died last Wednesday evening, Richard Cannon....Newberry Sentinel, 25th ult.

Issue of November 17, 1854 [USC]

Married on the 8th inst., by Rev. E. Lindsay, Mr. James Y. Luke to Miss Susan J. Hitt, all of Laurens District.

Married on the 9th inst., by Sterling Graydon, Esqr., Mr. Henry Eustace to Miss Elizabeth Price, all of this District.

Issue of November 24, 1854 [Duke & USC]

Married on the 19th inst., by Rev. R. F. Babb, Mr. Robertson Emmon to Miss Mary Bolt.

Died on 26 October in Greenville District, Mr. Jeremiah Hopkins, in the 60th year of his age...a devoted husband, an affectionate father.

Issue of December 8, 1854 [Duke & USC]

Married on the 20th inst., by Elihu Watson, Esq., Mr. Job Johnson to Miss Louisa J. E. Stapleton, all of Laurens District.

Married on the 30th ult., by Rev. C. B. Stewart of Laurens, James S. Peden to Miss E. M. Stenhouse, both of Greenville.

Died in Marion Co., Fla., on the 14 August, Mrs. Margaret A. Fleming, wife of James Fleming, in the 25th year of her age...born in Laurens District.

Two daughters of Mr. James Braddock,members of the Presbyterian Church, died Martha A. E. aged 23, and M. Elizabeth P. Braddock, aged 26. The latter on the 4th and the former on the 6th November.

Died of dysentery on Sunday morning, 29 October, Holly, second daughter of Mr. and Mrs. Cullen Lark, aged 1 year, 7 days.

Issue of December 15, 1854 [Duke & USC]

Married on the 27th ult by the Rev. W. H. Davis, Mr. J. W. Franks to Miss Jane Wilhite.

Married on the 7th inst., by Rev. E. Lindsay, Dr. R. C. Hunter to Miss L. F. Bonds.

Married on the 7th inst., by Rev. Abram Mitchell, Col.W. J. M. Jones to Miss S. E. Latimer, all of Laurens District.

Married in Pendleton, on Wednesday the 6th inst., by Rev. Thomas J. Earle, Thomas J. Warren Esq. of Camden, and Maria Louisa, daughter of Robert A. Maxwell, of the former place.

At the same time & place, by the Rev. T. L. McBride, Mr. J. R. Blake of Greenwood, and Miss Lizzie, youngest daughter of Robert A. Maxwell, Esq.

Married by Rev. J. W. McCall, Mr. T. D. Peden to Miss Lucinda, daughter of Charles & Parmelia Terry, all of Greenville District.

Died on the 10th inst., of Phthisis Pulmonalis, Miss Almira E. Raiford, daughter of Capt. D. S. & J. T. Raiford, in the 16th year of her age.

Issue of December 29, 1854 [USC]
    Departed this life on 8 November, Mr. Anthony Golding Campbell, of Spartanburg, in the 38th year of his age...elder of the Presbyterian Church...more recently elected to the Legislature.

Issue of January 5, 1855 [USC]
    Married on the 31st ult., by Rev. Thomas Taysor, Mr. R. G. X. Siebert, to Miss Elenor S. Auld, all of this village.
    Married on the 21st ult., by Rev. T. Robertson, Mr. Wm Hellams, to Miss Nancy M. Patten, all of Laurens District.
    Departed this life at his residence in Laurens District., on 25 December, of Pneumonia, S. T. Chandler, in the 35th year of his age, leaving a wife and 2 children.

Issue of January 12, 1855 [USC]
    Married on the 9th inst., by Rev. R. F. Babb, Mr. Henry M. Sprouse of Laurens to Miss Mary C. Hopkins of Greenville.
    Died at his residence in Laurens District, S. C., Nov. 27, 1854, Hezekiah Gray, in the 48th year of his age...Stewart of the M. E. Church.

Issue of January 19, 1855 [USC]
    Married on Tuesday, the 2d inst., by Rev. S. P. Getaen, DR. J. N. M. Fairbairn, formerly of Laurens, to Mrs Sallie A. Hall, of Hamburg.
    Married on the 16th inst., by J. M. Baxter, Esq., Mr. Dennis Lark to Miss L. C. Floyd, all of Newberry District.
    Died at his residence of typhoid pneumonia, Col. T. F. Farrow, in the 62nd year of his age, son of John Farrow, late of Laurens District, who served in the Revolution...never a member of any church....

Issue of January 26, 1855 [USC]
    Married in Kingston, Ga., on the 11th inst., by Rev. R. A. Milnex, Mr. T. B. Burris, of Anderson C. H., S. C., to Miss Bettie G. Johnson, second daughter of the late Dr. Mark M. Johnson.
    Married on the 23rd inst., by Rev. D. Wills, Mr. N. A. Greene, to Miss Sarah Bell, all of Laurens.
    Married on the 15th inst., by Rev. C. B. Stewart, Rev. Sewall Thomason, of Greenville, to Miss Mary A. Studdard, of Laurens.
    Departed this life, 24 December 1854, of typhoid pneumonia, Mrs. Sophia Power, wife of William Power, Esq., in the 33d year of her age...member of the Baptist Church for 8 or 10 years...leaves a husband and 5 children.

Issue of February 9, 1855 [USC]
    Departed this life on Thursday morning, Feb. 1, 1855, Jane W. Sullivan, wife of G. W. Sullivan, of Laurens District, and daughter of Sarah and L. A. Brooks, in the 34th year ef her age...leaves brothers and sisters, father, and a husband and seven children... scarecely eight months since she stood beside the death-bed of a daughter.
    Died on 20th January last, Mrs. Parmelia, wife of William Garett...leaves husband, mothers and 5 small children.
    Married on the 23d ult., by Rev. Lewis Ball, Mr. Lewis Rhenson, formerly of Laurens District, late of Pontotoc County, Miss., to Miss Nancy M. Lockhart of Chickasaw Co., Miss.
    Married on the 6th inst., at the residence of her father, John Simmons, by Rev. D. Wills., James Milnor, Esq., of Cassville, Geo., to Mrs. Susan M. Adamson of this place.

Issue of February 16, 1855 [USC]
    Married on the 8th inst., by Seaborn Parks, Esq., Capt. _____ D. Patten to Miss Margaret Robertson, all of this District.
    Married on Tuesday, the 6th inst., by Rev. T. Raysor, Mr. Stanback Baker [?], to Miss Ann Armstrong, all of this District.
    Died on Saturday, the 10th inst., Mrs. Milly Nabors in the ___ year of her age.
    Died on the 5th inst., in this District, Mrs. Margaret Mills, wife of Samuel Mills, aged about 60 years.
    Died on the 25th January last, at the residence of her brother _____ Cunningham, Mrs. Sarah Cummingham, aged 53 years.
    [The blanks in the above are due to the poor binding of this issue.]

Issue of February 23, 1855 [USC]
    Married on the 13th inst., by Rev. D. F. Hadden, Mr. Joseph M. McAteer to Miss Judith P. Franks.
    Married by the same at the same time and place, Mr. William L. Power to Miss Nancy A. Franks, all of this District.
    Married on Thursday, the 15th inst., by Rev. D. Wills, Mr. William E. Black to Miss

Antoinette E. Brown, all of this village.
 Died at his residence, Claremont, Laurens District, on the morning of the 14th inst., Gen. Thomas Wright in the 73d year of his age [long eulogy].
 Died on Sunday, the 18th inst., Mrs. Sarah Anderson, wife of Maj. E. Anderson, of this village, in the 68th year of her age...born in Union District, daughter of Samuel & Polly Jackson, removed to Laurens District, in 1827, and at the time of her death, the oldest lady in this village...married 50 years...member of the M. E. Church [long eulogy].

Issue of March 2, 1855 [USC]
 Died at the residence of Madison Milam, Cass Co., Geo., on the 15th Feb 1855, Mrs. Mary Milam, relict of William Milam, aged 68 years and 8 months...a residence of Laurens District, until the fall of 1850...a member of the Baptist Church for 35 years.

Issue of March 16, 1855 [USC]
 Married on the 14th inst., by Rev. David Wills, Dr. J. Lark of California, to Miss Sallie Lark of this District.
 Died in this place on the 9th inst., Weyman Holland Denton, in the 14th year of his age.
 Departed this life in Marion County, E. Florida, on the 8th of February, Mrs. Lizzie Agnew, wife of Dr. W. Agnew, daughter of Dr. John & Ann H. Sullivan, aged 28 years...left two children...member of the M. E. Church.
 Died in Mississippi, on the 23d Feburary last, in the 56th year of her age, Mrs. Sarah, wife of Andrew Middleton...born in Laurens District, daughter of Mathew and Margaret Hunter...member of the M. E. Church...leaves a husband, daughter, and two sons.

Issue of March 30, 1855 [USC]
 Married on the 21st inst., by Rev. W. B. Boyd, Mr. Robt. Scolds to Miss Jane Hamilton, all of this District.
 Died at her residence in Laurens District on the 7th February, Mrs. Amelia Mahaffy, wife of Wm Mahaffy, and daughter of Maj. William & Nancy Arnold, decd, of Greenville... member of the Baptist Church over 23 years at Rabun's Creek...an affective wife and tender mother.
 Died at the residence of Francis Beeks, in Laurens District, S. C. 19th March 1855, Dr. John Clardy, in the 36th year of his age, son of Michael and Ethalinda Clardy, leaving a widowed mother, brothers & sisters....admitted to the practice of medicine in 1848... joined the M. E. Church, 1846.

Issue of April 6, 1855 [USC]
 Married in this village, on Tuesday, the 3d inst., by   Rev. David Wills, Dr. E. L. Gunter of Newberry to Miss Ella Lark of this District.
 John B. Simpson, a worthy member of the Presbyterian Church at Friendship, died 17 February last, in the 72d year of his age.

Issue of April 20, 1855 [USC]
 Married at the residence of the bride's father, in Williston, S. C. on the 11th inst., by Rev. Simpson Jones, Mr. P. H. Larey of Orangeburg, to Miss Lorraine E., on ly daughter and child of W. B. Beazly & Mary L. Beazly, decd, and grand-daughter of the late Downs Calhoun, of Abbeville District.
 Married at Scuffletown, on Thursday, the 12th inst., by Rev. Z. L. Holmes, Mr. William Copeland to Miss Mary Ann McCarley, all of this District.
 Died at his residence, on Rabun's Creek, in this District, on the 7th of March, Capt. John Armstrong, aged 77 years...born & raised in Stokes County, N. C., only son of Col. John Armstrong, who fought bravely throught the Revolutionary conflict...member of the M. E. Church.

Issue of April 27, 1855 [USC]
 Married in this District, on the 19th inst., at the residence of Elihu Watson, Esq., by Rev. Thomas Raysor, Mr. Samuel W. Anderson to Miss Lizzie B. Hewitt, both of this village.

Issue of May 11, 1855 [USC]
 Married in Cassville, Geo., on Tuesday, 1st May, by Rev. JOHN S. Wilson, D. D., Mr. Joseph H. Pitman of Gordon County to Miss Laura C. Word, of Cassville, Geo.
 Married on the 26th ult., at the residence of Rev. C. B. Stewart, Mr. M. Garrett to Mrs. M. Peden, of Greenville District.
 Married on the 2d inst., by Rev. R. Robertson, Mr. Robert Stewart, to Miss Mary Dial, all of this District.
 Married on the 29th ult., by Rev. H. J. Glenn, Mr. Marion Lamb to Miss Frances Edwards, of Union District.

Issue of May 18, 1855 [USC]
Died in Laurens District, on the 9th inst., Mrs. Elizabeth Susan Simmons, daughter of Robert and Susan Hunter, and consort of James Watts Simmons, in the 29th year of her age ...lived at Martin's Depot [now Joanna, S. C.--BHH]...leaves a husband, parents, and an infant child.
Died on the 4th inst., Stobo James Lewis, infant son of George L. and Elizabeth Ann Dollar, aged 1 year, 1 month, and 6 days.

Issue of June 1, 1855 [USC]
Died on the 12th of May, Eliza Jane, youngest child of William and Rebecca K. Franks, aged 1 year and 9 months.

Issue of June 8, 1855 [USC]
Died of dropsy, on 25 May 1855, Mr. John Riddle, in the 82d year of his age.
Mr. Nimrod Overby is no more...departed this life at Swansy's Ferry on Tuesday, 22d ult....born Halifax County, Va., 9 April 1770, came to this State with his parents at age 16...has six children now living, many grandchildren, and nine great-grandchildren... member of the Baptist Church over 40 years...fought in the last war with Great Britain... was a man of good common sense, which George McDuffie once observed was the most uncommon kind of sense.
Died in Newberry District, on 16 May, at her father's residence (Capt. Chesley Davis), Mrs. Mary J. Martin, aged about 28 years...leaves an only son and many other relations.

Issue of July 20, 1855 [USC]
Departed this life on 21st June, Mrs. Catherine Puckett, wife of John S. Puckett, and daughter of Samuel & Nancy Boyd, in the 43d year of her age...attached herself to the Baptist Church at Poplar Springs...later joined the Methodist Church...left a husband and six children.

Issue of August 17, 1855 [USC]
Married on the 9th inst., by Rev. D. F. Hadden, Mr. S. S. Blakely to Miss Sarah Franks, all of Laurens.
Died at her residence in Laurens District, Mrs. Mary Owings, wife of William Owings, in the 65th year of her age, leaving a husband and children....

Issue of August 31, 1855 [USC]
Married on the 23d inst., by Seaborn Parks, Esq., Daniel Robertson to Martha Jones, all of this District.
Departed this life in this District on the 22d inst., Miss Louisa, daughter of Dr. John H. and A. L. Davis, in the 17th year of her age.
Died at her residence in Laurens District, on the 16th ult., Mrs. Lavinia Tucker, consort of Gen. S. Tucker, decd, in the 86th year of her age...member of the Baptist Church over 65 years.
Died on the 16th inst., of Scrofula mesenterica, John D. Long, only child of Mrs. Rebecca D. Long, in the 8th year of his age.

Issue of September 28, 1855 [USC]
Died in this District, on the 24th ult., Mrs. Matilda Simmons, aged 77 years...a consistent member of the Baptist Church.

Issue of October 12, 1855 [USC]
Married on the 4th inst., at the residence of Rev. C. Stewart in this District, Mr. G. Vaughn, of Baldwin Co., Geo., to Miss E. Jones, of Laurens, S. C.
Married on the 4th at the residence of her father in this village, by Rev. T. J. Pearce, Dr. A. M. Barnes to Miss M. C. Griffin.
Married at Madison, Geo., on the 3d inst., by Rev. C. M. Irvin, P. Watson Denton, Esq., of Columbus, Geo., to Miss Fannie J. Walker of the former place.
Married in this District, on the 9th inst., by Rev. Tolaver Robertson, Mr. William Alexander McCorkle, of North Carolina, to Miss Emily T. Odell, of this District.
Died in this District, on Thursday the 20th ult., Mary Louisa, 2nd daughter of Col. John F. and Eliza W. Kern, in the 5th year of her age.

Issue of October 19, 1855 [USC]
Married on Sunday morning, the 7th inst., by Rev. Mr. Hitt, at the residence of Mrs. Louisa F. Neely, Mr. Ransom Davenport to Miss Sarah Ann Jennings, all of Laurens District.

Issue of October 26, 1855 [USC]
Married on the 18th inst., by Rev. Z. L. Holmes, Capt. D. M. H. Langston to Miss Sallie J., daughter of Mrs. Robert Pitts, all of this District.

Hillary Foster died at Spring Hill, Ala., of yellow fever, on the evening of the 9th inst., aged 40 years. Thrice this family has been bereaved in less than a month.

Issue of November 2, 1855 [USC]
Married on the 23d inst., by Rev. E. Lindsay, Mr. J. N. Entricken of Laurens, to Miss N. A. Abrams, of Newberry.

Died at the residence of her brother, Andrew Burnside, near Hamburg, on Monday night, the 15th October, Miss Tabitha Burnside.

Departed this life on the 24th ult of Puerperal Convulsions, Mrs. Nancy Jane Leak, wife of Capt. Robert B. Leake, in the 27th year of her age...member of the Presbyterian Church at Clinton...gave birth to a tender offspring a few hours before she died, who expired before its mother, and was amtombed circled in its mothers arms...left a husband and two children.

Issue of November 9, 1855 [USC]
Married on the 1st inst., by Rev. Tolaver Robertson, Mr. J. S. J. Garrett to Miss Marry C. Burns, all of Laurens District.

On Thursday, the 25th ult., by Rev. Z. L. Holmes, Mr. Geo. Davidson to Miss Elizabeth, daughter of Mr. Robert Adair, all of this District.

Departed this life on the 14th October 1855, Amelia M. J. only daughter of Samuel E. and Margaret F. Barksdale, aged 17 months and 26 days.

Issue of November 30, 1855 [USC]
Married in Campbellton, Ga., on Wendesday evening, the 14th inst., by Rev. Noah Smith, Mr. William J. Garrett to Miss Caroline E., daughter of Col. Thos A. Latham, all of the same place.

Married on the 22d inst., by Rev. J. M. Runion, Perry Nobles of Laurens to Miss Margaret Ann Robertson of Greenville District.

Married on the 22d inst., by Rev. Z. L. Holmes, Mr. J. M. Young to Miss M. E. Stroud, all of this District.

Died at his residence, Pomaria, in Newberry District, Capt. John Summer, in the 77th year of his age...only son of Capt. Nicholas Summer, who was killed at Granby in the Revolution, son of Capt. John Adam Summer, pioneer settler in the Fork of Broad and Saluda Rivers...Capt. Summer was a senior elder of the Luther Church [long eulogy].

Issue of December 7, 1855 [USC]
Married on the 27th inst., by Rev. E. Lindsay, Maj. O. A. Watson of Laurens District, to Miss M. S. Johnston of Newberry District.

Married on the 27th inst., by Rev. E. Lindsay, Mr. John Miller of Laurens District, to Miss M. K. Pitts of Newberry District.

Died at Euharlee, Geo., on the 21st September, Mrs. Fannie H., consort of Dr. M. G. Williams, in the 24th year of her age...member of the M. E. Church for 2 years.

Mr. Robert Bell, born County Tyrone, Ireland, March 1796, emigrated to this county in 1818, age 22, became a member of Rocky Springs Presbyterian Church in 1824 and died 15 November 1855, leaving a wife and 4 children.

Issue of December 14, 1855 [USC]
Married on the 5th inst., by Rev. Z. L. Holmes, Mr. E. Y. Cunningham to Miss Martha S., only daughter of Mr. Lewis Duvall, all of this District.

Departed this life, on Friday, the 9th of November, at 11 o'clock, in Marion Co., East Fla., Mrs. Mattie A. H. Eichelberger, wife of Adam Eighelberger, and daughter of Dr. John and Mrs. Ann H. Sullivan, aged 21 years and 8 months. [long eulogy].

Departed this life on the 9th inst., Sarah Ann, only daughter of Capt. Thomas and Nancy Blakely, in the 14th year of her age.

Issue of January 4, 1856 [Laurens]
Died on the 12th December, Martha Ann, daughter of Albert and Martha R. Dial, aged 4 years, 2 months, and 7 days...only three years since they followed their first born, a bright little boy of nearly three summer to the grave.

Issue of January 11, 1856 [Laurens]
Death of Charles Allen, Esq.,...this venerable Revolutionary soldier died at his residence in this District on Saturday the 5th instant, in the 93rd year of his age... he outlived all of his family but one daughter, the wife of Rev. S. B. Lewers; she came from home in West Mississippi. [obituary in issue of 18 January.]

Another Gone! Mr. John Duncan, A Revolutionary Soldier, died in Jackson County, on the 8th. He was born in Randolph County, N. C. on 27th April 1764. He has been a resident of Jackson County for 60 years...was present at the battle of Kings Mt. Athens Banner.

Issue of January 18, 1856 [Laurens]
George Holland was killed by James Mc. Williams on Monday last [14 Jan]. We forbear giving particulars as we have received contrary report of them. Williams has fled.
Married on the 13th inst., at the residence of W. B. Henderson Esq., by Rev. J. B. Hillhouse, Mr. Charles H. White of Spartanburg to Miss Kate P. V. Henderson, late of Tennessee.
Married on Thursday, the 10th, by Rev. David Wills, Mr. Robt Cleaveland to Miss Mary only daughter of Maj. George Byrd, all of this District.
Married in Panola Co., Miss., on the 20th December 1855, by Rev. A. W. Young, Capt. Thos. Lewers of DeSoto, to Miss Martha M. Orr, of Panola Co., Miss.
Married on the 8th inst., by Rev. W. A. McSwain, W. B. Bell, Esq., of Martins Depot to Miss Rebecca E. C. Glymph of Glymphville, Newberry, S. C.

Issue of January 25, 1856 [Laurens]
The death of John Caldwell, Esq., occurred at his residence in this town on the 14th inst., in the 69th year of his age...an old and distinguished citizen....Newberry Mirror.
Married on Thursday, November 1, 1855, by Rev. Wm. B. Boyd, Mr. John A. Feltz to Miss Lizzie, daughter of Larkin Coleman, all of this District.
Married on the 12th of January by Rev. W. B. Boyd, Mr. Robert Hipps to Miss Catherine, daughter of Ephraim Pitts.
Married on Thursday, the 3rd January, by Rev. Z. L. Holmes, Mr. J. L. Hipp to Miss Catherine Cunningham.
Married on the 10th of January, by the same, Mr. C. F. Williams, to Miss I. E. Hunter, all of this District.
Married on Thursday, the 17th of January, by the same, Mr. Hugh Taylor to Miss Ann Boyce.
Married on Sunday, the 20th of January, by Rev. R. F. Babb, Mr. John A. Bolt to Miss Sarah Jane, daughter of Edmund Bolt, all of this district.
Died at her residence in Laurens District, on the 17th Novmeber 1855, after a painful illness, Mrs. Susan Luke, consort of Mr. Young Luke...born June 17, 1829 in Laurens District, and was raised by her pious grandmother...at the age of 26 she married Mr. Luke with whom she lived only __ months...her infant, only a few days old, died first.

Issue of February 1, 1856 [Laurens]
Married on the 18th December 1855, by Rev. James Duff, Mr. George W. Green, formerly of Laurens District, S. C., to Miss Nancy B. Mahon of Pontotoc Co., Miss.
Married in Yorkville, on Wednesday morning, the 23rd January, by Rev. J. Monroe Anderson, Dr. John W. Simpson of Laurensville, to Mrs. Jane C. Clowney of Union District.
Died at her residence near New Harmony in this District, on the 11th December 1855, Mrs. Nancy Halk, widow of John Halk, decd, in the 67th year of her age...long a faithful member of the Baptist Church of Christ.

Issue of February 8, 1856 [Laurens]
Married by Rev. J. B. Hillhouse, on the 16th January, Mr. Robert Goodwin to Miss Margaret Cunningham, all of Laurens District.
Married on Tuesday, the 15th January by Rev. Walsh, George W. Lewers, of Desoto, Miss., to Miss M. C. Caraway of Shelby County, Tenn.
Married on 29th November 1855, by Rev. H. Hawkins, R. E. Love to Miss Mary G. Lewers, all of DeSoto, Miss.
Died of Asthma, at her residence in Laurens District, on the 20th December 1855, Mrs. Hannah Higgins, consort of James B. Higgins, in the 72nd year of her age...she had been a consistent member of the Baptist Church at Warriors Creek upwards of 50 years...a kind, affectionate wife, a tender mother (though she had outlived all of her children) a kind grandmother (having all her grandchildren under her care)...leaves a husband, 5 grand-children, one brother, three sisters, and many other relations and friends.

Issue of February 22, 1856 [Laurens]
Married on the 13th February, by Rev. David Wills, Col. John D. Williams of Laurens, to Miss Ann Eliza Barnett, of Abbeville District.
Married on the 13th February, by Rev. D. F. Hadden, H Bryson Young, Esq., to Mrs. Martha Young, all of Laurens District.
Married on Thursday evening, the 14th of February, by Rev. W. A. Gamewell, John T. Craig of Laurens District, to Miss Laura, eldest daughter of James S. Boatwright of Columbia.

Issue of February 15, 1856 [Laurens]
Married at the residence of Rev. C. B. Stewart, on the 5th February, Mr. David Anderson to Miss P. C. Griffin.

Issue of February 29, 1856 [Laurens]
    Married on Thursday night, the 31st January by Rev. James C. Vaughn, of Newberry,
Dr. James P. Knight, formerly of Laurens District, to Miss Marie, daughter of Dr. Griffin
of Alabama.
    Obituary. William P., son of Samuel L. A. and Mary Powers, aged 5 years, 3 months,
and 26 days, on Dec. 22, 1855.

Issue of March 7, 1856 [Laurens]
    Married by Rev. J. B. Hillhouse, on the 21st ult., Mr. John T. Templeton to Miss
Mary Anne Templeton, all of this District.
    Died, of scarlet fever, in Laurens, S. C., January 22, 1856, John Derrick, infant
son of H. J. and Sarah Simpson, aged 11 months and 8 days.

Issue of March 14, 1856 [Laurens]
    Married on Thursday, the 6th inst., by Rev. W. B. Boyd, Mr. Thomas Toland to Miss
Catherine, daughter of Winder Hitch, Esq., all of Laurens.

Issue of March 21, 1856 [Laurens]
    Married on the 12th ult., by Rev. Wm. Fleming, Mr. O. P. Hill to Miss Sarah, daughter
of Wiley and Nancy Yeargin, all of Cherokee Co., Ala.
    Died of Typhoid Fever at her father's residence in this District, on the 28th of
February, Miss Susan, daughter of Elisha and Mary Hellams, aged 31 years...a consistent
member of the Baptist Church at Chestnut Ridge for two years...a kind and affectionate
daughter, a loving sisters...leaves father, mother, brothers and sisters.
    Died at her father's residence in this District on January 6, 1856, Miss Margaret
Ann, only daughter of Andrew and Sarah Middleton, in the 20th year of her age...joined
the M. E. Church in 1853...her mother a short time previous had gone to her reward...
leaves fahter and two brothers.

Issue of March 28, 1856 [Laurens]
    Died on the 8th of February last, at the residence of her father near Brewerton, in
this District, of scarlet fever, Sarah Elizabeth, only daughter of George and Cassie
Geral, in the 12th year of her age.

Issue of April 4, 1856 [Laurens]
    Died at his residence in this District, on 26th March, of typhoid pneumonia, Elihu
Garrett, in the 47th year of his age. His son David, about 20 years of age, died of
the same affliction, on Tuesday, the 18th ult, and his son John, about 22 years of age,
on Saturday night, the 22nd ult...left widow and children...member of the Baptist Church
since age 18.
    Died on the 6th ult., Silas T. Watson, aged 21 years and 2 months...a few months
only have elapsed since he was preceded to the silence of the grave by a lovely and interesting little sister...they sleep beside a mother who died while they were yet in
infancy.

Issue of April 11, 1856 [Laurens]
    Married on the 27th of March in Cassville, Ga., by the Rev. F. R. Goulding, Mr.
James W. Hance of Coweta Co., (formerly of Laurensville, S. C.) to Miss Sallie E. Latimer,
of the former place.

Issue of April 18, 1856 [Laurens]
    Died at her residence in Pontotoc County, Miss., on the 5th of April, after an ill-
ness of 12 months, Lewis Ball, Senior, in his 77th year...about 70 years of his life
were spent in Laurens District, S. C., 5 years in Mississippi, and 2 years in Virginia...
a member of the Baptist Church for 60 years.
    Died on the 30th March last, at the residence of T. R. Jones, in this District, of
Malignant sore throat, Mrs. Elizabeth, widow of Joseph Jones, in the 73d year of her age...
a strict and pure member of the M. E. church for 40 years.
    Died on the 11th inst., in Spartanburg District, Mrs. Mary Holcomb, a dear mother &
a friend...member of the Baptist Church for many years.

Issue of April 25, 1856 [Laurens]
    Married on the 22nd inst., by Rev. David Wills, Mr. H. N. Maddox, of Laurens to Miss
H. M. Miller of Spartanburg.
    Died at the residence of her father in Rockford, Coosa County, Ala., on the 31st day
of March last, Othella L. Arnold, aged 7 years, 8 months, and 11 days...burned severly
when her clothes caught fire at school and died four days later.

Issue of May 2, 1856 [Laurens]
    Married on the 29th inst., at the residence of the bride's father, Mr. John Simmons,

by Rev. David Wills, Mr. R. N. Lowrance, formerly of N. C. to Mrs. C. D. Badgett, all of Laurensville.

Issue of May 9, 1856 [Laurens]
Married on Tuesday, the 6th inst., by Rev. T. Robertson, Mr. Allen Dial to Miss Louisa Barksdale, all of Laurens.

Issue of May 16, 1856 [Laurens]
Married on the 20th of April by Rev. J. Townsend, Mr. Robt K. Paslay of Panola, to Miss Sarah Wooten, of DeSoto, all of Miss.
Married on Tuesday morning, May 13, by the Rev. DR. O'Connell, Mr. R. P. W. McCants to Mrs. Catherine E. Steen, all of Columbia.
Died on the 18th of April, Mrs. Jane Crisp, wife of Mr. John Crisp, daughter of Mr. Mathew Bryson, who has been for many years a Ruling Elder of the Presbyterian Church. She died in the 30th year of her age...for 11 years, member of the Presbyterian Church... leaves 4 little children and husband.
Died at his father's residence, in the upper part of Laurens District, on the 6th inst., James Young, 3rd son of R. K. and H. E. Owings, in the 20th year of his age.

Issue of May 23, 1856 [Laurens]
Married on Thursday night, the 8th instant, by Rev. R. Raysor, Mr. J. R. Tribble to Miss Lizzie N., daughter of R. Harris, Esq., all of this District.
Departed this life, on 10th April last, in the 42nd year of her age, Mrs. Sidney Dendy, wife of Marcus Dendy, of this District...left husband and children...she was for 15 years a member of the Baptist Church...lived her whole life in the vicinity in which she died...[long eulogy].

Issue of June 6, 1856 [Laurens]
Married on the 27th ult., by the Rev. Mr. Hadden, Mr. George L. Franks to Miss D. J. Blakely, all of Laurens.
Married on the 4th instant, by Rev. Z. L. Holmes, Mr. Thomas A. Toben of Baltimore, to Miss Lizzie J. McDowell, of this District.
Departed this life at this father's residence in this District, on the 21st of May, Elias H. Henderson, aged 21 years...belong the the Baptist Church at Mount Pleasant... member of Sabbath school for several years at Williamsville...left bereaved father, 7 brothers, one sister. His body followed a pious mother and one little brother and sister to the cold house of death...funeral preached by Rev. T. Robertson, 3rd Sabbath in June.

Issue of June 20, 1856 [Laurens]
Married on the 12th instant, by Alexander Acker (Rev.), Mr. William Donaldson of Greenville, to Miss Nancy E. Bolt of Laurens District.
Suicide. Mr. G. L. Dollar, a very worthy citizen of our District, committed suicide by hanging himself from a tree near his dwelling on Sunday morning last...he leaves a wife and large family of children, most of them quite young, in embarrassed circumstance of life.

Issue of July 4, 1856 [Laurens]
Married on the 25th of June by the Rev. Thos Raysor, Mr. John W. Terry to Miss Carrie E. Wooden, all of Laurens District, S. C.   Unionville Journal, please copy.
Death of Mrs. O. D. Eppes, consort of John W. Eppes, Esq., occurred on the 24th ultimo., in this town...daughter of Capt. John D. and Mrs. Susan Boyd, born May 28, 1825, married December 14, 1841 in the 17th year of her age...a wife and mother.

Issue of July 18, 1856 [Laurens]
Married on the 26th ultimo, by Rev. D. F. Hadden, Mr. W. S. Pearson of Spartanburg, to Miss Dorothy F. Little of Laurens District.
Died at the residence of James Tyson, near Wacahoota, East Florida (where she was going to school), June 23, Sarah W., second daughter of Dillon and Elizabeth A. Griffin (late of Laurens Dist., S. C.), aged 12 years, 1 month and 14 days.
Death of Mrs. Matilda F., consort of Maj. G. F. Mosely, on the 1st of July 1856, in the 27th year of her age...daughter of Gen. B. D. and Mrs. Sarah Garrison of Greenville District...her mother died when she was quite a young girl...member of the Baptist Church ...leaves a babe and husband.

Issue of August 1, 1856 [Laurens]
Married on the 3rd of July, by Rev. A. H. Tribble, Dr. S. S. Cunningham, formerly of Greenville District, to Mrs. Elender E., daughter of West, of Pickens County, Ga.
Died in Charleston , S. C. on 23 July, John A. Gyles, Esq., attorney at Law...for 10 years previous to his death helf office of R. W. Grand Secretary of the Grand Lodge of teh I. O. O. F. of S. C.

Issue of August 8, 1856 [Laurens]

Died on Sunday, the 20th July, at her residence near Rocky Ridge, Anderson Dist., S. C., Mrs. Mary C. Cooley, aged 32 years...leaving a husband and two little sons, with many relatives and friends...in 1842 she attached herself to the Baptist Church at Clear Springs in Greenville District...married and moved to Anderson District, moving her membership to a neighboring Church.

Died in the lower part of this District, of an affliction of the heart, Miss Frances J. Hill, daughter of Rev. Silas and Rebecca B. Hill and step-daughter of Gen. T. B. Griffin, aged 16 years...member of Bush River Church...to meet her departed father, little brothers and sister in heaven. Newberry Mirror, please copy.

[Bush River Baptist Church is located just across the county line from Laurens County in Newberry County.]

Issue of August 15, 1856 [Laurens]

Married on Wednesday evening, the 6th of August, at Rocky Mount by the Rev. J. B. Hillhouse, Dr. A. C. Shands, of Spartanburg District, to Mrs. M. E. Saxon of this District.

Died in Newberry District, on the 31st July, one of our most highly esteemed citizens Daniel Rudd in the 48th year of his age...left several small children, giving them to his brother, John Rudd, calmly and quietly fell asleep in Jesus. Newberry Mirror, copy.

Issue of August 22, 1856 [Laurens]

Mrs. Sarah Dorroh, died 30 July, at her residence in this district, in the 73d year of her age, leaving several children and grandchildren...united with the Presbyterian Church at Friendship at its organization in the year 1828...a wife for 19 years, a widow for 14 years.

Issue of August 29, 1856 [Laurens]

Married on the 7th August, by M. P. Evans, Esq., Mr. Wm Hammond to Miss Parthena Moore, all of this District.

Married on the 14th August, by the Rev. Mr. Whitemore, Mr. Hayne I. Klinck to Miss Margaret Anna Robertson, second daughter of Col. J. F. Robertson, all of Memphis, Tenn.

Issue of September 5, 1856 [Laurens]

Married on the 21st August, by Rev. Tolaver Robertson, Mr. Henry Chandler to Miss Louisa Walker, both of Laurens.

Married on Thursday evening, the 28th August, by Rev. Thos. Raysor, Maj. Elias Bearden, to Miss Lucind B. Leak, all of this District.

Death by typhoid fever of the following young persons from the bounds of the Rocky Springs Presbyterian Congregation in this District.

Mr. Clark Taylor, a son of Mr. Samuel Taylor.

Miss Martha, oldest daughter of the same.

Miss Jane Taylor, an only daughter of Mr. Robert Taylor, and for some time past a member of the Church.

Issue of September 19, 1856 [Laurens]

Married on the 11th September by Rev. W. Hitt, Mr. Henry Hill to Miss Ellen Hitt, all of Laurens District.

Married on the 19th August, by Rev. Wm. B. Boyd, Mr. Moses Madden of Louisiana, to Miss Elzeveen, daughter of Wm. and Rebecca Madden of this District.

Married on the 4th September, by Rev. Wm. B. Boyd, Mr. Thomas Rogers, to Miss Mathier McCleallam.

Married on the 11th September by Rev. Wm. B. Boyd, Mr. Edwin Vallentine to Miss Margaret, daughter of Elizabeth Boyd.

Issue of October 3, 1856 [Laurens]

Married on the 17th September by Rev. W. P. Martin, Mr. Berry E. Knight to Miss Nancy Jane Ballentine, all of Laurens District.

Married on the 16th September by the Rev. W. P. Martin, Mr. John H. Pyles, to Miss Harriett Minerva Boyd, all of Laurens District.

Married on the 18th September by the Rev. W. P. Martin, Dr. Wm. J. Ballentine to Miss Cleopatra Hassletine Victory Emeline Lafayette, youngest daughter of John and Mary Knight, all of Laurens District.

Married on the 25th September by Rev. A. Acker, Dr. R. S. Cheshire, formerly of Laurens, to Miss M. A. Acker of Calhoun, Anderson Dist.

Died in Benton County, Ala., of croup, on the 15th of August last, Hannah M., youngest daughter of Mary E. Fowler, aged 4 years, 6 months, 6 days.

Issue of October 10, 1856 [Laurens]

Died in Pontotoc Co., Miss., on 13th August last, Mrs. Letty Coleman, wife of J. H. Coleman, formerly of Laurens District, in the 62nd year of her age...member of the Baptist

Church for 21 years.
    Died at his residence in this district, September 14th, Thomas R. Ferguson, about 47
years of age...became a member of Bethany Church in 1849 under ministry of Mr. Lewers.

Issue of October 17, 1856 [Laurens]
    Died on the 1st of October of typhoid dysentery, Mary Elizabeth, second daughter of
John M. Crisp, aged 5 years and 6 months.

Issue of October 24, 1856 [Laurens]
    Married on Tuesday, the 21st October by Rev. Z. L. Holmes, Mr. Robert C. Dunlap to
Miss M. Hunter Black, all of Laurens District.

Issue of October 31, 1856 [Laurens]
    Married on the 16th October by Rev. H. H. Durant, Capt. Jas. Bailey of Greenwood,
to Miss Mary D. Hodges of Cokesbury.
    Married on the 23rd October by the Rev. T. Bertson, Capt. N. J. Allison, to Miss
Margaret Cunningham, all of Laurens District.
    Died at his residence in Carnesville, Ga., on the 18th of July last, of typhoid
pneumonia, Elijah T. Wilson, in about the 36th year of his age...leaves a wife and 3
children.
    Died suddenly on Saturday evening, the 18th October of apoplexy, or disease of the
heart, Mr. Albert Miller, aged 47 years, 5 months, 9 days...born and reared in Laurens
District...left wife and 8 children...member of the Methodist Church.

Issue of November 7, 1856 [Laurens]
    Married on the 30th of October by Rev. Tolaver Robertson, Mr. Wm. J. Patterson to
Miss Rebecca E. Fleming, all of Laurens.
    Married on the 23rd October by Rev. C. B. Stewart, at the house of Capt. James Tem-
pleton, Mr. John H. White to Miss Nancy K. Templeton, both of Greenville.
    Died on the 27th of October in the 5th year of his age, Campbell Preston, son of
Dr. William and C. B. Phillips.

Issue of November 28, 1856 [Laurens]
    Married on the 18th November by Rev. T. Robertson, Mr. N. L. Barksdale to Miss Mary
Burns, all of Laurens District.
    Married on the 20th instant, by the Rev. J. N. Bouchelle, Mr. P. D. Elliott of Miss
E. N. Little, all of Laurens District.
    Died on 3 November in the 54th year of her age in Laurens District, S. C., Mrs.
Rachel Copeland, consort of Maj. Samuel Copeland...member of the M. E. Church.
    Died near Kinards Turn Out, Newberry District, Mrs. Martha Oxner, in her 33d year...
she was born in Laurens District, daughter of Mrs. Hannah Meadows...her father died when
she was quite young...member of the Methodist Episcopal Church...leaves husband and 3
small children.

Issue of December 5, 1856 [Laurens]
    Married on the 20th November by the Rev. S. Donnelly, Dr. G. H. Waddell to Miss Clough
T. Sims, both of Abbeville.
    Married on the 27th November by the Rev. Tolaver Robertson, Mr. W. Cheek to Miss
Sallie Fowler, both of Laurens District.

Issue of December 19, 1856 [Laurens]
    Married on the 4th December by Rev. Z. L. Holmes, Mr. Wm. A. Nelson to Miss Lou
Dial, all of this District.
    Married on the 4th December by Rev. H. H. Durant, Mr. Edward Babb to Miss Emma J.
Drummond, all of Spartanburg District.
    Married on the 13th November by Rev. Tolaver Robertson, Mr. Henry Fuller to Miss
Sarah Culbertson, all of Laurens District.
    Married on the 16th November by Elihu Watson, Esq., Mr. Washington Thomason to Miss
Caroline Peden, both of Greenville District.
    Married on the 30th October by Rev. John McKittrick, Mr. Robert H. Hollingsworth of
Newton Co, Ga., to Miss Sarah, daughter of Susan and John Marbet, formerly of Newberry
Dist., S. C. but now of DeKalb Co., Ga.,
    Married on the 4th November by Rev. J. C. Vaughn, Dr. J. P. Knight of Newberry, for-
merly of Laurens District, to Miss Antoinette Jeter, of Union District.
    Died on the 26th September last, at the residence of her brother, Nathaniel Barksdale,
Miss Martha Barksdale...member of Church for 25 years.
    Died on the 6th December in the 20th year of her age, Mrs. Sallie Jane, wife of Maj.
D. M. H. Langston, daughter of Robert and M. E. Pitts.
    Died, Wm. Preston Wier, son of Dr. Thos. Wier, Friday night, 21st November last, at
the premature age of 17...member of the Presbyterian Church.

Issue of December 26, 1856 [Laurens]
Died at the residence of her father, near Van Pattons, in Laurens District, on Monday evening, the 15th December, Miles Robuck, youngest son of S. S. Roebuck, aged about 12 years.
Married on the 6th day of November by Rev. T. J. Pearce, Mr. Newton Pyles to Miss Parmelia Francis MdDowell, all of this District.

Issue of April 24, 1857 [USC]
Married on the 14th inst., by Rev. David Wills, Mr. J. Randolph Adams of Richland, to Miss Kate Henderson, of Laurens District.
By the same on the 15th inst., Capt. J. D. Garlington, to Miss S. E., second daughter of Col. John D. Williams, all of Laurens District.
Died at his residence in this District, on the 15th inst., John Milam, in the 85th year of his age...a native of Halifax County, Ga., emigrated to this state in his 21st year.
Died on the 13th inst., of scarlet fever, Leanore Emma, youngest daughter of Maj. A. J. Eigleberger, in the 8th year of her age.

Issue of June 26, 1857 [USC]
Married by the Rev. Wm. Cowder, of Early Co., Ga., Dr. W. H. Garlington, formerly of Laurens District, to Mrs. Lizzie Holms, daughter of Judge Spreights of Blakely, Ga.

Issue of July 3, 1857 [USC]
Married in Kingston, Geo., on the 25th ult., by the Rev. W. B. Telford, Mr. Benjamin F. Reynolds (formerly of Greenwood, S. C.), to Miss Mary Johnson, of Kingston, Ga.
Died on Monday evening, the 15th ult., Mrs. Rachel Pitts, wife of Mr. Ephraim Pitts, 74 years of age...a consistent Church member for about 30 years.

Issue of October 2, 1857 [USC]
Married on the 15th ult., by Rev. T. Robertson, Dr. M. C. Cox, to Miss Rebecca Martin, all of Laurens District.
Married on the 24th ult., by Rev. T. Robertson, Capt. R. Martin, of Laurens District, to Miss M. J. Hanna of Spartanburg District.
Married on Tuesday, the 29th by Rev. David Wills, Dr. S. F. Styles to Miss Lucinda L. Wright, all of Laurens.
Died at his residence, on Reedy River, on the 17th of September, Capt. James Dorroh, in the 55th year of his age...leaves a discomsolate companion.
Died in Cass County, Ga., on Tuesday, the 22d ult., Abigail Adeline, infant child of John A. and Mary B. Moore, formerly of Laurens District, S. C., aged 8 months and 20 days.

Issue of October 16, 1857 [USC]
Died on the 20th ult., of Dysentery, George Howe Stewart, son of Rev. C. B. Stewart.
Died on the 10th inst., of Cramp Colic, Isabella J., wife of Hosea Garrett, in the 28th year of her age...leaving a husband and two small children...member of Warrior's Creek Baptist Church for 10 years.

Issue of October 23, 1857 [USC]
Married on the 20th inst., by Rev. Tolaver Robertson, Mr. Jas. H. Irby, Jr., of Laurens to Miss Ourah Lyles of Newberry.
Died at his residence in the lower edge of this District, on Thursday, 1st SEptember, Mr. Robert Workman, aged about 79 years.
Died on the 12th ult., Barron R., son of H. R. and Minerva Shell, and 14 months and 13 days.

Issue of October 30, 1857 [USC]
Married on the 28th inst., by Rev. A. P. Martin, Mr. M. H. Hunter of Clinton, to Miss M. K. Patterson, all of Laurens.
Died of Typhoid Fever, on the morning of 1st October, Miss Florella M. Young, daughter of John and Naomi Young.
Died at her residence, Tumbling Shoals, Laurens District, September 25, 1857, Mrs. Temperance Sullivan...she had reached the age of 56, joined the Baptist Church in 1840. Her husband, Joseph Sullivan, died in Charleston in 1850.

Issue of November 20, 1857 [USC]
Robert Campbell, M. C. died 14 August 1857, in the 78th year of his age at Cross Hill. ...born Laurens District, 12 May 1780 of pious parents, and Scottish ancestry, & only three years after the birth of his relative, Thomas Campbell, the Modern Scottish Poet, and author of "Pleasures of Hope." for 41 years ruling Elder in the Presbyterian Church at Liberty Spring...began practice in 1802...[long eulogy].

Died at his residence in this Dsitrict, on the 18th inst., John Watts, in the 50th year of his age...leaves a wife and 7 children.

Issue of November 27, 1857 [USC]
Married on the 19th inst., by Rev. David Wills, Mr. H. P. Farrow, of Cartersville, Ga. &Miss Corrie F. Simpson, eldest daughter of Dr. John W. Simpson, of this village.
Married on the 19th inst., in Laurens District, S. C. by Rev. T. J. Pearce, Dr. J. W. Brown, of Lafaette, Miss., and Miss Rachel Bell, of the former place.
Married on the 19th inst. by Rev. Tolaver Robertson, Mr. Martin Riddle to Miss Parmelia Power, all of Laurens District.
Married on the 25th instant by Rev. D. F. Hadden, Wm. William Leaman, and Miss Agnes Austin, all of Laurens.
Married on Tuesday, the 24th inst., by Rev. Tolaver Robertson, Mr. Edward Boyd to Miss Martha Bolt, all of this District.
Died on the 27th ult., George W. Gary, in the 39th year of his age...a fond husband and parent...[eulogy].
Died on the 12th inst., Charles Bluford, son of George W. and Martha E. Gary, in his 9th year.

Issue of January 15, 1858 [USC]
Married on the 31st December by Rev. E. Lindsay, Mr. Daniel A. Monroe, to Miss Frances S. Griffin, all of Laurens District.
Married on Tuesday evening, January 12, by Rev. Silas Knight, Mr. G. W. Bass to Miss Isabella Nabors, daughter of Jno. Nabors.
Married on the evening of the 12th inst., by R. J. Sullivan Esq., Mr. Stephen Garrett, aged 76 years to Miss Sarah Lloyd aged 60 years, all of Laurens.
Married on the 10th inst., by William Powers, Esq., Mr. John D. Burns and Mrs. Jane G. Osburn, all of Laurens District.
Departed this life in this place, on the 9th inst., Mrs. Margaret Richardson, in the 48th year of her age,,daughter of John and Nancy Hunter, wife of Mr. O. Richardson, Sheriff of Laurens District...mother of 7 children...member of the Presbyterian Church [long eulogy].

Issue of January 22, 1858 [USC]
Married on the 23d ult., by Rev. Z. L. Holmes, Mr. J. O. Templeton to Miss H. E. S. Donnan.
By the same on the 14th inst., Mr. John Anderson to Miss Sarah J. Blakely, all of this District.
Died at his residence in Barnwell District, on Monday, the 12th January, Thomas Raysor in the 61st year of his age.

Issue of January 29, 1858 [USC]
Married by Rev. Toliver Robertson, on the 26th inst., Mr. Sidney J. Finley to Miss Sallie A. Motes.
Married on the 22d inst., by Rev. J. B. Hillhouse, Mr. J. A. Boggs of Anderson to Miss E. P. Stewart of Laurens District.

Issue of February 5, 1858 [USC]
Married by Rev. Tolaver Robertson, on the 27th ult., Mr. Jacob L. Rop, to Miss Fannie Higgins, all of Laurens.
Died at the residence of his son in law, Cullen Lark, in this District, on the 30th ult., after an illness of 16 days, Mr. James Cunningham, in the 66th year of his age...attached himself to the Baptist Church in early life...buried in Mt. Pleasant Cemetery by the side of his wife, whom he was bereaved of eight years ago...leaves an only child, a daughter. Tennessee Baptist, please copy.
Died of Typhoid Pneumonia, at the residence of her mother in Greenville District, Jan. 24, 1858, Mrs. Sarah Ann Jones, wife of Benjamin F. Jones, Jr., and daughter of John Mcd. and Mary Terry, in the 18th year of her age...member of the M. E. Church from childhood... married only two months.
Died at his residence in Chambers Co., Ala., on the 16th of last month, Andrew J. Blakely, in the 85th year of his age...son of William and _____ Blakely of this District, emigrated to Alabama 4 years ago...leaves a wife and 2 small children.

Issue of February 19, 1858 [USC]
Married on the 4th inst., by Rev. J. B. Hillhouse, Mr. Perry Dillard to Miss Clementine Poll, all of this District.
Married on the 9th ult., by Rev. N. R. Smith, Capt. A. G. Nelson of Laurens District, to Miss A. L. Bailey of Cass County, Ga.
Married on the 9th inst., by Rev. A. P. Martin, William McPherson to Miss Elizabeth F. Forgy, all of this District.

36

Married on the 10th inst., by Rev. Tolaver Robertson, Mr. James Downey to Miss Sally Hudgens, all of Laurens District.

Died at her residence in Laurens District, on the 20th December 1857, Mrs. Polly Geddings, wife of Jas Geddings, decd, and daughter of Col. Armstrong of the Revolution, aged 80 years...member of M. E. Church last 35 years.

Mrs. N. L. Johnson, consort of Andrew Johnson, died on the morning of the 11th inst., in the 41st year of her age...member of the M. E. Church...left a husband, children and relatives [long eulogy.]

Issue of March 5, 1858 [USC]

Married on the 27th ult., by Rev. T. Raysor, Mr. S. H. Tillery, to Miss N. E. Lark, all of Newberry District.

Issue of April 2, 1858 [USC]

Married on Thursday, the 25th inst., by Rev. W. B. Boyd, Mr. Samuel Austen to Miss Marry Reed, all of Laurens.

Married on the 24th inst., by Rev. R. H. Reid, Dr. C. A. Saxon of Laurens to Miss Martha A., daughter of Dr. Pinckney Miller, of Spartanburg District.

Issue of April 16, 1858 [USC]

Married in March last by M. P. Evins, Esq., Capt. Dempsey Armstrong, to Miss Mary Mahaffy, all of this District.

Married in March last, by the same, W. A. Adams, of Laurens, to Miss Caroline Gunnels of Greenville.

Issue of April 23, 1858 [USC]

Married at Pontotoc, Miss., on 23 February last, by Rev. Lewis Ball, Mr. N. W. Overby, formerly of this District, to Miss Caroline Grant, of Pontotoc.

Issue of May 14, 1858 [USC]

Married on the 2d inst., by Rev. J. D. Durham, Mr. Lewis Bolt to Miss Barbary Vaughan, all of Laurens.

Married on the 11th inst., by Rev. D. F. Hadden, Mr. George M. Auld to Miss Jane Franks, all of this District.

Issue of May 21, 1858 [USC]

Married on the 13th inst., by Rev. Rolaver Robertson, Mr. Achilles Dendy to Miss Mary Powel, all of Laurens.

Married on the 22nd of April by the same, Rev. Wm. B. Boyd, to Mrs. Lucinda Pain, all of Laurens.

Died on Sabbath, the 9th inst., at the Asylum in Columbia, George Ross Kennedy, a native of this District...requested that he be buried in Duncan's Creek Church, which was done. [Duncan's Creek Presbyterian Church is located near Clinton, S. C. George Ross
    Kennedy's grave marker can be found in the church cemetery.]

Died on the 30th ult., in the 25th year of his age, Mr. Warren Blakely, son of Mr. Wm. Blakely, Jr.

Died at his residence in Bienville Parish, La., Absolom Wade Puckett, in the 27th year of his age...native of Abbeville District, S. C. and became a member of Siloam (Baptist) Church in 1854...leaves parents, brothers, sister, wife and two lovely children.

Issue of May 28, 1858 [USC]

Married on the 15th of April, by Rev. J. A. Moody, Mr.D.T. Bobo, to Miss A. E. Hitch, of Sandy Springs, Laurens District, S. C.

Issue of June 11, 1858 [USC]

Married on Tuesday morning, the 8th inst., at Methodist Protestant Church, by Rev. S. B. Sutherland, Leonard Williams of Greenville, S. C. to Annie Olivia, youngest daughter of Maj. Wm. Laval, of Charleston.

Died on the 27th ult., Miss Elizabeth Ann Stewart.

Died on the 1st inst., at the res. of his mother, Pendleton, S. C. Major Patrick Calhoun, U. S. A., in the 38th year of his age.

Issue of June 25, 1858 [USC]

Married on the 3d inst., by Rev. S. B. Jones, Mr. Thomas Mahon of Laurens, to Miss Harriet Hodges of Cokesbury, Abbeville District, S. C.

Married on Sunday morning,the 13th inst., by Rev. W. P. Martin, Mr. Thomas Mahon to Miss Lauracy Woods, daughter of William Woods, all of this District.

Died at the residence of Maj. George Byrd, on the 10th inst., in the 15th year of his age, Leumas L. Z. Vance, son of the late Dr. Sam'l Vance.

Jefferson Wallace is no more...died onthe 17th inst., in his 25th year.

Issue of July 2, 1858 [USC]
    Married by the Rev. Z. L. Holmes, on Sabbath night, June 20, at the close of public
service, in the Presbyterian Church, Clinton, Col. B. S. Jones to Miss Linda Holland,
all of this District.

Issue of July 23, 1858 [USC]
    Departed this life on the 5th ult., at her residence in this District, Elizabeth,
wife of Robert Monroe, decd., in the 70th year of her age...member of the Presbyterian
Church...left four children and several grandchildren.
    Died on the 21st June, at the residence of his sisters, in this District, Mr. James
Fleming, in the 42d year of his age...member of A. R. Church at Bethel about 20 years.
    Robert Childress died at his residence in this District, on the 20th June. He was
taken [ill] on his birthday and suffered 3 weeks...aged 63 years and 3 weeks...left a
large family of children.
    Died on the 7th inst., in the 20th year of her age, Miss Sarah Jane Byrd.

Issue of August 13, 1858 [USC]
    Died in the vicinity of Due West, on 22 July of Cancer on the tongue, Mrs. Anna Had-
don, wife of Abram Haddon, in the 73d year of her age...oldest member,save the husband,
of the A. R. Church of Due West...born 24 February 1786...wife of an elder, mother of
11 children, nine of whom are still living, and all of whom, except Rev. D. F. Haddon,
of Laurens, S. C., reside in Abbeville District.

Issue of August 20, 1858 [USC]
    Died in Abbeville village, on the 12th inst., of Scarlet Fever, Mary Eliza, infant
daughter of Col. Henry W. and Mrs. Eliza A. Garlington of Laurens...born January 24,
1858, and soon afterwards she lost her mother & was received by an aunt of this place.

Issue of October 1, 1858 [USC]
    Married on the 19th ult., by Rev. A. M. Machen, Mr. Henry Redden to Melissa
Washington, all of this District.
    Died of Croup on the 20th inst., Alice Mackey, youngest daughter of G. M. and J. R.
Gunnels, aged 9 months and 28 days.

Issue of October 29, 1858 [USC]
    Married on the 26th inst., by Rev. Tolaver Robertson, Mr. Ludy K. Teague to Miss
Parthenia Eugenia Williams, all of Laurens.
    Married on the 14th by Rev. J. Burris, Mr. Elias T. Chambell and Miss Isabelle
Bolt, all of Anderson District.

Issue of November 12, 1858 [USC]
    Married on the 4th inst., by Rev. S. B. Jones, Mr. S. P. Simmons of Laurens C. H., to
Miss Anna R. Connor of Cokesbury, Abbeville District.

Issue of November 26, 1858 [USC]
    Married on the 18th inst., by Rev. J. B. Hillhouse, Mr. Samuel D. Cunningham, to
Miss Emily McDowell, all of this District.

Issue of December 3, 1858 [USC]
    Married on the 25th ult., by Rev. J. B. Hillhouse, Mr. R. W. West of Greenville, to
Miss A. M. Fielder, of Laurens.
    Married in the 25th inst., by Rev. Z. L. Holmes, Mr. W. J. Leak to Miss C. S. Little,
all of this District.
    Married on the 21st ult., by Rev. Tolaver Robertson, Benjamin Newman, to Miss Elizabeth
Henderson, all of Laurens.
    Married on the 23d ult., by the same, Mr. Milford Motes to Miss Frances Abrams, all
of Laurens.
    Married on the 25th ult., by the same, Mr. Washington Grant to Miss Elizabeth Moore,
all of Laurens.
    Married on the 25th inst., by A. P. Martin, Mr. William Patterson, to Miss Martha
Poole, all of Laurens.
    Married on the 25th ult., by Rev. D. F. Hadden, Mr. Robert Austin, to Miss Jane
Nichols, all of Laurens.
    Died, November 19th, George Barum, infant of W. H. And M. S. Sheldon.
    Died, in this town, on yesterday morning, Mrs. Antoinette E. Black, wife of Dr. W.
E. Black, of this place, and daughter of the late Rev. Samuel P. and Mrs. Jane Pressley.
    John Creswell Godfrey, died in thisvillage on 12 November last, aged 17 years...a
student of the University of Virginia.

Died on the 15th ult., at his residence in this District, Mr. Noah Smith, in the 67th year of his age...Mr. Smith and his first wife Sophia (who died in 1835) united with the Presbyterian Church at Rocky Springs about 35 years ago...buried at Bethany Church.

Died on Monday, the 8th ult., Mrs. Martha Burnside, wife of E. J. Burnside, aged 55 years, and 10 months...member of the Baptist Church...a kind wife and mother.

Issue of December 10, 1858 [USC]

Married on the 1st inst., by Rev. Tolaver Robertson, Col. G. F. Moseley, to Miss Harriet Lester, all of Laurens.

Died in this place, on the 2d inst., Mrs. Antoinette E. Black, in the 28th year of her age...member of the Presbyterian Church.

Issue of December 17, 1858 [USC]

Married on the 9th of December by Rev. A. Slover, Mr. Wm. T. Willson, son of A. H. Willson, formerly of S. C., to Miss Pollie Ragon, all of Tippah Co., Miss.

Issue of February 11, 1859 [USC]

Married on the 1st inst. by Rev. Tolaver Robertson, Mr. John J. Fowler, to Mrs. Sarah Henderson, all of Laurens.

Married on the 20th by the same, Mr. Warren Tribble to Miss Frances Copeland, all of Laurens.

Married on the 6th inst., by the same, Mr. George W. Hines, to Miss Rebecca Grant, all of Laurens.

Married on the 2nd inst., by Rev. C. B. Stewart, Mr. Henry Cox to Miss Mary Brasher, all of Greenville District.

Died at his residence in Chickasaw Co., Miss., on Sunday morning, January 9, 1859, Capt. George Bowen...born in the City of Charleston, 9 December 1784, his father died when he was a child...taken by a friend named Cunningham who raised him and trained him for business...sent to West Indies while still a small boy where he served in a counting-room for seven years...returned to Charleston and married Miss Tabitha Canant in 1810...distinguished himself in the Creek War in 1814...engaged in agriculture in Laurens District until 1839 when he moved to Mississippi...moved to Monroe County for a while...In 1848, his wife died...all children were married except a son...wife was a member of the Presbyterian Church...left 3 sons, 1 daughter (the other four children living in other states), and a number of granchildren...buried at Soule Chapel by the side of his wife.

Issue of February 25, 1859 [USC]

Married on the 17th inst., by Rev. C. B. Stewart, Mr. D. C. Stoddard, of Laurens, and Miss M. F. Harrison, daughter of R. C. and L. M. Harrison, of Greenville.

Died on the 15th inst., Mrs. Phoebe Farrett, wife of John Garrett, aged 45 years... leaves an aged mother, a kind husband and four small children.

Issue of March 11, 1859 [USC]

Married on the 22d of February, by Rev. Tolaver Robertson, Mr. Hargrove Miller to Miss Mary Coleman, all of Laurens.

Married on the 24th of February, by the same, Mr. Benjamin Young to Miss Eliza Hanna, all of Spartanburg.

Married on the 24th of February, by Rev. J. C. Vaughan, Mr. S. R. Puckett of Abbeville, to Miss Frances E. Austin of Laurens.

Departed this life on Thursday, Dec. 23, 1858, Mrs. M. E. Calhoun, consort of Col. P. L. Calhoun, and daughter of Dr. Thomas and Mrs. Margaret Teague...left a husband, children, mother, brother and sister. [buried in the Teague family cemetery near Clinton, S. C.].

Died in Cass Co., Georgia, on the 23d of February, Florence Rosalie, 2nd daughter of William J. and Louisa Benham, aged 3 years, 6 months, and 13 days.

Issue of March 18, 1859 [USC]

Married on the 10th inst., by Rev. S. Donnelly, Mr. James H. Bryson to Miss M. E. McGowan, all of this District.

Died of Apoplexy, near Young's Store, S. C. on Wednesday the 23d ult., Mrs. Anna Patton, in the 60th year of her age...[eulogy].

Issue of March 25, 1859 [USC]

Married on the 17th inst., by Rev. A. P. Martin, Mr. M. McDaniel of Georgia, to Miss Martha Downey, of Laurens.

Issue of April 8, 1859 [USC]

Married on the 20th of March, by Ellis Thompson, Esq., Mr. John Guin, to Miss Sealy Bramlett, all of Laurens.

W. S. Philips, only son of Dr. W. and C. B. Philips, died at Athens, Georgia, on the 15th ultimo of Pneumonia...in the 18th year of his age...in the Junior Class of the Univ.

of Georgia...wrote of beautiful eulogy on J. C. Calhoun, which was published in the
Laurensville Herald...Buried in family burying grounds in Laurens District, S. C.

Issue of July 18, 1859 [USC]
    Died on the evening of the 18th ult., of valvular diesease of the heart, Jefferson May,
in the 50th year of his age...born in Laurens District, and though he occasionally changed
his place of residence, yet his inclinations in this respect seemed circumscribed by the
limits of his native district...left son and daughter, mother and wife.
    Died of Rheumatism, in this District, on the 3rd inst., Mrs. Sarah Madden, consort
of William Madden, decd, aged 76 years...for 20 years, member of the Baptist Church.
    Samuel Chamblain Maddox, infant son of H. N. and M. A. Maddox, of Laurens District,
S. C. died 22 June, aged 1 year and 26 days.

Issue of August 5, 1859 [USC]
    Died at her residence in this District, of Typhoid Fever, on the 28th of July, at 15
minutes past 6 in the afternoon, in the 39th year of her age, Mrs. Martha Templeton Milam,
consort of Milton Milam...left a husband and 9 children....buried at Providence church..
funeral obsequies delivered by Rev. Mr. Holmes.

Issue of September 25, 1859 [USC]
    Married on the 15th inst., by Ellis Thompson, hsq., M. Y. Wolff, Esq., to Miss Fannie
Burns, all of this District.
    Married on the 18th inst., by T. J. Sullivan, Esq., Mr. James Loven to Miss Betty
Abercrombie, all of Laurens.
    Married on the 19th ult., by Rev. James F. Smith, Mr. G. W. Moore and Miss E. W. West,
both of this District.
    Married on the 21st inst., by Rev. David Wills, Mr. J. W. Eppes, of this village, to
Miss Sarah C. Pelot of Cokesbury.
    Married on the 18th inst., by Rev. Tolaver Robertson, Mr. Henry L. Fuller of Newberry,
and Miss Jennie Casey, of Laurens.

Issue of October 14, 1859 [USC]
    Married on the 6th inst., by Rev. Z. L. Homes, at the house of Dr. E. G. Simpson, near
Cross Hill, Mr. Charles h. Phinney of Florida, to Miss Martha C. Simpson of Laurens.
    Lula McGowan, eldest daughter of John J. and Mary McGowan was born 17 January 1841, and
died at the residence of her father near Cross Hill on the 6th inst...[long eulogy].
    Departed this life on the 24th August, at her residence in Chattooga Co., Ga., Mrs.
Elizabeth Strange, in the 48th year of her age...a member of the Presbyterian Church nearly
20 years...made a public profession of religion in Fairview Church, under the care of Rev.
Mr. Carlile...left a husband and children.

Issue of November 4, 1859 [USC]
    Married on the 1st inst., by Rev. Silas Knight, Jesse Teague, Esq., to Mrs. Elizabeth
Pinson, all of Laurens.

Issue of November 11, 1859 [USC]
    Married on the 3rd inst., by Rev. A. C. Stepp, Mr. James S. Bolt to Miss Melinda Pool,
all of Laurens.
    Married on the 26th of October last, by Rev. W. B. Boyd, Mr. William Hunter of Abbeville
to Miss Bettie Maxwell, of Newberry.
    David Louis Saxon, son of Joshua and Eliza Saxon, died at the residence of his parents,
Oct. 21, 1859, in the 29th year of his age...left father, mother, brother, and sisters.

Issue of December 2, 1859 [USC]
    Sallie M. Philips, died at her father's residence on the 19th November, in the 20th
year of her age...Providence took her only brother only 8 months before...a graduate of
Barhamville.
    Died at Euharlee, Cass County, Ga., on the 21st October, John Adrian Franks, son of
Samuel M. and Eliza J. Franks, aged 5 years and 5 days.
    Departed this life at her residence in Mecklenburg Co., N. C., on the 30th October
1859, Wm. Deweese, in the 62d year of his age... a native of Greenville District, son of
Rev. Jonathan and Elizabeth Deweese.

Issue of December 9, 1859 [USC]
    Married on the 1st inst., by Rev. J. C. Williams, W. L. Hudgens, Esq., of Laurens, to
Miss Corrie Klugh, of Cokesbury, Abbeville District, S. C.
    Died on the 10th of November, in this District, at the residence of the late John
Mason, M. E. Mason, in the 24th year of his age...an affectionate son, devoted brother....
Martin's Depot.
    Died of Apoplexy, on the 4th inst., at his residence near Clinton, Mr. Hugh McKelvy,

aged 56 years...left a devoted wife, a large family...more than 30 years a member of the M. E. Church. [His grave was removed to Rosemont Cemetery, Clinton, S. C. when the M. E. Church was moved.]

Issue of December 16, 1859 [USC]
Married on Tuesday evenin g, the 13th inst., by Rev. David Wills, Homer L. McGowan, Esq., to Miss Julia A. Farrow, all of this place.

Mrs. Lethe Ann Ragsdale, died at the residence of her father in Abbeville Dist., on the 8th of November...consort of John F. Ragsdale...leaves husband, father, and mother... a member of the Presbyterian Church.

Dr. James Henry Dillard...born 29 August 1807, died 28 November 1859...an elder of the church...[eulogy].

Issue of December 23, 1859 [USC]
Married on the 27th ult., by Ellis Thompson, Esq., Mr. Samuel Waddle to Miss Catharine Godfrey, all of this District.

Married on the 18th inst., by the same, Mr. William Patton to Miss Permelia Garrett, all of this District.

Married on the 23rd ult., by Rev. Mr. Walter, Dr. T. A. Power, formerly of this District, to Miss Eugenia Duckworth, of Anderson.

Died in Elberton, Ga., on the 11th inst., Samuel McFall, only child of J. Freeman and Rachel A. Auld, aged 11 months and 2 weeks.

Died at Laurensville, S. C., on Saturday, the 3rd inst., Eugene, eldest son of P. D. and E. N. Elliott, a little boy about 2 years old.

Issue of January 6, 1860 [USC]
Sad Accident. On last Wednesday Mr. Butler lost his life attempting to break the ice around the water wheel of Elihu Madden's mill, a few miles west of this place...leaves a wife and three small children.

Married on the 27th ult., by Ellis Thompson, Esq., Mr. Harrison Bryant to Miss Elizabeth Thomason, all of this District.

Married on the 25th ult. by ___ Hammond, Esq., Hasting Woods of Laurens to Miss P. Cook of Greenville.

Married on 22 December last, by Rev. David Wills, Mr. G. W. Shell of Laurens to Miss E. W. Hill, of Abbeville Dist.

Married on the 22d ult., by James Harris, Esq., Mr. R. M. Templeton, late of Laurens District, S. C. to Miss A. A. C. Morris of Chambers Co., Alabama.

Married on the 1st inst. at sunrise, by R. J. Sullivan, Esq., at his residence, Mr. Alexander Simpson of this District to Miss Isabella Armstrong, of Anderson District.

Died on the 7th of December at her residence at Greenville C. H., Mrs. Elizabeth Blackburn, aged 62 years...[eulogy].

Died of Typhoid Fever, on the 4th October 1859, at the residence of his father-in-law in Laurens District, Nathan Henderson, Reuben E. Davenport, aged 23 years, 5 months, and 2 days, youngest son of Capt. Francis Davenport, born and raised in this District...m. Miss Clary M. Henderson on the 21st of last January...baptized at Rabun's Creek Baptist Churc on 6 August last.   Line Creek, Nov. 30, 1859.

Issue of January 27, 1860 [USC]
Died on the 12th inst., Mrs. Rebecca Pitts, aged about 50 years.

Died on the 19th inst., near Pleasant Mound, infant son of Hosea and Lydia E. Garrett, aged 12 days.

Issue of April 13, 1860 [USC]
Married on the 5th inst., by Wm Stoddard, Esq., Mr. Albert Babb to Miss Nancy L. Abercrombie, all of Laurens.

Issue of April 20, 1860 [USC]
Married on the 27th March last, by Rev. Mr. Irvin, Dr. A. H. Nabers, formerly of Laurens District, to Miss Mary A. E. Tate, of McDowell Co., N. C.

Departed this life on the 23rd March last in Monroe Co., Arkansas, Mr. Jno. Compton, about 37 years of age...born and raised in Laurens District, moved to this country in the fall of 1856...leaves four little children.

Issue of May 25, 1860 [USC]
Married on the 17th inst., by Rev. J. J. Brantley, Jas. M. Baxter, Esq., to Miss Fannie C. Nance, daughter of Drayton Nance, all of Newberry.

Married on the 23rd inst. by Rev. Tolaver Robertson, Mr. James E. Anderson of Cokesbury, and Miss S. E. Fowler of Laurens.

Married on the 17th inst., by Rev. Tolaver Robertson, Dr. F. D. Coleman to Miss Othella D. Fuller, all of Laurens.

Departed this life on the morning of the 6th inst., Mrs. Nancy Lockhart, wife of John H. Lockhart...born in Newberry District, lived several years in Laurens District, until in 1851 when her husband emigrated to Russel Co., Ala., where she died...united herself with the Baptist Church at New Prospect, Laurens District, S. C.

Issue of June 8, 1860 [USC]
    Married on the 27th ult., by Wm Stoddard, esq., Mr. Thomas J. Watkins, to Miss Charlotte Abercrombie, all of Laurens.

Issue of June 22, 1860 [USC]
    Departed this life April 3, 1860, in Columbia, S. C. Mr. James Carter, in the 56th yar of his age...born in Laurens District, near Cross Hill...in the Spring of 1857, he moved to Kingston, Cass County, Ga., from which place he went to Columbia two weeks before his death for surgery...member of the Baptist Church, but had objection to closed communion, then united with the Presbyterian Church at Liberty Spring...ruling elder at the Presbyterian Church in Kingston.

Issue of June 29, 1860 [USC]
    Died on the 22d of June, Miss Elizabeth Catherine Boyd, daughter of Mr. Isaac Boyd, had just begun as a teacher of youth.

Issue of July 6, 1860 [USC]
    Married on the 14th ult., by Rev. C. B. Stewart, Mr. W. L. Hopkins of Greenville, to Miss M. Jane Anderson, of Laurens.
    Died of disease of the heart, at his residence in this District, Wm. Pool, Sr., in the 74th year of his age...born Feb. 21, 1787, died June 21, 1860...a plain, unassuming and successful farmer...a husband and father....Eden, Laurens, S. C., June 28, 1860.

Issue of July 27, 1860 [USC]
    Died on the 9th inst., at her residence in the city of Memphis, Tenn., Mrs. Sabra White, formerly Sabra McNees in the 67th year of her age...raised in this District and first married a Cook.
    Died on Wednesday, the 18th inst., at the residence of her uncle, Beaufort T. Watts, Miss Virginia Watts, daughter of Harriet & Braxton, in her 17th year. Bolton Farm, July 20, 1860.

Issue of August 10, 1860 [USC]
    Departed this life in Sevier Co., Ark., on the 16th July 1860, Susan Anna, infant daughter of James B. and Mary E. Clardy, aged 5 months and 16 days.

Issue of August 24, 1860 [USC]
    Departed this life at Chick Springs, on Saturday the 4th of August, in the 64th year of her age, Mrs. Nancy P. Farrow, of Charleston, relict of the late Dr. Samuel Farrow.

Issue of October 26, 1860 [USC]
    Married on the 14th inst., by the Rev. Jas. Smith, Mr. J. F. Saxon to Miss E. F. Wells, all of this District.
    Sarah Simpson Boyd, daughter of Mr. Isaac Boyd, departed this life, Thursday, the 11th inst.
    Sister Narcissa Fuller, consort of Jones Fuller, and eldest daughter of Thomas and Elizabeth Harris, departed this life, Sept. 19, 1860...born in Laurens District,died in Abbeville District, in the 53d year of her age, leaving a husband and five children, brothers and sisters.
    Died in Chattoogga Co., Ga., on the 14th ult., Mrs. Haney Ball, wife of Reuben S. Ball...born and raised in the upper part of Laurens District, joined the Baptist Church at Warrior Creek, in '51 moved membership to New Harmony...in '58 moved with her husband and family to Georgia.

Issue of November 30, 1860 [USC]
    Married on Tuesday night last, Nov. 27, by Rev. Z. L. Homes, DR. R. S. Dunlap, to Miss Sallie Black, all of this District.
    Died in York District, of Typhoid Fever, on the 10th inst., Mr. William B. Russel, in the 36th year of his age.

Issue of January 18, 1861 [USC]
    Married on the 12th of December last, by Rev. Robert McLees, Mr. L. K. Glasgow of Newberry to Miss Sue H. Hillhouse, of Anderson District.

Issue of January 25, 1861 [USC]
    Married on the 9th inst., by Dr. E. C. Ragsdale, Mr. Atchison Mahon to Miss Amanda

Woods, all of Laurens.
    Married on the 10th inst., at the residence of Dr. J. C. Sullivan, by Dr. E.C.
Ragsdale, Mr. Jesse K. Brockman, to Miss Kittie Bryson, all of Greenville, S. C.

Issue of February 1, 1861 [USC]
    Married on Tuesday, the 22d inst., by Rev. Dr. Williams, Capt. H. P. Griffith and
Miss A. P. Lanford, of Spartanburg.
    Married on the 24th of December 1860, by Wm. Stoddard, Esq., Mr. Tolaver Armstrong and
Miss Hannah Curry, all of Laurens.
    Married on the 7th of January, by the same, Mr. Thomas Putman to Miss Julia Curry, all
of Laurens.
    Married on the 24th ult., by Rev. Robert McLess, at the house of the bride's father,
Mr. John H. Copeland to Miss M. T. Phiney, all of Laurens.

Issue of February 8, 1861 [USC]
    Married on Thursday, the 31st January, by Rev. Z. L. Holmes, Mr. M. A. Cason to Miss
P. A. Simmons, all of this district.
    Married on the 30th ultimo, by Rev. John C. Williams, Mr. Marshall W. Motes to Miss
H. Carrie, daughter of Capt. Edmund and Mrs. Caroline Paslay.
    Married on the 4th January last, Mr. J. P. Stephens of Laurens, S. C. to Miss Mollie
Ross of Harrison County, Texas.
    Married on the 7th January, Dr. N. G. B. Henderson to Miss Nannie E. Abbott, eldest
daughter of Col. Jno. Abbott, of Panola Co., Texas.

Issue of February 15, 1861 [USC]
    Married on the 7th inst., by Rev. J. B. Hillhouse, Mr. R. L. Henry to Miss O. M.
Martin, all of this District.
    Married on the 27th ult., by Rev. C. B. Stewart, at Geo. Thomason's, Mr. Thomas N.
Leak of Laurens, to Miss N. C. Thomason, of Greenville.
    Married on the 30th ult., by the same, Mr. Jesse Knight and Miss Pernecy Long, all of
Greenville.
    Married on the 12th inst., by the same, at David Boyd's, at Fairview, S. C., Mr. J.
R. Godfrey of Greenville, to Miss Nancy A. Willis of Laurens.

Issue of March 1, 1861 [USC]
    Married on the 14th inst., at the house of Elihu Madden, Esq., by Rev. Silas Knight,
Mr. John H. Jones of Centreville to Miss Margaret S. Johnson, all of Laurens District.
    Departed this life, February 25th, at her home near Cross Hill, Laurens, S. C., Mrs.
Polly O'Neal, consort of Henry O'Neal...born December 29, 1794, aged 66 years, 1 month
and 26 days...twice married, and leaves by her former husband, one son R. F. Babb, a resident of Missouri. By her present husband, had seven children, five of whom--3 sons and
2 daughters--survive to mourn with their father. Cross Hill, February 26, 1861.

Issue of March 15, 1861 [USC]
    Married on the 7th inst., by Rev. N. P. Walker, Mr. DeForrester Miller of Pickens
District, to Miss Mellie F. Walker of Waterloo, Laurens District, S. C.

Issue of March 29, 1861 [USC]
    Married on the 21st inst., by Rev. G. C. Grimes, Mr. William A. Worthington to Miss
Rebecca E. Griffin, all of Laurens.
    Married on the 18th inst., at the residence of the bride's father, Col. P. L. Calhoun
of this District, by the Rev. D. D. Brunson, Mr. Robert h. Middleton to Miss M. Eugenia
Calhoun.
    Died at his residence in Laurens District, on Friday, the 8th of March, Mr. John Smith
...leaves a wife and a large family of children, some of whom have arrived at manhood...
[eulogy].
    Died at his residence in Ouachita Co., Arkansas, on January 9, 1861, William Brown, in
the 67th year of his age...born and raised in S. C., lived a good many years in North
Mississippi, and for the last few years in Arkansas...a member of the M. E. Church for 30
years...leaves wife, sons and a daughter. WILLIAM MOORES, Jan. 1861.

Issue of April 5, 1861 [USC]
    Died at the residence of Col. John Hudgens, on the morning of the 1st instant, John
Henderson Hudgens, in the 23rd year of his age...buried with Military honors on the 2nd
inst.

Issue of April 12, 1861 [USC]
    Married on the 9th inst., by Rev. W. P. Hill, Dr. J. L. McClintock of Laurens, and
Miss C. A. Crews of Greenwood, Abbeville, S. C.

Issue of April 12, 1861 [contd.]
Married on the 26th ult., by Rev. Mr. Barnett, at the residence of the bride's mother, Dr. Madison Drummond and Miss Sallie H. Allen, all of Spartanburg.
Married on the 1st inst., by G. H. Wofford, Esq., Mr. J. B. C. Bass and Miss Emaline Varner, all of Spartanburg.

Issue of May 17, 1861 [USC]
Died on the 22d ult., at the house of Maj. A. J. Griffin, in Arkansas, his son John K. Griffin, in his 17th year...my heart was still bowed down in sorrow at the death of D. F. Gary, a doting mother's only son, the only care of a loving wife and fond sisters. He fell at his post, a member of Capt. Garlington's State Guards. John K. is no more. He is now with his cousin Duff and grandfather, for whom he was named....AN UNCLE.

Issue of June 7, 1861 [USC]
Married on the 28th ult., by Rev. D. F. Haddon, Rev. J. C. Boyd of Newberry and Miss M. F. McClintock, of Laurens.
James R. Tribble departed this life at Martin's Depot, on the 29th inst., at his residence...an elder in the Presbyterian Church.

Issue of June 21, 1861 [USC]
Married on the 18th inst., by Rev. DR. Lee, W. S. Gregory of Union, to Miss Frances Permelia Ferguson, of Laurens.
Died of Puerperal Fever, on Tuesday, the 11th inst., at her residence near Tylersville, S. C., Mrs. Sarah Louisa Craig, wife of J. S. Craig, Esq., and daughter of Joshua and Eliza Saxon, in the 33d year of her age.

Issue of June 28, 1861 [USC]
Died in this village, on the 19th inst., Emma Esabella Philson, daughter of W. F. and Jane E. Philson, aged 18 months.
Died in Pontotoc, Mississippi, on the 2d inst., Mrs. Elizabeth B., wife of J. F. Green.
Died on the 7th inst., at her residence near Waterloo, in this District, Mrs. Mary Finley, widow of John Finley, decd, in the 79th year of her age.

Issue of July 5, 1861 [USC]
Married on the 22d May, by Rev. F. D. Smith, Zimri Henderson to Miss Sallie L. Wier, all of Calhoun Co., Ala.

Issue of July 12, 1861 [USC]
W. D. Watts, Esq., died at Glenn Springs, 5 o'clock, Wednesday evening [July 10]. Upon the first call of his country to arms, gave up two sons and an overseer....[later mentioned as Judge Watts.]

Issue of August 2, 1861 [USC]
Died at his residence in Newberry District, in the 69th year of his age, of Typhoid Diarrhoea, Mr. George Speak, on the 7th inst., born and raised and lived--with a few years exception--in Newberry District...leaves a wife and 5 children...member of the Baptist Church.

Issue of August 9, 1861 [USC]
Died in Laurens District, S. C. on the 30th ult., in the 85th year of her age, Mrs. Mary Simpson, widow of Mr. J. B. Simpson, a soldier in the War of 1812 [eulogy].

Issue of August 16, 1861 [USC]
Married on the 11th inst., by ___ Briggs, Esq., Mr. James Bobo of Union District, to Miss Asenith Pool, of Laurens District.

Issue of August 30, 1861 [USC]
Died at the residence of his father, near Pleasant Mound, Laurens District, S. C., on Saturday evening, the 24th inst., Henry P. Ball, of the Laurens Briars, 3d Regt., SCV in the 19th year of his age...leaves parents, borther and sisters.

Issue of September 6, 1861 [USC]
Married on the 29th ult., at the residence of John Workman, of Laurens District, Lt. A. M. Johnson, of Co. F. 3d Regt, S. C. V., to Miss Mary E. Workman.
Died in this town, on the 30th ult., James Lewis Parks, infant son of Mr. and Mrs. A. R. Parks.
Died at the residence of her husband, in Greenville, S. C. on the 19th ult., Mrs. Eliza W., wife of Col. John F. Kern, and daughter of Mrs. Eliza W. and the late Dr. Robinson M. Earle...aged 33 years, 4 months, and 13 days...at age 20 joinged Greenville Baptist

...on 16 May the following year, she married Col. John F. Kern of Laurens...[long eulogy].

Issue of September 20, 1861 [USC]
Married by W. D. Mayfield, Chaplain, 3d Regt., S. C. V., on the 12th inst., at the residence of John Duncan, Mr. Baruch Duncan of Newberry, to Miss Sallie Murrel of Arkansas.

Hickerson Barksdale, died in the 68th year of his age, on the 11th ult., left a wife and five children...member of the Baptist Church at Hurricane...[eulogy].

Issue of September 27, 1861 [USC]
An infant child of Mr. and Mrs. H. J. Pearson, aged 4 months and 21 days, was taken from its parents on the 24th August last.

Issue of November 1, 1861 [USC]
T. McDuffie Templeton, died at Mrs. E. Peden's, his mother-in-law, at Greenville, S. C., on Saturday, the 19th inst., B. December 20, 1834...member of Rocky Springs Church, Laurens District...married Miss M. C. Peden, 24 April 1860...transferred his membership to Fairview, Greenville, S. C....became a member of Boazman's Co. in Hampton's Legion, and went to Virginia and contracted the fatal disease.

Marcus Lafayette Langston fell in the battle of Oak Hill, on the 10th of August... son of Thomas and Emily Langston of Laurens District...born about 1834. After his father's death, his mother married Joseph Shaw, Esq., who, with the family, moved to Georgia... came to Washington, Hempstead County, Arkansas, three years ago with the trade of a mechanic. His paternal and maternal ancestors were Whigs in the Revolution of 1776...member of the Baptist Church...[long eulogy].

Issue of November 15, 1861 [USC]
Married on the 5th inst., by Rev. D. F. Haddon, Mr. E. E. Lindsey of Tennessee, and Miss N. L. Taylor of Laurens.

Died on the 31st ult., near Waterloo, Omie Ann McCrady, daughter of Robert and Jane McCrady, aged 26 years, and 13 days...member of A. R. Church 8 years.

Rev. Hilliard Judge Glenn died at his residence in this district, on Sunday evening, the 27th ult., a volunteer in the Confederate army...a member of the Methodist Episcopal Church.

James Watts, son of John and Elizabeth C. Watts, born 14 August 1842, died of measles, at Camp Butler, near Aiken, S. C., 15 October 1861, entered S. C. College December 1859 [eulogy].

Issue of November 22, 1861 [USC]
Departed this life of Typhoid Fever, on Sunday, 19th November 1861, Miss Eliza Daniel, eldest daughter of p. M. Daniel, Esq., aged 18 years...member of the Methodist Episcopal Church....

[next extant issues are in 1866]

Issue of November 9, 1854 [UNC]
    Death of A. G. Campbell...died at his residence on Wednesday, the 8th instant, about
1 o'clock AM after an illness of some ten or twelve days--his disease was Typhoid Fever.
Our community has lost one of her best citizens, and our District, a faithful Representa-
tive.

Issue of November 23, 1854 [UNC]
    Tribute of Respect to Wm Jefferson Bowden by the O'Neall Section, No. 28.

Issue of January 18, 1855 [UNC]
    Married on the 16th inst., in the Methodist Church at this place by Rev. Wm. M.
Wightman, D. D., Dr. J. L. Wofford to Miss L. E. Pettit, recently of Virginia.

Issue of October 11, 1855 [UNC]
    Death of Col. Wm. T. Nuckolls occurred, we learn from an Obituary in the Unionville
Journal, on the 27th ult., at his residence in Union District, in the 55th year of his
age...Col. Nuckolls represented the Old Congressional District to which this District
formerly belonged, for three consectuive terms in the U. S. Congress.

Issue of October 25, 1855 [UNC]
    Married on the 18th inst., by William Lipscomb (jr.), Esq., Mr. Samuel M. Kirby to
Miss Elizabeth Blanton, all of Union District.

Issue of May 1, 1856 [UNC]
    Married on the 22d inst., by Rev. David Wills, Mr. H. N. Maddox of Laurens to Miss
H. M. Miller of Spartanburg.
    Married on the evening of the 17th inst., by Rev. Mr. Gaillard, Mr. William Thompson
of Charleston to Miss Anna E. Stall[?] of Greenville.

Issue of August 21, 1856 [Duke]
    Died at Spartanburg on Friday the 8th inst., Cora Henry, daughter of T. Stobo and
Laura H. Farrow, aged 13 months and 12 days.

Issue of January 8, 1857 [USC]
    Married on the 3rd ult., by the Rev. Simpson Drummond, Mr. Cyrus S. Greenleaf to Miss
Mary A. Holcombe, all of Spartanburg District.
    Married on the 4th ult., by the Rev. John L. Norman, Mr. Garland Allen to Miss Mary
A. Layton, all of this District.
    Married on the 18th ult., by the Rev. Jno. H. Ezell, Mr. Miles H. Ferguson to Miss
Loueza A. Rogers, all of Spartanburg District.
    Married on the 18th ult., by John H. Walker, Esq., of this District, Mr. Amos Nix to
Mrs. Nancy Sealy, both of Union District.
    Married on the 21st ult., by John H. Walker, Esq., Mr. Benjamin Wells to Miss Nancy
Waldrip, all of this District.
    Married on Wednesday evening, the 24th ult., by the Rev. J. D. McCullough, Col. F. S.
Gillespie of Marlboro District, to Miss S. A. Lockwood, only daughter of Wm. & E. S.
Lockwood of Spartanburg C. H., S. C.
    Married on the 1st inst., by Rev. R. H. Reid, Mr. John Hadden and Miss Mary Pearson,
all of Spartanburg District.
    Married in this place on last Tuesday evening, by Rev. J. G. Landrum, Jas. M. Bowden
to Miss Virginia Nolly of Madison County, Mississippi.

Issue of July 9, 1857 [USC]
    Died on Sabbath morning the 21st June, Mr. Robert McCarley in the 59th year of his
age...brought up by pious Presbyterian parents in Ireland...emigrated here at age 19....

Issue of August 13, 1857 [USC]
    Married at the United States Hotel in Augusta, Ga., on the 2nd of July by the Rev.
Mr. Hard, Mr. J. W. Gamble, late of the Calder House, Charleston, and Mrs. Virginia H.
Sheen, of the same city.
    Married on the 29th ult., by the Rev. Jos. Rochell [Bochell?], Mr. Jas. McCravy of
Spartanburg, to Miss Kittie S. Speake of Newberry.
    Married on Sunday evening, the 2d instant by Rev. Thos. Ray, Mr. Bennett Whitlock to
Miss Frances A. Hawlow, all of Unionville.

Issue of September 3, 1857 [USC]
    Married on the 30th ult., by A. E. Smith, Esq., Mr. James Swarford to Miss Lucinda
Guardiner, all of Spartanburg District.

Issue of September 10, 1857 [USC]
Died at the Franklin House, Tuscumbia, Ala., Sunday evening, July 26, 1857, after a protracted illness of 18 days in his 25th year, Samuel M. Green, a native of Spartanburg, S. C.

Issue of September 17, 1857 [USC]
Died on the 6th inst., at the residence of Dr. F. M. Tucker, in the lower part of this District, Miss Louisa A. Barnett, eldest daughter of Javan and Rachel Barnett, in the 20th year of her age...completed her English education at Spartanburg Female College...zealous member of the Baptist Church for three years.

Issue of October 8, 1857 [USC]
Married on Thursday, October 1, by John H. Walker, Esq., Mr. Samuel S. Johnson to Miss Nancy Bowen---all of this District.

Issue of October 15, 1857 [USC]
Tribute of Respect to F. D. Lytle by Eumathian Society.

Issue of October 22, 1857 [USC]
Married on Thursday evening, the 15th inst., by Rev. Chas. Taylor, Wm. J. Brem to Miss S. M. Gilliard [?], all of Spartanburg Village.
Married on the 8th inst., by the Rev. W. H. Lauton, Dr. Thos. C. Poole of Spartanburg, to Miss Emma C. Way, only daughter of Mrs. C. Mallard, of St. James, Goose Creek, S. C.
Married at her father's residence, Edgefield District, S. C., on the 6th inst., by the Rev. Dr. Bradly, Mr. Drury T. Vaughn of Newberry District, to Miss E. Statira, only child of Col. John and Mrs. Ann Huiet.

Issue of October 29, 1857 [USC]
Departed this life on Sunday morning, the 6th of September last, of diarrhea, Mrs. Millie W., consort of J. H. Garrison, in the 29th year of her age, leaving an infant child five months old...member of the Independent Presbyterian Church...born in Union District...lost her father when quite young....

Issue of November 12, 1857 [USC]
Married on the 27th October, by Rev. A. A. James, Major Henry McDowell of Spartanburg District, S. C. to Miss Ann Alexander of Union District.

Issue of November 19, 1857 [USC]
Married near Wadesboro, N. C., Octo. 28th by Rev. T. R. Walsh, the Rev. Hilliard C. Parson of the S. C. Conference, to Miss Cornelia Frances, daughter of W. R. Lea, Esq., of Anson County.
Married on Tuesday evening, the 10th inst., by the Rev. C. P. Gadsden at St. Phillips Church, Charleston, Thomas B. Clarkson, Jr., of Richland District, to Miss Septima L., youngest daughter of the late Rev. N. B. Scieven [sic].
Married on the 11th inst., by Rev. S. C. Pharr, D. D., Dr. J. Brown Gaston of Montgomery, Ala., to Miss Sallie J. Torrence of Cedar Grove, Mecklenburg County, N. C.

Issue of November 26, 1857 [USC]
Tribute of Respect to J. R. Stoops by Morgan Lodge, No. 19, I. O. O. F.
Tribute of Respect to Jno. R. Stoops by Spartan Lodge, No. 70, A. F. M.
Married on the 19th inst., by the Rev. A. W. Walker, Mr. Lemuel Burnett to Miss Mary Cothran, all of Spartanburg District.
Married at Society Hill on Tuesday, the 10th inst., by the Rev. Richard Furman, Zimmerman Davis, Esq. of Charleston, S. C. to Miss Cornelia J., daughter of the late Dr. John K. McIver of the former place.

Issue of December 3, 1857 [USC]
Married on Tuesday the 24th ult., by Rev. Washington Baird, Mr. T. R. Jackson of Spartanburg, to Miss Mattie J. Goudelock of Union District, S. C.
Married on the 18th of November, by John H. Walker, Esq., Mr. Stephen T. Sexton to Miss Laura Ann Jane Landrum, all of this district.
Married on the 19th ult., by Rev. David Wills, Mr. H. P. Farrow of Cartersville, Geo., to Miss Corrie F. Simpson, eldest daughter of Dr. J. W. Simpson of Laurens.

Issue of December 10, 1857 [USC]
Married on Sunday morning, the 29th ult., by John H. Walker, Esq., Mr. Levi Madison Stone, of Coffee County, Ala., to Miss Jane Eveline Waldrip of Spartanburg District.
Married on Thursday evening, the 3d inst., by Rev. U. Sinclair Bird, Wm. B. Carlisle, Esq., Assistant Editor of the Courier, to Arabella, third daughter of Wm. Bird, Esq., all of Charleston.
Married on the 25th ult., by the Rev. Mr. McCormick, Mr. James L. Barry of Arkansas (formerly of York), to Miss Sue Carlisle of Chester.

Issue of December 24, 1857 [USC]
    Died at her residence in Spartanburg Village on Thursday, 17 December 1857, Mrs.
Sally M. Hall, in the 68th year of her age, after a painful illness of six weeks...eldest
daughter of Dr. Jacob R. Brown, an officer in the Revolution, married Henry Reese Hall
about the year 1810 and had ten children, all of whom died young and unmarried except
one daughter who lived to marry, had one son, and died also in early life.... At the
death of her husband about 25 years ago, Mrs. Hall was left with a family of small children, and an estate in Laurens District...She leaves only a grandson.

Issue of March 24, 1859 [UNC]
    Married at Bethel Church, Sunday, the 13th inst., by Rev. J. G. Landrum, Mr. E. B.
Bowen of Williamston, to Miss Fannie A. Farrow of Spartanburg.
    Departed this life, March 19, 1859, Elizabeth Colman, infant daughter of Dr. Wm. T.
and Mrs. Mary E. Russell, aged 2 months and 21 days.

Issue of January 4, 1860 [USC]
    Died at the residence of her husband in Spartanburg District, S. C. on the 5th of
December 1859, Mrs. Elizabeth Cunningham Evins, daughter of the late Gen. Thomas and Mrs.
Martha Moore...wife of Col. Samuel N. Evins...in her 63d year...member of Nazareth Pres-
byterian Church.
    Death of Mrs. Addie Wright...on Friday the 9th inst., we laid Miss Addie Wright in
her tomb...age 16...Woodruff's, S. C., Dec. 22, 1859.
    Married in Crawfordsville, S. C. on the 22d December 1859, by Rev. W. C. Kirkland,
Col. J. H. Vandike to Mrs. Elizabeth Caldwell, all of this Dist.
    Married by Rev. A. A. James on 22 December 1859, Mr. James L. Owen to Miss Susan Ann
Kirby, all of Spartanburg District, S. C.
    Married on 6 December 1859, by Jno. H. Walker, Esq., Mr. Anthony Shands to Miss Fran-
ces Madilla Landrum, all of Spartanburg District.
    Married by Jno. H. Walker, Esq., on the 27th December 1859, Mr. Morgan Young Sexton
to Miss Sallie Caroline, only daughter of Capt. Asail and Elizabeth Littlefields.

Issue of January 11, 1860 [USC]
    Married in Rutherfordton, N. C., on the 28th ult., at the Presbyterian Church by the
Rev. N. Shotwell, Mr. James B. Morris to Mrs. M. A. Gaither.
    Married by the Rev. M. Baker at Marietta, Ga., on the 29th ult., Mr. William Russell
to Miss Harriette R. Brumby, daughter of Prof. R. T. Brumby, recently of Columbia, S.C.
    Married at Anderson on the 27th December by Rev. A. A. Morse, Mr. T. J. Glover of
Orangeburg, to Miss E. Toccoa, daughter of Judge J. N. Whitner of Anderson.

Issue of January 18, 1860 [USC] (day of publication changed from Thurs. to Wed.)
    Died at his residence near Woodruff's on the night of 15th December, Mr. Samuel
Pilgrim in the 53rd year of his age. He sleeps now near the home of his childhood, having
been born and raised near the same spot...for six years, member of the Baptist Church at
Bethel...funeral discourse by Rev. Mr. Landrum...leaves wife and two little children.
    Married on the 10th inst., by Rev. Mr. Vann, Maj. S. D. Goodlett, editor of the
Greenville Patriot to Miss Mary, eldest daughter of Col. W. S. Lyles of Fairfield Dist.

Issue of January 25, 1860 [USC]
    Married on the 9th of January, 1860, by Elias Wall, Mr. Thomas J. Rollins to Miss
Susan Barnett, all of this district.
    Married on the 22d December 1859, by Elias Wall, Esq., Mr. F. W. Ray to Miss M. J.
Ray, all of this district.
    Married on the 22d December 1859, by Elias Wall, Esq., Mr. Columbus Brannon to Miss
Rhoda Bishop, all of this district.
    Married on the 10th of January 1860, by Elias Wall, Esq., Mr. Simpson Umphries [sic]
to Miss Missouri Horton, all of this district.

Issue of February 1, 1860 [USC]
    Died on the 25th January 1860, Henry Lorimer, son of G. and Rachel Ann Hicks, aged
11 years, 4 months, 20 days.

Issue of February 15, 1860 [USC]
    Death of a Young Carolinian Abroad...on the morning of the 7th ult., Thomas Aston
Coffin, son of T. A. Coffin of Charleston, S. C. in Berlin.

Issue of February 22, 1860 [USC]
    Married on the 19th inst., by Randolph Turner, Esq., Mr. Thomas Kimbrell to Miss Mary
Camp, all of Spartanburg District.

48

Departed this life in Hempstead County, Arkansas, on the 4th ult., Mr. Theophilus Thorn, aged about 50 years...born in the northern part of Spartanburg District and resided there until about 9 years ago...leaves many relatives and friends in this district.
    Died on the 19th of September 1859 in the same county and state, Mrs. Mahala _____, second daughter of Mr. Thorn, leaving a husband and four children.

Issue of February 29, 1860 [USC]
    Married at the residence of the bride's father on Thursday, the 16th inst., by the Rev. James Boyce, D. D., Mr. W. S. Brice to Miss Mattie E. Simonton, all of Fairfield District.

Issue of March 14, 1860 [USC]
    Married on Thursday the 8th inst., by Rev. R. H. Reid, Mr. Elijah McMullen and Miss Mary Ann Muray, all of Spartanburg.

Issue of March 21, 1860 [USC]
    Died in consequence of a painful accident, Feb. 20th 1860, at his father's residence in York District, S. C. Robert, son of Mr. Robert and Mrs. Jane Flemming, aged 3 years and 4 months.

Issue of April 4, 1860 [USC]
    Married on the 29th ult., at Woodruff's, S. C. by A. B. Woodruff, Esq., Mr. William Pinckney Bragg, to Mrs. Mavel C. Roebuck, all of Spartanburg.
    Married on the 25th ult., by John H. Walker, Esq., Mr. BEnjamin West of Union Dist., to Miss Permelia E. Campbell, of Laurens District.
    Married at the same time & place by the same, Mr. Wm. H. Patton of Laurens District to Miss Nancy Casey, of Spartanburg District.

Issue of April 11, 1860 [USC]
    Married on the 24th February 1860, by Rev. B. Bonner, Mr. John Sarratt to Miss Eliza Morgan, all of Spartanburg District.
    Died on the 17th ult., in the 39th year of her age, Mrs. Esther Vise, wife of John S. Vise, leaving six little children...member of the Baptist Church.

Issue of April 25, 1860 [USC]
    Married on the 19th inst., by Rev'd R. H. Reid, Mr. Samuel W. Miller of Texas, to Miss Elliot C. Drummond of Spartanburg District.

Issue of May 2, 1860 [USC]
    Tribute of Respect from Spartanburg Female College to their teacher Mrs. Ella L. Blake, who died 23 April 1860.
    Died in this village on the 24th ult., Theodore Lawrence, son of Henry J. and Anne Eliza Mouzon, aged 2 years, 8 months, and 13 days.
    Died at Campobella, near Pendleton village, on the morning of the 18th ult., Colin, eldest son of Archibald C. Campbell, aged 20 years, 9 months, 18 days.
    Died of Pneumonia, in Pontotoc County, Miss., on the 10th of March, John Willy, infant son of John J. & Mary A. Miller, aged 7 months and 23 days.

Issue of May 9, 1860 [USC]
    Married on the 29th ult., by Agner E. Smith, Esq., Mr. William Jefferson Saterfield to Miss Mary Ann Johnston, all of this District.

Issue of May 16, 1860 [USC]
    Departed this life at his residence in Spartanburg Village, on Saturday the 12th instant of apoplexy, Jefferson Choice, Esq., in the 50th year of his age...born in Greenville Dist., on the 29th April 1811, studied law with his brother Capt. William Choice at Greenville...admitted to the bar in 1833.

Issue of May 30, 1860 [USC]
    Married on the evening of the 24th inst., by Rev. Richard Woodruff, Mr. William A. Todd of Panola County, Mississippi, to Miss Mary A. Woodruff of this district.
    Married on Tuesday morning, the 22nd inst., at Camp Hill, at the residence of Dr. Winsmith by Rev. C. F. Jones, Col. John R. Sondley of Newberry to Miss Carrie Smith.

Issue of June 6, 1860 [USC]
    Died at Bivingsville, S. C., May 23rd, aged 18 months and 1 day, Susan Lois, youngest child of N. N. and S. D. Haynes of that place.
    Died on the 28th of April last, at the residence of her husband in Spartanburg Dist., Mrs. Mary Gaston, wife of James N. Gaston...born 3 August 1778, united with Nazareth Presbyterian Church.

Issue of June 27, 1860 [USC]
    Married on the 14th inst., by the Rev. J. J. Brantly, D. D., Mr. Robert H. Land,
formerly of Spartanburg, to Miss Bettie P., daughter of Dr. R. C. Griffin of Edgefield.

Issue of July 4, 1860 [USC]
    Married on Sunday the 1st[?] inst., by Jno. Bankston Davis, Esq., Mr. W. M. West to
Miss Sarah Ann White, all of Spartanburg District.

Issue of July 11, 1860 [USC]
    Married in this town on Thursday morning, the 5th inst., by Rev. A. H. Lester, Col.
Joseph Walker to Miss Sue E. Wingo.

Issue of July 25, 1860 [USC]
    Married on the 8th inst., by Elias Wall, Esq., Mr. David Petet to Miss Louisa Powel,
all of this District.
    Married in Hendersonville, N. C. on Tuesday the 10th inst., by Rev. Mr. Bird, Mr.
Will S. Hamby (formerly of Rutherfordton, N. C.) to Miss Beatrice M., daughter of Wm.
Bryson, Esq., of Hendersonville, N. C.

Issue of August 8, 1860 [USC]
    Married at Cedar Springs, Spartanburg District, August 2, 1860, by Rev. Edwin Cater,
Mr. Jas. C. Templeton of Laurens District, to Miss Margaret Jane Hagins of Lancaster
District, S. C.
    Married on Sunday the 5th inst., by Abner E. Smith, Esqr., Mr. H. Pierce to Miss
Sarah Cannon, all of this District.
    Departed this life, August 7th, 1860, Sarah Rebecca, youngest daughter of D. R. and
N. S. Hudson, aged 1 year, 3 months, 16 days.

Issue of August 15, 1860 [USC]
    Obituary: Charlie Chalmers, infant son of Rev. W. T. and Mary Farrow, on the 13th
inst., at their residence in this town.
    Departed this life at Chick Springs on Saturday the 4th August, in the 64th year of
her age, Mrs. Nancy P. Farrow of Charleston, relict of the late Dr. Samuel Farrow.

Issue of August 22, 1860 [USC]
    Married on Thursday evening in the Presbyterian Church of this place, by Rev. Edwin
Cater, the Pastor, A. T. Davis, Esq., Editor of the Carolina Spartan, to Miss Anna
Hamilton, all of this place.
    Tribute of Respect to Junius W. Thomson, by Spartan Lodge, No. 70, A. F. M.

Issue of September 5, 1860 [USC]
    Married by Elias Wall, Esq., on the 26th ult., Mr. Littleberry Gilbert to Miss
Jenetta Kimbrell, all of Spartanburg District.
    Died at the residence of his parents in this village, on Wednesday the 29th ult.,
John David, infant son of John W. And Amanda Maxwell, aged 2 years, 10 months, 5 days.

Issue of September 12, 1860 [USC]
    Married by the Rev. Wm. Curtis, LL. D., on Tuesday evening, the 4th inst., Mr. L. M.
Gentry, of this place to Miss Julia A. Camp of Limeston Springs.
    Married on Tuesday, September 4, 1860, at Fairfield, near Nashville, at the residence
of the bride, by Rev. Dr. Howell, J. D. B. DeBow of Louisiana, to Martha E., daughter of
the late John Johns of Nashville, Tennessee.
    Married on the 19th of August, by the Rev. Lanceford Padget at the residence of George
W. Smith, Mr. James Smith to Miss Lotty Blackwell, all of Spartanburg District.
    Married by the same at the residence of Thomas Shields, on the 6th inst., Mr. James
Henderson to Miss Lucinda Steadman, all of Polk County, N. C.
    G. B. Styles died at home near Woodruff's, S. C., Thursday, the 14th ult.

Issue of October 3, 1860 [USC]
    Died at the residence of his mother in Spartanburg village, on the 28th of August,
last, of consumption, John B. Golding, only surviving son of Dr. A. F. Golding, decd.,
and C. Matilda Golding, in the 27th year of his age.

Issue of October 10, 1860 [USC]
    Married on 7 October 1860, by Elias Wall, Mr. Jason Steadman of Polk Co., N. C. to
Miss Harriet Shields of Spartanburg District.
    Married on the 27th of September by Rev. D. F. Haddon, Mr. James Anderson of Spartan-
burg and Miss Jane Mills of Laurens.

Issue of October 24, 1860 [USC]
    Married on the 18th inst., by Rev. C. Murchison, Dr. P. P. Butler of Spartanburg to Miss Arsinoe of Unionville.

Issue of October 31, 1860 [USC]
    Married at Granby-Street Methodist Church, Norfolk, Va., on Wednesday morning the 24th October 1860, by Rev. J. R. Finley, D. D., Mr. John A. Henneman of Spartanburg, S. C., and Miss Louise Rate of Norfolk, Virginia.
    Married on the 25th inst., by Rev. Whitefoord Smith, D. D., Mr. R. R. King of Clarendon District to Miss Mary Bivings to this place.
    Married on the 18th inst., at the Presbyterian Church, Pendleton, by Rev. T. L. McBryde, H. J. Smith, Esq., and Sallie E., eldest daughter of J. W. Cobb, all of Anderson District.
    Married on Sunday morning, the 28th of October 1860, by Elias Wall, Esq., Mr. Edmund Belcher to Miss Nancy Edgins, all of Spartanburg District, S. C.
    Died at the residence of her father, on Wednesday morning, the 26th of September 1860, Miss Sarah[?] E. J. Anderson, daughter of John and Nancy Anderson...joined the Presbyterian Church.

Issue of November 7, 1860 [USC]
    Married on Tuesday evening the 30th October, by Rev. R. H. Reid, Mr. William L. Morgan and Miss Emily Frances Smith, all of Spartanburg District.

Issue of November 14, 1860 [USC]
    Married on Wednesday evening, the 7th of November, by Rev. A. W. Walker, Mr. Thomas B. Anderson of Laurens, to Miss Fannie M., only daughter of Rev. A. W. and Mrs. L. W. Walker of Spartanburg, S. C.
    Married on Tuesday evening last week, by the Rev. R. H. Reid, Mr. Simeon Dillard of Greenville, to Miss Mary Rebecca Anderson of Spartanburg District.

Issue of November 21, 1860 [USC]
    Married on the 15th inst., by Elias Wall, Esq., Mr. Edmund Manning Bishop to Miss Avaline Brannon, all of this District.

Issue of November 28, 1860 [USC]
    Married on Tuesday morning, the 6th inst., by Rev. O. A. Darby, A. S. Douglass, Esq., editor of this paper to Miss Mary E. Byers of Union District.
    Married on the 12th November 1860, by Rev. M. C. Barnett, Mr. W. H. Walker and Miss M. E. Roundtree, all of this district.

Issue of December 12, 1860 [USC]
    Married on the 1st ult., by Rev. J. S. Ezell, Mr. Thos. Gardener to Miss Mary Ann Price.
    By the same on the 13th ult., Mr. J. R. Warmuth to Miss Elizabeth Logan.
    By the same on the 27th ult., Mr. Doctor F. McDowell, son of Wm. McDowell to Miss Sarah W., only daughter of Mrs. Elly Turner, all of Spartanburg District.

Issue of December 19, 1860 [USC]
    Died, near Woodruff's, on the 3d November last, the little infant daughter of Green Lee and Julia Lanford, aged 21 days.

Issue of January 2, 1861 [USC]
    Married in Yorkville, S. C., December 27, 1860, by Rev. R. Y. Russell, Wm. Mcd. Palmer of this place to Miss Sallie J. Tomlinson of Yorkville, S.C.

Issue of January 9, 1861 [USC]
    Married on the 27th of December by Rev. R. H. Reid, Mr. John M. Thomas to Miss Matilda Jane Smith, both of Spartanburg District., S. C.
    Married on Thursday, the 27th December by Elias Wall, Esq., Mr. ----- McKinney to Miss Emiline Burnett, all of Spartanburg District.
    Married on the 11th December 1860, by Rev. Mr. Jacobs, Mr. A. C. Moore of Spartanburg District, S. C. to Miss Mary J. Foster, of Alabama.
    Died on the morning of the 19th ult., Maj. Andrew Barry in the 73d year of his age. His father was a Scotch Irishman and emigrated from Pennsylvania to the Tyger River in Spartanburg District in 1760...was elected to the first bench of elders in Nazareth Presbyterian Church at its organization in 1772...held seat in State Legislature....

Issue of January 16, 1861 [USC]
    Died of Comsumption, January 1, 1861, Mrs. Anna P., wife of Mr. James H. Goss, in the 30th year of her age...member of the Presbyterian Church.

Issue of February 6, 1861 [USC]
    Married on the 28th ultimo, by Rev. Mr. Connor, Mr. Wm. K. Blake, President of the
Spartanburg Female College, to Miss Marina G. Jones of Edgefield.

Issue of February 27, 1861 [USC]
    Married on the 24th inst., by Elias Wall, Esq., Mr. Wm. Cleveland Bonhan, to Miss
Elizabeth Cannon, all of Spartanburg District.
    Married on the 24th inst., by Elias Wall, Esq., Mr. L. Henry Low, to Miss Judea
Cannon, all of Spartanburg District.
    Tribute of Respect to Mr. Wm. Maxwell Hall by Calhoun Society of Wofford Co llege....
contracted disease at Fort Moultrie.

Issue of March 6, 1861 [USC]
    Departed this life on the evening of 27th January, 1861, Mrs. Eliza Cash, wife of
Capt. Benjamin Cash, aged 43 years, 11 months...leaving a husband and ten children.

Issue of March 27, 1861 [USC]
    Married on Tuesday, the 19th inst., by Rev. Whiteford Smith, D. D., Rev. W. W. Duncan,
formerly of this place, now of the Virginia Conference, to Miss Medora Rice of Union
District.

Issue of May 15, 1861 [USC]
    Married on Tuesday morning, the 14th inst., by Rev. R. H. Reid, Mr. William Means of
Florida to Miss Margaret Evins of Spartanburg District.

Issue of May 22, 1861 [USC]
    Married on Wednesday morning, the 15th inst., by W. F. Parker, D. D., Mr. J. Bayles
Williamson of Spartanburg, S. C. to Miss L. E. Porter of Leicester, N. C.
    Died at his residence in this district of Pneumonia, J. W. Cooper, in the 74th year
of his age...was a mild Calvinist, attached to the views of Andrew Fuller....head of
family.

Issue of June 12, 1861 [USC]
    Married on the 28th ult., by Rev. R. H. Reid, M⁻. Franklin Smith of Union District,
to Miss Rosa Ann Coan of Spartanburg District, S. C.
    Tribute of Respect to the Hon. Francis Hugh Wardlaw, by members of the Spartanburg
Bar.

Issue of June 26, 1861 [USC]
    Married on Sunday, the 23d inst., by C. P. Petty, Esq., Mr. Thompson Humphries to
Miss Nancy Minerva, second daughter of Mr. Joab Bryant, all of Spartanburg District.
    Married on Tuesday morning, the 25th inst., by Rev. J. G. Landrum, Dr. W. E. Dean to
Miss Anne E. Camp, all of Spartanburg.

Issue of July 3, 1861 [USC]
    Married on the 28th ultimo, by Rev. J. H. Thornwell, D. D., Rev. A. F. Smith of
Mississippi to Miss Carrie M. Golding of this place.

Issue of July 10, 1861 [USC]
    Mrs. Ellender D. Snoddy died at her residence in this district, on the 24th ult., in
the 44th year of her age...member of Nazareth Presbyterian Church...lost a loving daughter
in 1854.

Issue of July 24, 1861 [USC]
    Died at the residence of Mr. John Thomas near Allgood P. O. in this District, on the
1st inst., Mrs. Molly Guthrey, consort of Fred. Guthrey, decd...died in her 90th year,
the last of our acquaintance here connected with the days of '76...mother of 6 sons and
5 daughters, all of whom are dead but five. She has but one child, Mrs. Thomas living
in this county, and three grandchildren, one of whom is the wife of Rev. J. S. Ezell.
One of her sons, Samuel Guthrey was promoted to Judge of the Inferior Court in Arkansas.
Another--Edmond--who has both legs amputated, when last heard from was a wealthy planter
in Texas. Her father, Mr. Louallen, lived within 3 or 4 miles of the battleground. She
was with her little brother 17 January 1781, and heard the battle. Her father was killed,
mistaken for a Tory...she joined the Baptist Church.

Issue of July 31, 1861 [USC]
    Married on Sunday, the 28th inst., by Rev. C. Lee, Mr. Isaac Padgett of Rutherford
Co., N. C., to Miss Jane Satterfield of Spartanburg District, S. C.

<u>Issue of August 14, 1861</u> [USC]

Advance Forces of the Army of the Potomac, Vienna, Va., August 4, 1861: Died at Charlottesville, Va., 19th July 1861, William Smith, son of Caswell E. and Unity C. Smith of Spartanburg District, S. C.....member of Cross Anchor Volunteer Company...in the 21st year of his age.

Tribute of Respect to Joseph B. McVay, from Morgan Light Infantry, Camp Pettus, Va., August 2, 1861.

<u>Issue of October 2, 1861</u> [USC]

Married on the 29th ult., by Rev. W. T. Farrow, Mr. D. G. Finley to Miss Mary Wilkie, all of Spartanburg District.

<u>Issue of October 9, 1861</u> [USC]

Jesse Jefferson Robuck expired at Hospital at Lynchburg, Va., Friday, 27 September 1861...wrote to his brother John P. Robuck...member of Co. J, Capt. Kennedy, 3rd Regt., S. C. V., enlisted at age 19...to be buried at the Bethel church-yard.

<u>Issue of October 16, 1861</u> [USC]

Married on Wednesday, 2d October at the residence of the bride's father in Bennetts-ville, S. C., by the Rev. Mr. Wilson, James D. ANderson, of Spartanburg to Miss Sallie S., daughter of Col. C. S. Dudley.

<u>Issue of November 6, 1861</u> [USC]

Married on the 6th ult., by Jno. H. Walker, Esq., Mr. William M. Rhodes, to Miss Mary M. Allen, daughter of Rev. Jesse Allen, all of Spartanburg District.

Married on the 16th ult., by William H. Foster, Esq., Mr. Moses Turner, to Miss Nancy Nickols, all of Spartanburg District.

Married on the 27th ult., by Rev. Hilliard Haynes, Mr. Newman McDowell, to Miss Margaret Chapman, all of Spartanburg District.

Married on the 31st ult., by Rev. J. G. Landrum, Mr. C. H. McMillen, to Miss Mary Jane Dixon, all of Spartanburg District.

<u>Issue of December 4, 1861</u> [USC]

Married on the 1st inst., at 10 p'clock AM, by the Rev. W. F. Pearson, Mr. Elias Flemming to Miss Amanda Hawkins, all of Spartanburg District.

Married on Thursday, the 21st of November, by Rev. R. H. Reid, M. C. C. Sartor of Union, to Miss Cornelia Brandenburg of Spartanburg District.

Died at her residence in this district, on Monday morning, the 21st November, Mrs. Nancy Steadman, wife of Mr. B. H. Steadman, in the 41st year of her age...for ten years member of the Baptist Church...leaves husband and 8 children.

<u>Issue of December 11, 1861</u> [USC]

Married on the 5th instant, at 4 o'clock AM, at the residence of the bride's father, by Rev. A. M. Shipp, D. D., Rev. Clarence McCartha of Columbia, S. C. to Miss S. Janie Farrow of Spartanburg, S. C.

William T., son of Hesekiah Hughes and a member of the Brockman Guards, fell at his post in camp, on the 26th ult., a victim of Typhoid Fever...born and reared in Spartan-burg District, 21 years old and 3 months...member of the Methodist Church more than a year...Camp Ripley, S. C.

<u>Issue of January 1, 1862</u> [USC]

Obituary. W. A. Woodruff in the 24th year of his age, at the distant seat of war near Centreville, on the 24th ult....member of Co. K, 3d Regt, S. C. V....brought home to sleep with his father.

<u>Issue of January 29, 1862</u> [USC]

Mrs. Elizabeth Austin born in Spartanburg Dist., May 22, 1840, died in Greenville Dist., Jan. 4, 1862...joined the Baptist Church at an early age...married Nov. 22, 1860 to Mr. Thomas Austin.

<u>Issue of February 12, 1862</u> [USC]

John Poole, a member of the Morgan Rifles, Capt. Bomar, died in camp on the coast.

<u>Issue of March 5, 1862</u> [USC]

Died on the 27th ult., at the residence of this father, Mr. Woodward Allen, near Cedar Springs, Mr. James Allen, aged 20 years...died of Typhoid Fever...member of Spartan Rifles, Capt. Walker, 5th Regt., S. C. V.

Issue of December 22, 1843 [Library of Congress] (1st issue)
William Wingo departed this life at the residence of his brother in Spartanburg Village, on the 26th of Sept. last. Scarcely had he reached his twenty-first year. For two years previous to his death he had been engaged in the prosecution of the study of medicine.
Died on the 1st day of September last, Benjamin Thomas Cottrell, infant son of Zadock and Elizabeth Cottrell, aged 7 months.

Issue of March 6, 1849
Died of Pneumonia, on Friday evening last at his residence in this District, another worthy citizen, David Cooper Esq.

Issue of March 27, 1849
Married at Thomasville, Geo., on Sunday morning the 25th ult., by the Rev. S. Potter Hon. D. McCrimmon of Abbeville, Ala., to Miss Mary Ann, daughter of Rev. I. L. Potter, of the former place.

Issue of March 13, 1849
Married on the 8th inst., by Rev. J. G. Landrum, Mr. A. P. Caldwell to Miss Barbary A. Bomar, all of Spartanburg District.
Col. David Crosby, one of the Representatives in the Legislature from Fairfield District, died of typhoid pneumonia on the 22d ult.

Issue of April 3, 1849
Another Revolutionary Hero Gone!
Reuben Newman, Sr., died at his residence in the lower part of this district, on the 26th instant, aged about 98 years--if we mistake not born and raised in Granville Co., N. C. Sometime after the close of the War, he became a citizen of Spartanburg....member of the Methodist Episcopal Church.. He has left an extensive relationship to mourn his loss.

Issue of April 24, 1849
Tribute of Respect to David Cooper-, Eq., by the Lower Battalion of the 36th Regiment.
Died of Winter Fever, at the residence of William Richies in Navasso Co., Texas., Captain A. H. Hanna, late of Spartanburg District, after an illnes of eight days. He has left an aged mother and numerous relations to mourn his loss.
From the Greenville Mountaineer
Departed this life on Monday, 9 April, at her residence in Spartanburg District, Mrs. Mary Woodruff, wife of Thomas Woodruff, Esq. and daughter of the late Richard Harrison, Esq.--aged 64 years. She was a descendant of one of the oldest and most respectable families in this part of the State...member of the Baptist Church at Bethel.

Issue of May 8, 1849
Died on the 17th ult., at the residence of his father, Joseph J. Gaston, after one week's illness, in the 22nd year of his age.

Issue of May 31, 1849 [day of issue changed to Thursday from Tuesday]
A Coroner's Inquest was held in this place on Tuesday last on the body of a servant of J. W. Hudson, Esq....He had been reared by his mistress Mrs. Martha T. Hudson, and had been instructed by her in reading and writing. Upon the death of his mistress, grief for her loss drove him to this act of despair. Fairfield Herald. May 26th

Issue of June 28, 1849
Died on the 22d of this inst., at Bivingsville, Mrs. Susan B. Thomas, in the 23d year of her age...attached herself to M. E. Church. She has left a husband and little daughter.
Died in Columbia, in the Asylum, on the 12th inst., the Rev. Dr. Adams, of Diarrhea. He was a long resident of this District.

Issue of July 5, 1849
The 9th Brigade of S. C. M. mourns the loss of Capt. J. F. M. Taylor.
Departed this life on Wednesday, the 27th inst., Mrs. Louisa A., wife of Thomas B. Collins, leaving a large family to mourn her loss....[torn].

Issue of July 26, 1849
Departed this life, the 6th of June, in Spartanburg District, Mrs. Sarah Jane, consort of F. S. Furguson, Esq., aged 22 years...attached herself to M. E. Church, South... she was an affectionate mother and dutiful wife.

54

Issue of August 2, 1849

Died on the 26th inst., at the Village of Spartanburg, Dr. Samuel Farrow in the 63d year of his age, after a painful illness of 5 months and 20 days....took an active part in the War of 1812, as his father had done in the Revolution....Elder of the Presbyterian Church...sleeps beside a son and a daughter.

Issue of August 30, 1849

Departed this life on the 10th August 1849, at his residence in Spartanburg District, Mr. George Nicholls, in the 43d year of his age, leaving a wife and three children.

Issue of September 6, 1849

Died at his residence in Wittsburg, Saint Francis County, Arkansas, Isaac Wofford, on the 8th August 1849, aged 58 years, a native of Spartanburg District...in 1837 moved to Pickens Co., Ala., until 1841, removing thence to Arkansas.

Issue of September 13, 1849

Died on Monday, the 20th August, near Mt. Sarratt Iron Works, Spartanburg District, Margaret T. Porter, consort of R. S. Porter, in the 55th year of her age...raised in Rutherford County, N. C....member of Presbyterian Church...on Dec. 29, 1842, she was received into the Methodist Episcopal Church, by Rev. S. Townsend.

Issue of September 20, 1849

Married on Packolet, on Thursday evening, the 13th inst., by Elias Wall, Esq., Mr. Henry Cantrell to Miss Ann Kimbrell, all of Spartanburg District.

Issue of October 11, 1849

The sympathy of our community was excited on Sunday morning last toward some waggoners who drove into Town bearing the body of Bird Lannier, who died two hours before. He had left his home near the Village of Pendleton a few days before on his way to Rolling Mill...[torn].

Issue of October 18, 1849

Died at his residence on South Pacolet in Spartanburg District, on the 20th Sept. 1849, Christopher Golightly, in the 78th year of his age. The deceased was amongst the oldest of our citizens, having been raised in this District, and for 34 years had resided on the spot where he died. He attached himself to the Baptist Church in early life. He had raised a large and respectable family, many of whom are now citizens of this District. He gave most of his sons a classical education.

Issue of October 25, 1849

Departed this life on Saturday, the 6th of October 1849, Mrs. Mary A. Snoddy, consort of Dr. Samuel N. Snoddy of Pickens, Co., Ala., and daughter of Allen and Mary A. McClendon of Butts Co., Ga., aged 25 years, 8 months, and 16 days. She was a devoted member of the Presbyterian Church.

Issue of November 8, 1849

Married on the 20th of October 1849, by John Linder, Eq., Mr. John D. Cannon to Miss Leonarah Rush, all of Spartanburg District, S. C.

From the Laurensville Herald

Died at his residence in Laurensville on the 18th inst., Patillo Farrow, in the 54th year of his age, after a protracted illness of 63 ydas, of typhoid fever. Col. Farrow was the son of a Revolutionary soldier, born in Spartanburg District 1st Sept 1797. He was sent to South CArolina College and was a member of the S. C. Bar, practiced law about 15 years at Laurens Court House. Some eight years before his death, he became a member of the Presbyterian Church. He has left a widow and a large family.

Issue of November 15, 1849

Died in this village on the morning of the 9th at the residence of Wm. B. Seay, Charles Mouzon, a native & citizen of Charleston, S. C.

Issue of November 29, 1849

Married on the 22nd inst., by Rev. M. Durant, Mr. John Brown to Miss Jane Bradley, all of Spartanburg.

Married on the 22nd inst., by James Cooper, Esq., Mr. Noah Bell to Miss Eliza Byers all of Spartanburg.

Issue of December 6, 1849

Married on Thursday, the 29th ult., by Rev. J. G. Landrum, Mr. Marion Bloomfield Duncan of Spartanburg, to Miss Permelia Ann, daughter of Col. James Jeffries of Union District.

Issue of January 31, 1850

Married on the 24th inst., on Pacolett Bend, by the Rev. Mr. Farrow, Leiut. Clements P. Thomson, to Miss Nancy E., eldest daughter of Reuben Lindsay, all of Union District.

Married on the 24th inst., by Rev. D. Hilliard, Mr. William M. Grisham of Greenville District, to Miss Sarah Jane Nesbitt, eldest daughter of Joseph and Elizabeth Nesbitt of Spartanburg District.

Married on the 17th inst., by Rev. W. Drummond, Thos. Woodruff, Esq. of Spartanburg, to Mrs. Polly Hawkins, daughter of the late Rev. Lewis Rector of Greenville.

Issue of February 7, 1850

Married on Tuesday, the 15th ult., by Rev. D. Humphreys, Mr. Theodore G. Trimmier to Miss Mary L., daughter of Dr. M. Thomson, all of Anderson District.

Issue of March 14, 1850

Married on the 7th inst., Pacolett Bend, by the Rev. Mr. Farrow, Dr. John R. Lyons to Miss Nancy R., eldest daughter of Mr. Wm. H. Thomson, all of Union District.

Married on the 7th inst., by Rev. Samuel Townsend, Mr. John W. Arnold to Miss Mary Richardson, both of Laurensville.

Married on the 7th inst., by D. Hilliard, Mr. Isham Roberson to Miss Martha Wood.

Married on the same day, Mr. Benjamin Wood to Miss Elizabeth Roberson, all of Spartanburg District.

Issue of April 18, 1850

Married on the 11th inst., by the Rev. David Hilliard, Mr. William S. Turbyfield, and Miss Sarah F. Robertson, all of Spartanburg.

Issue of May 16, 1850

Married on last Tuesday evening [May 14], by Rev. Mr. Moss, James Farrow, Esq. to Miss Caroline Henry, daughter of the late Major James Edward Henry, all of Spartanburg.

Issue of May 23, 1850

Died, very suddenly, at his residence near Pickneyville, in the 46th year of his age, John Gist, the last lineal descendant of the Hon. Joseph Gist...served one term in the House of Representatives in the State Legislature.

Issue of June 6, 1850

Died at the residence of her father, on the 17th May, Miss Nancy Jane, daughter of Mr. James Alexander in the 21st year of her age. She was a member of the Baptist Church.

Issue of June 13, 1850

Died at his residence on North Pacolet, on the 19th ult., Mr. Robert Wall, in the 73rd year of his age. A native of Virginia, but a citizen of Spartanburg for more than 40 years...member of the Baptist Church.

Issue of June 27, 1850

Married on the 16th inst., by Rev. John WAtts, Mr. Samuel Switzer to Miss Sarah Miller, all of Spartanburg District.

Married by the Rev. S. Morgan, at 6 o'clock AM, on the 8th inst., Mr. Clayton J. Clark to Miss Nancy A., daughter of Hiram and Elizabeth Lockhart, at her father's near Limestone Springs, S. C.

Issue of July 25, 1850

Married on the 16th inst., by John H. Walker, Esq., Mr. John Fielder of Spartanburg District, to Mrs. Jane Fulton of Laurens District.

Issue of August 22, 1850

Married on the 15th inst., by J. C. Caldwell, Esq., Mr. John E. Cox to Miss Caroline Cox, all of Spartanburg.

56

Issue of September 5, 1850

Married on the 1st inst., by Rev. Mr. Laney, Mr. Andrew Tanner to Miss Amy Charlotte Cannon.

Married on the 27th ultimo, by Joel Cannon, Esq., Mr. John Chapman to Miss Lucy Ann Macca.

Issue of October 3, 1850

Departed this life at her residence in Spartanburg District, Mrs. Emma C. Farrow (consort of J. W. FARROW) on the 22d August 1850, in the 52nd year of her age, leaving a husband and five children.

Issue of October 10, 1850

Married near Laurens C. H., on the 26th ult., by Rev. E. F. Hyde, Mr. James Lewers to Miss Caroline Elizabeth Little, all of Laurens District.

Issue of October 24, 1850

Departed this life on the first of Oct. inst., Mrs. Sarah King, consort of John King of Revolutionary memory, aged 76 years and 14 days. Mrs. King (Lemaster) was born in Amherst Co., Va., Sept 17, 1774...came to this country in early life and married Mr. King from Louisa[?] Co., Va., in Spartanburg District on 2 March 1790. They settled near Rich Hill where they have raised a large family and remained until their death. Mrs. King joined the Methodist Episcopal Church, and remained a member for 50 years.

Issue of October 31, 1850

Married on Thursday evening, the 22d inst., by the Rev. John G. Landrum, Hilliard Thomas, to Martha Carolina, daughter of Elisha Poole, all of this District.

Issue of November 7, 1850

Died in Rutherford Co., N. C. on the 20th October last, the only daughter of H. F. and Letetia G. Vernon, aged 1 year, 5 months, and 21 days.

Issue of November 21, 1850

Died at her residence in Spartanburg District, on the 12th inst., Mrs. Nancy Cluff Sims, in the 60th years of her age, a native of Virginia.   J. G. L.
    The Mountaineer and Southern Baptist, please copy.

Issue of December 5, 1850

Death of Rev. Benjamin Wofford...departed this life on Monday morning last [Dec. 4] at half past 6 o'clock...has been a minister of the Methodist Episcopal Church nearly half a century...His remains were buried at his former residence near Chapel, now by the side of Mrs. Anna Wofford.

ANOTHER OLD HERO GONE

Our patriotic Volunteer Company under the command of Lieut. Elford, attended the funeral services, over the grace of Mr. James Seay, the last soldier of the regular army of the Revolutionary War who lived in Spartanburg. He died on Monday last, and was about 100 years of age...scars received at Brandywine and Eutaw Springs.

Issue of December 19, 1850

Married on Sunday evening, the 8th ult., by the Rev. Simpson Drummond, Mr. S. S. Robuck, to Miss Mary M. McHugh, all of Spartanburg District.

Died on the 8th inst., at Union Court House, Juan, son of h. H. and C. T. West, aged 2 months and 28 days.

Died at the residence of his son Mr. Woodward Allen, in this District, on Thursday evening, Mr. Caleb Allen, in the 61st year of his age...member of the Baptist Church.

Issue of January 9, 1851

Married by Mr. Durant on the 31st December, Mr. D. R. Zimmerman to Miss Georgia Ann Muscoga, all of this District.

Issue of January 23, 1851

Married in this District on the 26th ult., by A. Bonner, Esqr., Mr. Wm. Irvin to Miss E. Bridges, daughter of Stephen Bridges, of this District.

Married on the 5th instant, by the same in this district, Mr. Hugh Ray to Miss Susanna Humphris.

Married on the 9th instant, by the same near Grassy Pond, in this district, Mr. J. Wood of Rutherford, N. C. [sic] to Miss Mary Huskey of this distrcit.

Married by John Linder, Edq., in this district, on the 14th ultimo, Mr. Lacey Withers to Miss Hannah Crocker, daughter of J. Crocker.

Married by William Walker, Esq., on the 31st December 1850, Mr. Alberry Hammet to Miss Frances Kirby, daughter of Mr. Thomas Kirby, all of this district.

Married by William Walker, Esqr., on the 12th inst., Mr Daniel McHam to Miss Kissiah Satterfield, all of Spartanburg.

Married on the 16th inst., in this Town by J. B. Tollison, Esq., Mr. John Maxwell of Virginia, to Miss Amanda, youngest daughter of J. N. and L. T. Murray.

Married by Rev. J. G. Landrum on the 21st inst., Mr. Henry Turner to Miss Frances, youngest daughter of Burnold and Ann High, all of this district.

Issue of January 30, 1851

Tribute of Respect by Unionville Troop of Cavalry on Saturday, 18th inst., to William A. Q. Sims, decd.

Married at College Hill, Ohio, on Christmas-eve by Rev. Mr. Benton, Mr. James S. Cooke to Eliza J. Howard, all of College Hill.

Married on the 23rd inst., by Rev. T. Robertson, Mr. James M. Woodruff of Spartanburg District, to Miss Adline Lockhart of Laurens.

Issue of February 6, 1851

Married on Tuesday, 23rd Jan., by Rev. John G. Landrum, Col. O.E. Edwards of Spartanburg, to Miss R. Jane Gary of Laurens District.

Issue of February 13, 1851

Married on Tuesday, the 4th inst., by Rev. JOHN. G. LANDRUM, Mr. Miles Nesbitt to Miss Pauline Brewton, all of Spartanburg District.

Issue of March 27, 1851

Married on Sunday, the 23rd inst., by J. C. Caldwell, Esq., Mr. J. B. Bane to Miss Rebecca Bellman, all of this District.

Married on the 25th inst., by William Walker, Esq., Mr. William T. Dye, to Miss Jane Low, all of this town.

Married on April 10, 1851

Married by E. Wall, Esq., on the 23d March, Mr. James Turner to Miss Martha, daughter of James Burnett, all of this District.

Issue of May 1, 1851

ANOTHER REVOLUTIONARY PATRIOT FALLEN

Darby Reagan, a citizen of Spartanburg District, resident about 15 miles north West of this Town, departed this life April 16, 1851, age of 100 years, 11 months, 6 days. He was born 10 May 1750, in the county of Cork, West of Ireland. He emigrated to America in his 14th year, resided for some time in Georgia; moved to S. C., resided·for a time in Newberry District, and finally removed to Spartanburg. He was draughted [sic] as a soldier in the Revolution and fought unders Gens. Clark and Wayne. He was interred amidst the tears and regrets of about 200 relations and friends.

Issue of May 22, 1851

DEATH OF GOLDING TINSLEY

Another Revolutionary Patriot has fallen. On Sunday the ___ inst., at his residence in Spartanburg District, the aged & venerable man calmly fell asleep. He had attained the age of 96 years...survived the bloody massacre of Hay's defeat. He was buried at Cross Anchor with military honors.

Died in Walker County, Ga., recently, Mr. William Copeland, aged about 70 years. Mr. Copeland was an old citizen of this District...left a widow and many children.

Issue of May 29, 1851

Departed this life on the 11th inst., Mr. Golding Tinsly...born in Virginia & emigrated with his father to Newberry Dist....[quite a long obituary.]

Issue of June 5, 1851

Married on the 27th May, by Rev. Samuel Green, Mr. W. H. Caldwell to Miss Elizabeth A. Moore, all of Spartanburg District.

Mr. Solomon Bobo of Cross Keys, Union District, S. C., was found dead in bed on the 24 May last, aged about 60 or 61 years. Mr. Bobo was bereaved of his wife about six years ago by sudden death.

Issue of July 10, 1851

Departed this life on the 5th inst., at Cedar Spring, Spartanburg District, Mrs. Elizabeth White, aged 72 years, widow of Wm White of Union District....for 50 years she had been a pious & orderly member of the Baptist Church

Issue of July 17, 1851

Married on Sunday morning, the 13th July 1851, by John Linder, Esq., Mr. Isham H. Brown to Miss Mahala Ann Rush, all of Spartanburg District, S. C.

Issue of July 31, 1851

Died in this District, on the 29th inst., George Henry, son of David and Louisa Houghston, aged 18 months.

Issue of August 7, 1851

Married on the 23d ult., by Mark Bennett, Esq., Mr. James F. Brockman and Mary Francesm daughter of Mr. Benjamin Greer, all of this District.

Issue of August 14, 1851

Dr. G. R. Trimmier, formerly of Spartanburg, S. C., died at his residence in Lenoir, Caldwell Co., N. C., on the 24th ult., aged 27 years and 19 days.

Issue of Augusta 28, 1851

Died on the 17th inst., of Cholera Infanthm, John Calvin, son of Gen. A. C. and Emily T. Bomar, aged 14 months.

Issue of September 11, 1851

Died on the 15th inst of Consumption, at the residence of Miss Margaret Peden in Spartanburg, So Ca., Moses White Peden. He was a native of S. C., emigrated to Georgia a few years ago. He was a member of the Baptist Church. He has left a widow and two small children.

Died on the 25th ult., Mr. John Heatherington, Sner., born in Ireland, Tyrone Co., in the year 1782 and came to America 1815. Several years ago, he joined the Methodist Episcopal Church.

Issue of September 18, 1851

Married on the 28th ult., by Rev. Tolaver Robertson, Mr Wilson Kellar to Miss Lamb, both of Spartanburg District.

Married on the 21st ult., by Rev. J. L. Young, Mr. Isaac Adair to Miss Eliza A. Dillard, all of Laurens.

Issue of September 25, 1851

Married on the 17th inst., by Z. Lanford, Esq., Mr. William Henderson to Miss Elizabth, daughter of Richard S. Woodruff, all of Spartanburg District.

Issue of November 27, 1851

Death of James Edward Henry, second son of the late Mr. James Edward Henry, on Friday evening last in the 19th year of his age.

We regret to learn from the Laurensville Herald, that Dr. Hugh Saxon departed this life on Saturday the 13th inst.,at his residence in Laurens District, in the 54th year of his age. The third son of Lewis and Sally Saxon, born on Raibun's [sic] Creek, where his mother now resides. His father was a patriot in the Revolutionary War, and won the rank of Captain.

Married on the 19th inst., by Rev. J. H. Walker, Dr. J. Crawford Woods to Miss Mary Ann, daughter of James Alexander, all of this District.

Issue of December 4, 1851

Mr. Jesse Cleveland departed this life about 11 o'clock last night.

Issue of December 11, 1851

Mr. Jesse Cleveland departed this life in this place on the 3rd inst., in his 67th year, born in Wilkes County, N. C., 8 Feb 1785. He was engaged in the Mercantile pursuits in this town. He leaves a widow, children and numerous relatives.

Married on Wednesday the 3d inst., by Rev. C. Veard of Glenn's Spring, Mr. Joseph B. Cottrell of Charleston to Miss M. Louisa Jennings,daughter of Rev. John Jennings of Union District.

Married on Thursday, the 13th ult., by Rev. A. McCorquodale, Rev. E. J. Meynardie, of the S. C. Conference, to Miss Elinore, eldest daughter of Adam T. Walker of Chester C. H.

Married on Wednesday evening, the 26th ult., by Rev. E. J. Meynardie, Mr. J. Barber Ferguson, to Miss Nancy S., eldest daughter of the late J. R. Buchanan, all of Chester District.

Married on Tuesday, the 25th ult., at Edgefield C. H., by the Rev. Mr. Graham, Mr. A. M. Perrin, to Miss Emily, daughter of the late Col. P. M. Butler, all of Edgefield District.

Married on the 11th ult., by Rev. Wm T. Capers, Dr. Nathaniel Clark of Virginia, to Miss Hannah Catharine Weyman, daughter of the late Maj. Tm Turpin of Greenville Dist.

Married on the 13th ult., by Rev. Wm T. Capers, Rev. S. M. Green of Sumpter [sic], to Miss Laura Richmond Hulsenback, daughter of the late Maj. Wm Turpin of Greenville District.

Issue of December 18, 1851

Died on Friday, 21 Nov., in the 17th year of his age, James Edward Henry, son of the late Maj. James Edward Henry.

Died at Unionville on Saturday the 13th inst., Miss Louisa Jane, eldest daughter of John and Eliza Gibbs, aged 17 years, 11 months, and 4 days.

Issue of June 9, 1853

In February last, near Cross Anchor in this Dist., a North Carolina waggoner by the name of Haffner (Heffner) was most brutally murdered in his camp....

Issue of June 23, 1853

Death of Mrs. L. C. Preston. She died on Saturday evening last at Summer Home, near Columbia, wife of Hon. Wm. C. Preston.

Died on the 7th instant at the residence of his Father Dr. A. F. Golding, in the village of Spartanburg, A. R. Golding of Union District, in the 35th year of his age, leaving a wife and three small children.

Issue of June 30, 1853

Married on the 16th instant, by H. Wofford, Esqr., Alexander Aiken to Miss Marinda Taylor, all of Spartanburg District.

By the same on the 26th inst., Mr. F. Newman of Ga., to Miss Harriet Striblin of Spartanburg District.

Issue of July 7, 1853

Married on the 30th of June, by J. F. Sloan, Esqr., Mr. N. M. Quinn of Spartanburg, and Miss Jane M'Bride of Union District.

Issue of July 14, 1853

Married on the 27th instant, by A. Todd, Esq., Mr. William Taylor to Miss E. J. Spillers, all of Anderson District.

Died on the 7th of June last, at the residence of her husband in Walker County, Ga., Mrs. Martha Foster, consort of James Foster, formerly of Spartanburg District, leaving a husband and two small children.

Issue of July 21, 1853

Married on the 12th instant, by Rev. John G. Landrum, Dr. Thomas P. Dean to Miss Mary B. Davis, all of this District.

Issue of July 28, 1853

Death of A. M. Little. He died yesterday at 17 minutes past 12, and was buried yesterday evening at 4 o'clock by the Spartanburg Volunteer Company with the honors of war. The sermon was preached at 3 o'clock AM[sic] by the Rev. John G. Landrum. He came to our town a few weeks since and remained at the Martin Spring for a fortnight. He was carried here by his friend, T. Jarman Elford...At 16 or 17 he joined the Palmetto Regiment as it was departing for Mexico.

Death of Major S. A. Goodman. The editor of the Illustrated Family Friend, at the residence of E. W. Henry, Esq., at Charlotte County, Virginia.

Issue of September 1, 1853

Died at the residence of her husband, Foster Clark, on Pacolet the 31st July last, Mr Mary Ann Clark, daughter of Foster Jackson, in the 37th year of her age...member of the Presbyterian Church.

Issue of September 15, 1853

Married on the morning of the 31th inst., at the residence of Thomas B. Collins, Esq., by the Rev. Dr. Howe of Columbia, DR. A. G. Campbell and Miss Mary Collins.

At the same place and hour, by the Rev. DR. Howe, Rev. A. A. James and Miss Sarah Collins, all of this place.

Issue of September 22, 1853

Died in the village of spartanburg, on the 14th inst., Benjamin Franklin Cunningham, son of William Cunningham, Esq., of Greenville District, in the 22nd year of his age.... member of the Baptist Church for three years.

Issue of October 6, 1853

Departed this life at his residence near Cannon's Camp Ground, in this District, on the morning of the 26th of September, Joel Cannon, Esqr., aged 51 years. He has left a widow and nine children. His mother, brothers and sisters survive.

Issue of October 13, 1853

Married on Wednesday evening the 5th inst., by the Rev. R. H. Reid, Maj. Samuel Snoddy to Miss Rosa, eldest daughter of Silas Benson, all of this District.

Died on the 6th ultimo, at the residence of her son, near Woodruff's, Mrs. Hannah Pilgram, in the 67th year of her age...member of the Baptist Church at Bethel.

Tribute of Respect by the 37th Regiment of S. C. Militia to Lt. Col. Isaac Neighbors.

Issue of October 20, 1853

Died at the residence of Mr. H. F. Vernon, on North Pacolet, on the 10th Sept., Mr. James Blackwell of Rutherford County, N. C., aged 72 years, 7 months and 19 days. He was not a member of any church, but his predilections pointed to the Baptist denomination.

Issue of October 27, 1853

Married on the 4th inst., by Rev. E. Lindsay, Woodbury H. Farrow to Mrs. Mary A. Rook, all of Newberry.

Issue of November 3, 1853

Married on Tuesday evening, November 1st, by the Rev. R. H. Reid, Mr. Oliver Moss to Miss Mary, youngest daughter of Capt. John Snoddy, all of this District.

Issue of December 1, 1853

Married on the 24th ult.,by J. C. Caldwell, ESqr., Dr. John W. Crenshaw of Anderson, to Miss Lizzie M. Finch of this District.

Issue of December 15, 1853

Death of Mrs Bethland Foote Butler, on Friday evening (the 2d inst.), at the residence of her only surviving child, the Hon A. P. Butler. She was the relict of Gen. William Butler of the Revolution. She was born in Virginia in 1764, but had lived from early youth in S. C. She had nearly reached the age of 89. from the Edgefield Advertiser.

Issue of January 5, 1854

Married on the 22d December 1853, by J. C. Caldwell, Esqr., at the home of Col. W. T. Tanner, Mr. Jesse Gray of Laurens District to Mrs. Nancy Tanner of this District.

Issue of January 19, 1854

Married on Thursday evening, the 8th December, by John H. Walker, Esqr., Mr. Elihu C. Littlefields to Miss Mary Jane Chumley, all of Spartanburg District.

Married on Wednesday evening, the 14th December, by John H. Walker, Esqr., Mr. Thomas Huff of Union District, to Miss Mary Tinsley of Spartanburg District.

Married on the 20th December last, by Rev. J. G. Landrum, DR. A. M. Dantzler to Miss J. A. Hatchett of this District.

Issue of January 26, 1854

Married at the Walker House, on Tuesday evening the 24th instant by the Rev. John G. Landrum, Miss Martha J., third daughter of Wm Walker Esq. (W. H.), to Mr. J. Miles Lee, eldest son of Stephen Lee, Esqr., formerly of Charleston, S. C.

Died on the 16th November last, at the residence of her husband, Mrs. Jane Wright, consort of William Wright, in the 46th year of her age, leaving a husband and 13 children to mourn her loss...buried at Bethel Church. Funeràl preached by Rev. Warren Drummond and Rev. Drury Scruggs.

Issue of February 2, 1854

Obituary. Mrs. Anna Wofford McCravy, consort of Capt. John W. McCravy, and daughter of Mr. and Mrs. Samuel W. Tucker of Spartanburg District, was born Aug 8, 1830, and died November 27, 1853.

Issue of February 23, 1854

Married on the 14th inst., by the Rev. Mr. Smith, Mr. J. P. F. Camp to Miss Julia Ann, daughter of Abner & Charity Smith, all of this place.

Issue of March 9, 1854

Married on Sunday morning the 26th Feb last., by John H. Walker, Esqr., Mr. Leonard Oshields, to Miss Mary Powell, all of this District.

Married in this District, on the 14th ult., by A. Bonner, Esq., Mr. Wm. McCraw and Miss Elizabeth Harris.

By the same, on the 16th ult., Mr. Richard Scruggs and Miss Narcissa Martin.

By the same, on the 28th ult., Mr. Stephen Humphries and Miss Julia Ann Wilson.

Issue of March 16, 1854

from the Columbus Times

Alexander Mark Robins, the Deputy Sheriff of Muscogee County, was shot down on the 27th inst., in the streets of Columbus...killed by David Wright.

Issue of March 30, 1854

Died at his residence in this District, on the 15th inst., Jorial Barnett, aged 52 years, a consistent member of the Baptist Church for over 20 years...funeral preached by Rev. J. G. Landrum.

Died, of Catarrhal Fever, on the 22nd inst., in this District, Edward, infant son of Rev. M. C. and Nazareth Barnett, aged 11 months and 22 days.

Issue of April 6, 1854

Married in this District, on the 30th ult., by A. Bonner Esqr., Mr. Lemuel Scruggs to Miss Mary Davis.

Married in this District, on the 28th March, by Z. Lanford, Esq., Mr. Willis Bragg to Miss Mina Simpson, daughter of Samuel Simpson, Sr.

Died in Lincoln,County, Ky., Feb. 19, 1854, Mrs. Permelia T. Crow, wife of James Crow, Esq., in the 49th year of her age.

Issue of April 13, 1854

Married on Thursday evening, the 16th ult., by the Rev. R. H. Reid, Mr. Thomas McMullen to Miss Hester Ann Wingo, all of this District.

Married on Thursday evening the 4th inst., by the same, Mr. David Wingo, to Miss Martha E. Wingo, all of this District.

Married in Greenville District, on the 5th inst., by Rev. Dr. C. Lee, Mr. Jabez Gilreath to Miss Rose Carolina, daughter of Dr. Manning Austin.

Issue of May 4, 1854

Died on the 31st March last at his residence in Spartanburg District, Mr. Robert Dickson, in the 79th year of his age...born in Ireland and emigranted to Carolina, about the time he attained to manhood and settled in this District...member of the Presbyterian Church at Nazareth. Hymn "Unvail thy bosom faithful tomb" sung at his funeral.

62

Issue of May 11, 1854
Death of Rev. James M. Webb. Died on the 24th ult., at Rutherfordton, N. C. age 50 years...minister of the Baptist Church.
Married on the 9th inst., by Rev. C. Lee, Mr. Felix Clayton to Miss Nancy Jane Monroe, all of Spartanburg village, S. C.

Issue of May 18, 1854
Married on the 16th inst., by Rev. Mr. Wells, Thomas Stobo Farrow of Laurensville and Miss Laura A. daughter of the late Maj. James Edward Henry, of our town.

Issue of May 25, 1854
Married in Columbia Thursday evening, the 18th inst., by the Rev. George Howe, D. D., Mr. William H. Weller to Miss Louisa A. Dial, all of Columbia.
Married in Sumter on the 4th inst., by the Rev. Dr. Thomas Smyth, Dr. H. H. Huggins of Sumter District, and Miss Louisa E., only daughter of Jesse R. Gray, of Charleston.
Married on the 25th April, at Cedar Hill, Georgia, by the Rev. Mr. Reese, the Hon. R. B. Rhett of South Carolina, to Miss Catharine Dent.
Married in Bennettsville, Marlborough District, on Thursday evening, the 4th inst., by Rev. A. Thomas, Mr. Joshua H. Hudson, formerly of Chester to Miss Mary A. Eiller, all of Bennettsville.
Married on 30th April 1854, by Thos. H. Osteen, Esq., Mr. John H. Courtney, to Miss Martha Norton, all of Sumter District.
Married on Wednesday evening, the 3d inst., by Rev. Dr. D. W. Cuttino, Mr. Joseph B. White, Jr., to Miss Esther H., second daughter of John China, Esq.
Died at Spartanburg C. H., So. Ca., on Saturday evening at sun-set, May 20th 1854, Alice, third daughter of Maj. H. J. and Mary O. Dean, aged 16 months and 22 days.
Died on the 17th inst., at Glenn Springs, Harriet Augusta, wife of Prof. G. F. D'Vine, daughter of Isaac Sharland, Esq., of Bath, Somersetshire, England.
Died at Bivingsville, on 14 Jan last, Robert, eldest son of n. N. and Susan D. Haynes, aged 11 years and 26 days.

Issue of June 1, 1854
Married on the 11th inst., by the Rev. Camillus Jeter, Mr. Charlie Moore of this District, to Miss S. E., daughter of B. M. and L. T. Chapman, of Union District.
Departed this life on Saturday, 27th inst., Leonella Frederica, infant daughter of G. W. H. and C. S. Legg, aged 5 months and 1 day.

Issue of June 8, 1854
Died on May 23d 1854 at her late residence in Spartanburg District, Mrs. Mary Linder, widow of Lee Linder, Esq., decd., aged about 63 years.

Issue of June 15, 1854
Departed this life at his residence near Mt. Zion, Spartanburg District, on __ May 1854, John Chapman, Jr. in the 50th year of his age...member of the Baptist Church.
Murder. We learn says the Newberry Sentinel, of the 7th inst., that Oliver Towles was murdered on Monday morning near Dr. Bobo's. He was overseer for Dr. John E. Bobo.

Issue of July 6, 1854
Died at his residence in Union District, on the 31st May, Thomas M. Vise, in the 27th year of his age.

Issue of July 13, 1854
Died on the 26th ult., at the house of her father, W. R. Perry of Limestone Springs Hotel, in her 51st year, Mrs. Sarah S. Morgan.
Died on the 19th of June, of Typhoid Fever, William K. Cooper, 16 miles east of Carnesville, Ga., a native of this District.
Departed this life at Livingston, Ala., on the 28th ult., Mrs. Louisa Ann, wife of Rev. George W. Boggs. She was born in Anderson District, on the 20th of January 1821, and was the eldest daughter of Col. D. K. and Mrs. Jane E. Hamilton. She was married to Rev. George W. Boggs in December 1847 and resided until 3 or 4 years past at Dayton.

Issue of July 20, 1854

Obituary. Mrs. Nancy T. Cannon, consort of Hon G. Cannon, passed away at home in Spartanburg District, July 10th being 34 years of age, wanting 11 days...a member of the Methodist Church.

Departed this life on the 9th inst., at his residence on Tyger River, Captain E. Webster, leaving a wife and four children.

Issue of July 27, 1854

Died on Tuesday morning, the 11th inst., at her residence in this District, Mrs. Susan Ann King, wife of G. H. King, and only daughter of John and Nancy Leatherwood. Her son Merdock, aged 5 months, died four days after.

Issue of August 3, 1854

Monument "Erected by the Ladies of Spartanburg to the Memory of the 'Brave Palmetto Boy' ALLEN H. LITTLE who died in this place July 27th 1853" At the age of 16 he volunteered in the late war with Mexico.

Departed this life, on the 22nd July, at his residence in this District, Mr. Nathaniel Vise, in the 18st year of his age...entered the Baptist communion in 1850.

Died at his residence near Mt. Zion, So. Ca., on the 27th June 1854, Henry Jamison, at 92 years. He was born near the city of Carlisle, Pa., 22 Feb 1762, and about the time of the Revolution his father left Pennsylvania and settled in Spartanburg District, about two miles from the place at which his son lately died. He married Ann Goodlett who died in 1847. Of his children, he leaves only a daughter.

Died on Saturday morning, the 22nd July, Sarah Elizabeth Snoddy, daughter of the late John Snoddy, Jr. decd & Elender Snoddy, aged 7 years 2 months, and 15 days.

Issue of August 10, 1854

Died on the 3d inst. in this District, after an illness of 5 days, Lloyd, only child of Robert and Jane Flemming, aged 8 months and 24 days.

Married in camp, near Nebraska Centre, June 19th, Mr. Alba Sherman & Miss Mary Swan by Hon. A. W. Babbitt, Secretary of Utah....[a long account.]

Issue of August 24, 1854

Death of a Georgia Lieutenant. Among the killed at a recent fight with the Indians of New Mexico, was Lieut. J. E. Maxwell of the 3rd Regiment of infantry. His parents reside near Athens, Ga....killed on June 20th.

Died at his residence in this district, June 10, 1854, Rev. Azariah Vise, in the 55th year of his age. He united with the Baptist Church in the 18th year of his age, and the following year married Miss Jane Poole. He has left an aged and afflicted companion and four children.

Issue of September 7, 1854

Died in Atlanta, Ga., on the morning of August 21, at 10 minutes before 5 o'clock, Robert Andrew, son of Dr. Benjamin F. and Sarah E. L. Bomar, aged 2 years, 8 months, and 5 days.

Married on Tuesday evening, the 5th inst., by Rev. J. G. Landrum, John L. Petty to Miss Lucinda M. Briant.

At the same time & by the same, Mr. Benson Martin to Miss Hester Turner.

Also on the 29th, by Rev. J.G. Landrum, Mr. Abel Wingo to Miss Mary Wilson, all of this District.

Issue of September 14, 1854

Married on the 12th inst., by J. C. Caldwell, Esq., Mr. Martin Turner to Miss Francis C. Knight, all of this District.

Issue of September 21, 1854

James Franklin was killed near Newberry C. H., a few days since in a drunk shooting match frolic.

Died at his residence on the 4th insta., on Tyger River, Andrew Caldwell, in the 77th year of his age of malignant diarrhea...member of the Presbyterian Church at Nazareth.

Died on the 13th inst., in the 70th year of his age, Mr. John Sarrat, Sen'r, residing near Broad River, in the lower edge of this District....member of the Baptist Church.

Died at Limestone Springs on the 5th instant, in his 79th year, Capt M. Gaffney... born in Ireland, he sailed from Dublin for New York in his 22nd year and has left a journal of his Voyage...member of the Baptist Church of Providence.

Issue of October 5, 1854

Death of Luzerne Rae. Every friend of Deaf Mute instruction in this country will regret to hear of the death of Mr. Luzerne Rae, of the American Asylum in Hartford. The event took place on Friday and was remarkably sudden. His age was about 43.

Issue of October 12, 1854

Died at her father's residence, Spartanburg District, on the 7th September, Mary Jane, only daughter of Major William and Mrs. Francis C. Hoy, aged 10 months. Scarce a year has passed since the grave closed over a beautiful and promising son, Edward Dean Hoy.

Issue of November 2, 1854

Married on Thursday evening, the 26th inst., by the Rev. R. H. Reid, Dr. William C. Kilgore of this District, to Miss M. C. Sullivan of Laurens District.

Issue of November 9, 1854

Death of A. G. Campbell. On Tuesday night last between the hours of 12 and 1 o'clock He was like by all.

The State vs. Peter Gosnell. Murder. He was convicted of the murder of JAMES HORN, the father of his wife.

Issue of November 23, 1854

Married on the 5th instant, by Rev. N. P. Walker, Mr. James Clark Templeton formerly of Laurens, to Miss Arena Adaline Cooper, of this District.

Married on Thursday, the 9th inst., by Rev. R. H. Reid, Mr. Alexander Wakefield to Miss Rebecca, youngest daughter of Hiram Bennett, Esq., all of this District.

Married on the 15th instant, by H. Wofford, Esq., Mr. James J. Lucas, to Miss Alice Story, all of Spartanburg.

Departed this life at the residence of Mr. WM. S. Mills, in Rutherford County, N. C., on the 30th October, Mrs. Maria R. Miller, relict of the late James V. Miller, deceased of Spartanburg. For many years, she was a member of the Baptist Church. About eight years ago, death removed from her, and from her children, an affectionate husband and a loving father.

Issue of December 7, 1854

Married on Tuesday evening, the 5th inst., by the Rev. R. H. Reid, Mr. E. M. Cooper, of Laurens District, to Miss Margaret P. Caldwell, of this District.

Married on the same day, by J. C. Caldwell, Esq., Mr. Alberry McAbee to Miss Jane A. Tollison, of this District.

Died at her residence in Marshal county, Miss, November 16th, Mrs. Elenor Wilkins consort of Aaron Wilkins, and daughter of Capt. John and Rachel Jefferies of Union District, South Carolina, aged 59 years, 5 months and 1 day....a member of the Methodist Church.

Died in Marshal County, Miss., October 11th, James Jefferies Wilkins, aged eleven months and 11 days, infant son of M. J. and S. L. Wilkins, grandson of James Jefferies of South Carolina.

Issue of January 4, 1855

Married on Tuesday evening, the 21st of November, by John H. Walker, Esq., Mr. Samuel Hindman to Miss Vienna Moore.

By the same on Thursday, the 23d November, Mr. Thomas F. Houghston to Miss Mary Darby.

By the same on Tuesday evening, the 12th of November last, Mr. Samuel M. Waldrip to Miss Nelly Beason, all of Spartanburg District.

Obituary. Absalom Walker, died at his residence near Cedar Springs, on the morning of the 21st instant, having breathed the breath of life 74 years and 11 months. Born in North Carolina, came early in life to Union District, where he married Miss Susannah Jackson, daughter of Frederick Jackson. August 1810, they were baptized together into the Church at Padget's Creek by Rev. Thomas Greer. In that year, they moved their membership to Lower Fair Forest. Twenty-six years ago they moved to the place where he died. [Absalom Walker was the father of William Walker, A. S. H.]

Died at his residence, near Hobbysville, on the 28th December, Mr James Layoon in the 44th year of his age. In 1832, he became a member of Cedar Shoal Baptist Church, and was later a Deacon.

Issue of January 25, 1855

Married on Tuesday evening, the 23d instant, by the Rev. John D. McCullouhg [sic], Mr. Thomas T. Brown of Columbia, to Miss Carolina C. Blassingame of Spartanburg.

Issue of January 18, 1855

Married on the 16th inst., in the Methodist Church in this place, by the Rev. Wm. M. Wightman, D. D., Dr. J.L. Wofford of this town to Miss L. E. Petit, late of Virginia.

Married on the 14th inst., by J. B. Tolleson, Esqr., Mr. Vernon Tollins to Miss Harriet Bishop, all of this District.

Issue of February 1, 1855

Married on Thursday evening, the 25th inst., by Wm. Lipscomb, Jr., Esq., Mr. Newton M. Kirby to Miss Catharine S. Kirby, all of this District.

Married on the 25th ult., by the Rev. J. G. Landrum, Mr. Wm. Hobby to Miss Parmelia, eldest daughter of Mr. Harrison Drummond, all of this District.

Issue of February 8, 1855

Mrs. Louisa T. Chapman, wife of Mr. B. M. Mobley, departed this life on the 18th ult., a member of the Baptist Church nine or ten years.

Issue of February 15, 1855

Married on Thursday, the 1st February, by Wm. H. Atkinson, Esq., Mr. John G. Abbott of Spartanburg District, to Miss Harriet, eldest daughter of John J. McCullough of Edgefield.

Tribute of Respect to Bishop Capers [of the M. E. Church], born St. Thomas Parish, S. C., 26 Jan 1790...[long account of his life.]

Issue of February 22, 1855

Joel Smith, Esq., formerly a member of the House of Representatives from Abbeville District, died suddenly on Monday morning last at his residence at Stony Point.

                                                                    Carolina Times

Issue of April 5, 1855

Died at 5 o'clock on Thursday morning, the 15th inst., in the 44th year of her age, Mrs. Margaret Wakefield, wife of M. P. Wakefield, leaving a husband, five little daughters and a family of adopted children...member of the Presbyterian Church at Nazareth.

Died at the house of Mr. J. R. Frey, in Spartanburg District, South Carolina, on the 9 December last, Mr. Joseph Wellets, in the 48th year of his age, a native of Philadelphia, a Courier and Finisher by trade.

Issue of April 19, 1855

Married in Boston, on the 4th inst., by the Rev. Dr. Stow, Mr. James Lloyd Miller to Miss Sarah M. Smith, recently teacher in the Spartanburg Academy.

Married on Thursday, the 12th inst., at her father's residence in Spartanburg District, by A. E. Smith, Miss Susan Littlejohn to Mr. J. H. Cantrell, late of Alabama.

Issue of May 3, 1855

A personal recounter occurred at Hendersonville, N. C. on Thursday, the 26th ult., between Dr. Jones and a Mr. Fant, resulting in the death of the latter.

Issue of May 10, 1855

Death of Rev. James Dannely...died last Saturday, the 28th ult., at his residence near Lowndesville.

Married at Unionville, S. C., May 1, 1855, by the Rev. J. H. Saye, Giles J. Patterson, Esq., of Chesterville to Miss M. J. Gage of the former place.

Married at Anderson on the 1st inst., by the Rev. William T. Capers, Prof. P. Bayssoux Stevens of Citadel Academy, Charleston, to Miss Mary S. Capers, youngest daughter of the late Bishop Capers.

Died at his residence of Pneumonia, in this District, on the 22nd inst., Fortunatus H. Legg, Esq., in the 67th year of his age...born in Prince William County, Virginia, but a citizen of Spartanburg District, nearly forty years. He was bereaved of his first wife, shortly after coming to this district, by whom he had one surviving son, Major G. W. H. Legg, Intendant of the Town of Spartanburg. His second wife--his surviving widow--is the daughter of John Chapman, Sr., who lives at the great age of 94 years. By his last wife he had 4 sons and 3 daughters, all still living. One son is Dr. J. Columbus Legg, Union District. The deceased was a member of Oak Grove Baptist Church.

Died on Sunday morning, the 6th inst., in the 11th year of his age, C. Sumter, son of Daniel G. and M. Finley.

Issue of May 17, 1855

The Hon. D. J. McCord, died at his residence in Columbia...one of the oldest citizens of Columbia, having removed hither about 1804.

Married in Yorkville, on Wednesday morning, the 9th inst., by Rev. J. M. H. Adams, Hon. Daniel Wallace of Jonesville to Mrs. Emily H. Starr of Yorkville.

Died at his residence in this district, on the 30th ult., Edward Bomar, in the 89th year of his age...born in Halifax Co., Va., emigrated to Spartanburg District, in 1796. He had two wives--the first, the mother of his children died more than 20 years ago. The second still lives. He was a member 66 years of the Baptist Church. He came to Spartanburg with his young family 60 years ago. He was a member of Bethlehem Church, and later Mt. Zion. He was with others and Rev. Thomas Bomar, a founder of Mt. Zion.

Died in the Village of Spartanburg, while on a temporary visit to her sister, Mrs. Nesbitt, on the 19th ult of measles, Angeline Brewton, daughter of David Brewton, in the 32nd year of her age. She leaves her parents and an only brother and sister.

Issue of May 24, 1855

Death of a Student. On Monday last, Mr. J. J. Hall of Fairfield, died...a student of Wofford College.

Death of An Editor. F. W. Symmes, Jr., Asst. Editor of the Keowee Courier, died Monday evening the the residence of his father, Dr. F. W. Symmes in Pendleton.

Married on the 1st inst., by Elias Wall, Esq., Mr. William C. Bishop, to Miss Elizabeth Bullington.

Married on the 5th inst., by Elias Wall , Esq., Mr. John Spencer to Miss Catharine Eastler.

Married on the 16th inst., by Elias Wall, Esq., Mr. John Nolen to Miss Sarah Taylor all of this District.

Issue of May 31, 1855

Massena Taylor, Esq., died at his residence in Greenville Dist., on the 23d inst., of consumption, formerly Sheriff of that district.

Death of an old citizen. Mr William Reed, Esq., resideing about 3 miles from this village. He was an octogenarian--having lived to see his 80th year.

Mr. Hollman Smith, SR., was murdered by slaves, near his residence near the Rolling Mill, on Monday last, in this District.

Issue of June 14, 1855

Died at the residence of John Snoddy, in this district, in the 23d ultimo, Mrs. Elizabeth Snoddy in the 84th year of her age. Born 4 March 1772 in Abbeville District, and resided there until she was 19 when she married Capt. Sam Snoddy and moved to Spartanburg District. She was a member of the Presbyterian Church 64 years.

Issue of June 21, 1855

Departed this life on the 1st inst., at the residence of Mrs. A. Bomar, of our town, Thomas, son of Mr. and Mrs. T. O. P. Vernon, aged 3 years and 24 days.

Died on the 27th ult., of measles, at the residence of his father in this District., John B. Drummond, son of the Rev. Simpson Drummond, in the 18th year of his age.

Died in Newberry, on Saturday night last, the 9th inst., William Andrew, youngest child of W. A. (Rev.) and Elizabeth McSwain, aged 4 years, 2 months, and 25 days.

Issue of July 5, 1855

Tribute of Respect by Pleasant Grove Division, No 5, Sons of Temperance...on the death of Robert B. Wood, who died on Wednesday the 20th ult....June 23.

Married on the 28th ult., by A. E. Smith, Esq., Mr. Fielding Sandford Turner to Miss Martha Jane Cash, all of this District.

Married on Tuesday evening, 26th June, by Rev. J. G. Landrum, Mr. Adolphus P. Cansler of Lincolnton, N. C. to Miss Nancy W. Bobo, of this district.

Married on Tuesday evening, 26th June, Rev. T. Robertson, Mr. Jacob M. Holmes, of this district, to Miss Lucy A. Hammet, of Laurens District.

Died at her residence in this District, on the 24th of May last, Mrs. Elizabeth Wingo, in the 83d year of her age...born in Amelia Co., VA., and became the wife of Abner Wingo. In 1800 they removed to Spartanburg. In 1811, her husband died leaving his wife & family of small children. She was the mother of 9 children, 4 of whom are living. grandmother of 54, great grandmother of 81, and great great grandmother of two.

Issue of July 5, 1855

Death of Edmond Jones Henry, one of the proprietors of the <u>Spartanburg Express</u>, ...died at the late residence of his parents, on Saturday, the 7th inst., aged 26 years.

Married on the 6th inst., by William Lipscomb, Esqr., Mr. John Balke of Miss Elizabeth Harris, all of this District.

Issue of July 19, 1855

Maj. Robert Sims of Unionville, died in that village on Monday last.

William Abernathy, age 18 or 19, residing near Cross Anchor, hung [sic] himself on Thursday, the 12th inst.

Married on the 17th inst., by REv. David Hilliard, Mr. Hazel Hicks, Esq., to Mrs. Elizabeth Martin, all of this place.

Married on Sunday morning, by Elias Wall, Esq., Mr. Jesse Belcher to Mrs. Melinda Bush, all of this District.

Issue of July 26, 1855

Married in Union District, on the 22d, inst., by The Rev. Thos. Curtis, D. D., Robt. A. McKnight esq., and Miss Amanda M. Palmer, all of that idstrict.

Married by John H. Walker, esq., on Sunday evening the 20th May last, Mr. James Casey to Miss Frances Littlefields, all of this distrct.

Married by the same on Monday evening, the 25th of June last, Mr. Jason Canady to Mrs. Lucinda Carter, all of this District.

Married by the same on Thursday evening the 28th June last, Mr. John S. Gideons to Miss Anna P. Rampley, all of this district.

Married by the same on Wednesday evening, the 4th of July inst., Mr. William Gray of Laurens Dist., to Miss Polly Ann Gentry, of this District.

Married by the same on Sunday evening, 22d July inst., Mr. William Gillespie to Miss Polly Ann Couch, all of this District.

Issue of August 2, 1855

Died on July 20, 1855, Jemima, wife of L. Hewitt and daughter of J. W. and N. Williams, in the 40th year of her age...member of the Baptist Church...She has left 4 children.

Died on Tuesday morning, 17th ultimo, of bowel infection, Edward, youngest son of L. P. and Elizabeth Tinsley, aged 10 years.

Issue of August 9, 1855

Miss Delana Fowler departed this life at Bivingsville, on 30th July in the 28th year of her age. She joined the M. E. Church in July, 1847. Her body rests in the church yard.

Issue of August 16, 1855

Married on the 9th instant, by A. B. Foster, Esq., Mr. Isham Foster to Mrs. Arabelsy Garrett, all of this district.

Died in this district, of dropsy, on the 8th inst., Mrs. Patsey Brannon, consort of John Brannon, in the 70th year of her age. She has left a numerous train of friends and relatives.

Issue of August 23, 1855

Tribute of Respect to Bro. W. F. Smith, by Spartan Lodge, No. 70, A. F. M.... 17 Aug.

Died at the residence of her husband, near Spartanburg, on the 16th inst., of bilious fever, Mrs. Delilah Brannon, wife of Jefferson Brannon, in the 29th year of her age...a good wife, affectionate mother.

Issue of August 30, 1855

[Torn]...Married ____ Smith esq., on the 8th inst., ___ ry to Miss Martha Jane Tillot.

Died at his Father's residence, ___ July 30, Dr. Benjamin F. Lindsay, in the 25th year of his age.

Died at his residence near Woodruff's, on Saturday evening, August 18, Capt. Isaac Woodruff in the 49th year of his age...member 18 years of Baptist Church at Bethel.

68

Issue of September 6, 1855

Married in State Line M. H., on the 15th July, by the Rev. W. Curtis, Mr. T. Ezell and Miss Elizabeth Lane, all of Spartanburg District, S. C. Shelby Intelligencer.

Died on Tuesday, the 20th inst., at Lancaster, Pa., in the 35th year of her age, Mrs. Eliza Susannah Tucker Mills, consort of Clark Mills, of South Carolina.

Died at his father's residence near Hobbysville in this District, on Sunday morning, the 5th August, Mr. J. P. Hanna, in the 33d year of his age.

Died in Spartanburg District, S. C., on Monday night, August 20, 1855, Margaret Elizabeth, youngest and second daughter of W. K. P. & Julia Ann Madorah Chidwell, aged one year, four months and four days.

Issue of September 13, 1855

Tribute of Respect to Major R. G. H. Thomas, Brig. Quartermaster of 9th Brigade SC Milita.

Died whilst on a visit to her brothers in Polk County, N. C., on the 26th August of apoplexy, Miss Susan West of Spartanburg District, S. C. aged 33 years...member of the Methodist Church for many years.

Died at her residence in Abbeville, Alabama, on the 14th of August 1855, Mrs. Rebecca R. Clendenen, aged 55 year, relict of Jas. Clendinen, late of York District, S. C., deceased.

Issue of September 20, 1855

Mrs. Elizabeth Littlejohn, wife of Dr. Thomas Littlejohn, departed this life af Kirby's Springs, on the 5th of September 1855, aged 30 year and 25 days...born of religious parents, James Cooper, Esq., and wife--and in her 17th year attachéd herself to the M. E. Church...married on 16th February 1845...she was a wife and step-mother ...buried in Littlejohn family burial ground...children Betty, Medora, Minerva, James, Kenneth, Charlie, Lucy....

Issue of September 27, 1855

Married on Tuesday evening, the 21st August, by the Rev. Mr. Edwards, Mr. William J. Gibson of Alachua, County, Fla., to Miss Eliza J. Fleming, also of the same place, but formerly of Laurens District, S. C.

Married on the 10th inst., by A. E. Smith, Esqr., Mr. Henry Pettit to Miss Melissa Rollins, all of Spartanburg District.

Issue of October 4, 1855

Tribute of Respect to Maj. H. J. Dean and E. Jones Henry by Clerk of Court.

Tribute of Respect to J. K. Briggs, ef Union, a student at Wofford College.

Died at the residence of her mother in Union District, on the 3d inst., Mrs. Cicely A. Sims, widow of William Sims, decd, daughter of Mrs. Mary Mobley, in the 30th year of her age.

Issue of October 11, 1855

Capt. Alexander Stuart of this District died near Blackstock Depot, on Wednesday last of consumption...served in the Mexican campaign. Winnsboro Register.

Issue of October 18, 1855

Tribute of Respect to James W. Rogers by Calhoun Lodge, No. 81, A. F. M. at Glenn Springs.

Died at Oxford, Benton Co., Ala., on Wednesday, the 3d inst., Mr. Obadiah Vise, formerly of Spartanburg District, aged about 54.

Died in Spartanburg, on Tuesday the 9th inst., Daniel Mobley, of Union District, in the 22nd year of his age.

Issue of October 25, 1855

Married on the 18th inst by William Lipscomb, Jr., Esq., Mr. Samuel M. Kirby to Miss Elizabeth Blanton, all of this District.

Died on Saturday, October 20, at the residence of James K. Means, Esq., in this Dist., Dr. M. W. McRee of Spartanburg, aged 24 years, 1 month, 3 days.

Issue of November 15, 1855

Married in Chester District, on Tuesday, 30 October by Rev. Wm Banks, Mr. Elijah Wright of Spartanburg Dist., to Miss Elisa E., daughter of Mr. John Tims.

Issue of November 22, 1855
Married on Tuesday evening, the 13th inst., by Rev. Bishop Andrew, D. D., Rev. W. W. Moon of Charleston to Miss Lucy J. Rogers of Sumter District.

Issue of November 29, 1855
Married on the 25th inst., by J. M. Elford, Esq., Mr. J. Laurence Williams, to Miss Caroline Haines, all of Spartanburg District.

Issue of December 6, 1855
Married on Monday evening, the 5th of November, by John H. Walker, Esq., Mr. Nathan L. Daley of Tippah Co., Mississippi, to Miss Angeline Holcombe of Spartanburg District.
Married by the same on Friday evening, 30 November, Mr. Mansel Cooper to Miss Melinda Cooksey, all of this District.

Issue of December 13, 1855
Married on the 11th inst., by Rev. Mr. Landrum, Mr. Aaron Bell to Miss Sarah Jane Brown.

Issue of January 17, 1856
Married on the 18th December, by Rev. John G. Landrum, Mr. James Bishop to Miss Adelina L. Wolf.
Married on the same day, by Rev. John G. Landrum, Mr. Edmund Bishop to Miss Eleanor McDowell.
Married on the 20th December, by E. Wall, Esq., Mr. Augustus Morris to Miss Harriet Seay.
Married on the 20th December, by John G. Landrum, Mr. Columbus H. White to Miss Mattie Bishop.
Married on 8th January by Rev. Benjamin Page, Mr. John Belcher, to Miss Caneada Piehoof.
Married on 9th January, by Rev. Benjamin Page, Mr. Bevly Bush to Miss Mary White, all of this district.
Married on 20th December in Polk County, N. C., by Thomas Edgington, Esq., Mr. John Melton to Miss Selenor Mills.
Funeral Notice. Friends of Mr. and Mrs. James Farrow are invited to the funeral of their infant son, Patillo, today at 10 A. M. at their residence.

Issue of January 31, 1856
Married at Huntsville, Texas, on Tuesday, the 4th December, by Rev. Mr. Estill, C. H. Jackson, originally of Spartanburg, S. C. to Mrs. Carra Jones, formerly Miss McDonald, all of Polk County.

Issue of February 7, 1856
Married on the morning of the 5th inst., by the Rev. C. Taylor, D. D., John W. Carlisle, Esq., to Miss Laura C., daughter of Simpson Bobo, Esq., all of Spartanburg.
Married on the 31st January, by Rev. Dr. C. Lee, Mr. Henry Tate of Yalobusha[?] Co, Miss., to Miss Mary P. McCarter of Spartanburg District.
Married by John H. Walker, Esq., on 27th December last, Mr. Thomas Waldrip to Miss Nancy Ramsey.
Married by the same, on Thursday 17th January, Mr. Elijah Watson to Miss Mary Gentry.
Married by the same, on Wednesday evening, the 9th January, Mr. Robert Watson to Miss Senilla Alewine.
Married by the same, on Thursday, the 3rd January, Mr. Elias Stroud to Miss Thoda Monjoy.
Married by the same on the same evening, Mr. William Turner to Miss Susan Nabors.
Married by Harvey Wofford, Esq., on Thursday, the 24th January, Mr. Elihu Moore to Eliza Casey, all of Spartanburg District.

Issue of February 21, 1856
Married at Anderson, on the 15th of January, by Rev. I. Scott Murray, Maj. Jo. Berry Sloan to Miss Mary R., second daughter of Elias Earle, Esq.
Married at Asheville, N. C., on the 29th January by Rev. Dr. Chapman, Mr. Joseph R. Osborn, and Miss Penelope Twitty, all of this place.

Issue of February 28, 1856
Married on the 14th inst., Mr. John M. Griffen of Spartanburg District, to Miss Hattie M. Mahaffie, late of Greenville District, S. C.

Issue of March 6, 1856 [fragmentary issue at Spartanburg County Library]
Died in great peace, near Glenn Springs, on Tuesday, 19th February, Mrs. E. I. Beard, wife of Rev. C. S. Beard.

70

Issue of March 20, 1856
Married on the 8th inst., by Elias Wall, Esq., Mr. William Ragan to Miss Ann Foster.
Married by the same, on the 8th , Mr. William Manus to Miss Mary Ragan, all of
Spartanburg District.
Married on Wednesday, February 6th, by John H. Walker, Esq., Mr. James A. Rook to
Miss Linney Campbell.
Married by the same, on Sunday morning, Februar 17th, Mr. Jonathan Gentry, to Miss
Emily E. Rampley.
Married by the same on Tuesday evening, the 4th of March inst., Mr. James Phillips to
Miss Louisa Casey, all of Spartanburg District.

Issue of April 10, 1856
Departed this life at Pendleton, S. C., on the 21st ult., Mrs. Emily Campbell, wife
of Archibald Campbell, aged 38 years.

Issue of April 17, 1856
Married on Tuesday evening, the 8th inst., by Rev. Wm Curtis, Mr. P. O. Lemmons to
Miss Emily Jane, eldest daughter of S. A. and Harriet Camp, all of this District.

Issue of April 24, 1856
Married in Union District, on Thursday, the 10th inst., by Rev. W. W. Carothers, Mr.
J. H. Garrison of Spartanburg District, and Miss Milly W. McCulloch, of the former place.
Died in this District, on the 11th inst., Mrs. Mary Holcomb, leaving three dear
children...member of the Baptist Church.

Issue of May 8, 1856
Married on the 8th day of April, by Elias Wall, Esq., Mr. John Elder to Miss Elizabeth
Cantrell, daughter of George Cantrell.
Married by the same, on the same day, Mr. Hiram Owens, to Miss Sarah Belcher.
Married on the 30th April, by the same, Mr. Harlin Hughey to Miss Elizabeth Elder.
Married on the 1st of May, by the same, Mr. Elisha Turner to Miss Elizabeth Belcher.
Married on the 1st of May by Rev. J. G. Landrum, Mr. James P. Clement to Miss Rebecca
Hughey, all of this District.
Married in Unionville, by Rev. A. A. James, Mr. Wm R. Lipscomb of Spartanburg District
to Mrs. Nancy Elmina Jefferies of Union District.
Died on the 15th April 1856, at her residence near Cross Anchor, Mrs. Sarah Ann,
consort of M. Taylor...member of the Baptist Church...leaves a husband and two orphans.

Issue of May 15, 1856
Married on the 10th inst., by Joseph M. Elford, Esq., William Thomson, Esq. to Miss
Johanna Rollins, all of this District.
Married near Boiling Springs, on the 1st inst., by Rev. J. G. Landrum, Mr. James Cle-
ments, to Miss Rebecca Hughey.
Married on the 30th ult., by Elias Wall, Esq., Mr. Harlin Hughey to Miss Elizabeth
Elder, all of this District.
Married on the 12th inst., by Rev. Wm T. Farrow, Mr. Isaac Tinsley, to Miss Mahala
Nolen, all of this district.
Married by J. B. Tolleson, Esq., on Thursday, the 8th inst., Mr. Martin Smith to
Miss Cynthia Kirby, all of this district.
Died on the 8th inst., near this village, Jonnie Ross, son of Rufus and Amanda Poole,
aged 4 years, 4 months and 26 days.
Died on the 1st inst., at the residence of her father near Cedar Springs, Miss Martha
Cooper, daughter of James W. Cooper, Esq., in the 26th year of her age...member of
Methodist Episcopal Church.

Issue of May 22, 1856
Married by J. B. Tolleson, Esq., on the 8th inst., Mr. James Gossett to Miss Caroline
Smith, all of this District.

Issue of May 29, 1856
Married on the 21st of May, by Rev. S. Lander, Rev.G. H. Wells, editor of the Western
Eagle to Miss E. A. Weber of Shelby, N. C.
Married on the 20th instant at Granby, by the Rev. Mr. Gamewell, Mr. Jno. Duncan of
Spartanburg, and Miss Maria Cayce of the former place.

Issue of July 10, 1856
Died in Russel County, Ala., about the 20th ult., Rev. J. J. Salmond, of measles...
born and raised in Spartanburg District, and preached for over 25 years...Baptist Church.

Issue of July 17, 1856
Married on Tuesday, the 15th inst., by Rev. G. B. Tucker, Mr. J. F. V. Legg of Spartanburg, to Mrs. M. J. McConnel, of Fairfield, S. C.
Married on Sunday morning, the 13th inst., by A. R. Aughtrey, Esq., Mr. Eli McMahan of Union District to Miss Frances P. Sims of Laurens District.

Issue of July 24, 1856
Married on the 26th ult., by Rev. D. F. Hadden, Mr. W. S. Pearson of Spartanburg to Miss Dorothy F. Little of Laurens District.
Married on Thursday evening, the 22d inst., by G. W. H. Legg, Esq., Mr. Thomas Durham and Mrs. Eliza Black, all of Spartanburg.

Issue of July 31, 1856
Married in Greenville District, S. C. on Tuesday, the 15th inst., by Rev. Mr. Buce, Mr. T. J. Scaife of Unionville, S. C. to Miss E. E. Joyce of Greenville District.
Married at Boydton, Mecklenburg County, Virginia, on the 9th inst., by Dr. Wm A. Smith, President of Randolph Macon College, Mr. David R. Duncan of Spartanburg to Miss Virginia Nelson, of the former place.
Married in Spartanburg, on the 29th of June by Rev. Mr. Lancaster, Mr. Oliver Ross of Spartanburg ot Miss Nancy A. Henson of Greenville, S. C.

Issue of August 7, 1856
Married on Sunday morning, the 3d inst., by the Rev. Charles Taylor, Mr. John W. Low to Miss Ira H. Clements, both of this district.
Died at her father's residence in this District onthe 20th July, Minerva N. J., daughter of Rufus and Nancy Lancaster.
Departed this life, on the 23rd[?] July 1856, John Smith, B. S. who was born 1790 in Pennsylvania, and emigrated with his father and mother to Lincoln County, N. C., where he lived untill 1838, then moved to Spartanburg District. For several years lived at Bivingsville, until he became crippled, then moved to Crawfordsville on Middle Tyger where he died...joined the Methodist Church.
Died of diarrhea at Cowpens' Furnace, on the 24th July 1856, Joseph Simpson, son of Jesse and Hester Hollis, aged 1 year and 2 days.

Issue of August 14, 1856
Died on the 21st June last, Mrs. Louisa Ann, wife of Capt. James Waddell, aged 32 years ...leaves husband, aged parents and two small children.

Issue of August 28, 1856
Married on Sunday the 17th inst., by J. E. Belotte, Esq., Mr. Jonathan R. Casey, formerly of Spartanburg, to Miss Elizabeth Howard of Anderson District, S. C.
Died on Thursday, the 21st inst., Mrs. F. A. Gillaspie, in the 55th year of her age... member of the Baptist Church.
Mrs. Eliza Brew, late consort of Wm J. Brew, departed this life on the 5th inst., in her 23d year...member of the Baptist Church.

Issue of September 4, 1856
Married on the 14th August last, by Rev. M. C. Barnett, Dr. Joseph W. West to Miss Sallie A. Borrough, all of this district.
Married on Tuesday morning, the 18th August, by Rev. Wm Martin, Dr. Stringfellow of Florida, to Mrs. Sarah A. Wright, all of Unionville.
Married at the same time, Mr. W. J. Scaife to Miss M. Addie Dogan, all of Unionville S. C.

Issue of September 11, 1856
Married in Laurensville on Thursday evening, the 28th of August, by Rev. Thos. Razor, Maj. Elias Bearden to Miss Lucinda B. Leak, all of that district.
Died on Wednesday, the 3d of September, Eugenia V. Smith, daughter of Willis Smith, aged 8 years and 7 days.

Issue of September 18, 1856
Married on the 24th ult. by Harvey Wofford, Esq., Mr. John Johnson to Miss Elizabeth Frail, all of this district.
Married on the same day, by Sum Summer, Esq., Mr. Green Rogers to Miss Eliza Taylor, all of Spartanburg District.
Married on the 31st ult., by Harvey Wofford, Esq., James M. James of Georgia, to Miss Jane Smith of Spartanburg District.
Married on the 7th inst., by J. W. Wilkes, Esq., Mr. James Mattison to Miss Sarah Farrow, all of this District.

72

Issue of September 18 [contd.]
Married on the evening of the 14th inst., at the residence of Dr. R. E. Cleveland,
by J. M. Elford, Esq., Mr. James Bryant to Miss Adeline Patterson, all of this district.
Married on Monday, the 15th inst., at Epps Spring Camp Ground, by Rev. S. Dickson,
Mr. M. R. Davis of Spartanburg, to Miss M. B. Champion of Cleveland Co., N. C.
Married on Sunday the 14th, by A. Bomar, Esq., Mr. Alvin McCraw of Cleveland, N. C.
to Miss Caroline Clary of Spartanburg.
Married on Tuesday the 2d inst., by the Rev. Wm. Curtis, Mr. David Gramling to Miss
Harriet C. Ellis, all of Spartanburg.
Died at the residence of her son William at Epps Springs, Shelby, N. C. on Wednesday,
the 10th inst., Mrs. Mildred Patterson, widow of the late Edward Patterson, of Spartanburg,
S. C., in the 55th year of her age. Mildred Lewis was born in Rutherford Co, N. C. on
7 May 1799.-.at age 19 married Edward Patterson, then a resident of Pacolet Springs in
Spartanburg District, where they lived until about 1837, when he bought land and built
near Spartanburg C. H., where he died shortly thereafter, leaving Mrs. Patterson and 12
children, none of whom were grown. Shortly after his death, another daughter was born,
making 8 daughters and 5 sons...member of the Methodist Church.
Died at the residence of her son, Dr. B. F. Bomar, Atlanta, Ga., on the 27th July
last, Mrs. Elizabeth C., consort of the late Rev. Thomas Bomar, in the 73d year of her
age...member of the Baptist Church...leaves a great number of grandchildren and great-
grandchildren.
Died on the 6th inst., in Spartanburg District, Augustus Perry, only and infant son
of David S. and C. E. Burton, aged 5 months and 6 days.

Issue of September 25, 1856
Married on the evening of the 21st inst., by J. M. Elford, Esq., Mr. Elias James of
Union District, to Miss Missouri Low of Spartanburg.
Married in Abbeville, on Tuesday evening, the 9th inst., by Rev. Dr. Boyd, Mr. J. F.
C. Dupre to Miss Mary P., daughter of Rev. G. W. Huckabee, all of that district.
Died in Asheville, N. C., on Sunday night, the 24th ult., William Francis, infant son
of Miles and Martha Lee of Spartanburg village, S. C., aged 1 year,7 months,and 24 days.

Issue of October 2, 1856
Married on the 30th ult., at the residence of her father, John Bomar, by Rev. J. G.
Landrum, John Earle Bomar and Miss Louise Bomar, all of Spartanburg.
Married on the evening of the 28th ult., by B. F. Bates, Esq., Mr. James Crocker to
Miss Nancy Lee, daughter of Rev. Jeremiah Lee, all of this district.
Married on the 28th ult., by Elias Wall, Esq, Mr. Dolphus Irivn[sic], to Miss Louisa
Horn, all of Spartanburg District.
Married on Thursday, the 25th ult., by Geo. W. H. Legg, Esq., Mr. Thomas J. Dillard
to Miss Rosana Chapman, all of Spartanburg District.
Married on the 22d ult., by Elias Wall, Esq., Mr. Arnold Forester, to Miss Caroline
Smith, all of this District.

Issue of October 9, 1856
Randolphsville, Polk Co., Texas, Sept. 9, 1856. Dr. John A. Morgan, died 8 Sept 1856.
Tribute of Respect by Eureka Lodge 161 [A. F. M.].
Married on Sunday evening, the 5th October by W. H. Bagwell, Esq., Mr. Marshall Kirby,
to Miss Martha Devine, all of Spartanburg.
Died at the residence of her son in Greenville, on the 18th ult., Mrs. Jane Brice, in
the 79th year of her age...member of Nazareth Presbyterian Church over 60 years...married
in 1802, mother of 12 children, seven of whom are now living.
Died at his mother's residence on Thursday morning last, Thomas A. Gaston, in the 32d
year of his age.

Issue of October 16, 1856
Died on the 30th September, Elizabeth Angelita, 2nd daughter of G. A. and A. F. Smith,
aged 3 years and 10 months.

Issue of October 30, 1856
Married on Tuesday evening, the 28th inst., by the Rev. Wm. T. Farrow, Mr. John Belton
Free of Union District to Miss Lousarah Maybry of Spartanburg District.
Married on the 23d inst., by Wm Walker, Esq., Mr. H. H. Turner to Miss Ann Y. Chapman,
daughter of Beverly Chapman, decd., all of this district.

Issue of November 6, 1856
Died on the 30th ultimo, near Cowpens, Mr. John Hicks in the 51st year of his age...
member of the Baptist Communion.

Issue of November 13, 1856
    Died at the residence of Maj. William Hunter, in this District, on Sabbath evening,
the 19th October, Mr. Gabriel Madison Hobby, in the 41st year of his age...received a
fracture on the head from the kick of a horse at the age of 20 months and has had convulsions ever since...member 25 years of the Baptist Church at Bethel...[long eulogy and
medical history].

Issue of November 20, 1856
    Married on Sunday, the 9th inst., by Elias Wall, Esq., Mr William Wilson to Miss Eliz-
abeth Ezell, all of this District.
    Married by the same on the 13th inst., Mr. Harrison Brannon to Miss Harriet, daughter
of William Seay, all of this district.
    Married at Greenwood, on the 6th inst., by Rev. E. T. Buist, M. G. Anderson, Esq., of
Spartanburg District, and Miss Sallie, daughter of Gen. James Gillam of Abbeville District.
    Married on Wednesday, the 5th inst., by Rev. Thomas Mitchell, Mr. W. S. Oliver to
Miss M. A. Easterling, all of Georgetown.
    Married in New Gloucester, Me., on the 22d ult., J. L. Hatch, Esq., (Editor or the
Charleston Standard) to Miss N. Cushman of Gloucester.
    Died of fever on the 13th ultimo, at the residence of Maj. T. H. McCann, at Slabtown,
Anderson District, S. C., Andrew J. Coan, son of Wm Coan of Spartanburg, S. C., aged 18
years...was studying under Rev. J. L. Kennedy...[eulogy].

Issue of November 27, 1856
    Married on the 23d inst., by Rev. M. C. Barnett, Mr. Alex. Bullman to Mrs. Jane
Hunt, daughter of Isham Hurt, Esq., all of this District.

Issue of December 11, 1856
    Married on Thursday evening, the 4th inst., by H. H. Durant, Mr. Edwin H. Bobo, to
Miss Emma Drummond, daughter of Jared Drummond, Esq., all of this District.
    Married on the 7th inst., by Rev. H. H. Durant, Mr. Jas. M. Clark and Miss Agnes Dye,
all of Spartanburg District.
    Married at the Methodist Church in Yorkville, on Thursday morning, the 27th November,
by Bishop J. O. Andrew, Rev. A. H. Lester and Miss Margaret C. Miller, both of Yorkville.
    Married at Lancaster C. H., on the 25th ult., by the Rev. D. P. Robinson, Mr. Edward
Meng, of Union, S. C. to Miss F. A. Hammond of Lancaster.

Issue of December 18, 1856
    Married on Sunday morning, the 14th inst., by Rev. Dr. C. Lee, Dr. Lee L. Smith to
Miss Mary Jane, daughter of William Smith, decd, all of Spartanburg.

Issue of December 25, 1856
    Married on Tuesday evening, the 23rd inst., by Rev. H. H. Durant, Mr. Davis Gassaway
of Union, to Miss J. Hannah Bogan of this District.
    Married on Tuesday, the 18th inst., by Rev. R. H. Reid, Mr. Ephraim Few of Greenville
to Miss M. L. Seay of this District.
    Married on the 14th inst., by Rev. J. G. Humbert, Miss Nancy Caroline Riley to Mr.
Enoch B. Gambrell, all of Laurens District, S. C.
    Married on Tuesday evening, the 23rd inst., by Rev. R. H. Reid, Mr. Samuel C. Means,
Esq., of Florida, to Miss M. A. Moore of this District.
    Married on the 23rd inst., by Rev. J. G. Landrum, Dr. O. G. Chapman, and Miss Sallie
Wingo, all of Spartanburg District.

Issue of January 1, 1857
    Married on Wednesday evening, December 24, by Rev. J. D. McCollough, Col. F. S. Gilles-
pie of Marlboro District, to Miss S. A. Lockwood, only daughter of Wm and E. S. Lockwood,
of Spartanburg C. H., S. C.

Issue of January 8, 1856
    Married on Tuesday evening the 6th inst., by Rev. J. G. Landrum, Jas. M. Bowden, Esq.,
to Miss M. Virginia, eldest daughter of John N. Nolly of Madison Parish, La.
    Married by the same on the 4th inst., Mr. Madison   to Miss Elizabeth Ballenger,
all of Spartanburg District.
    Married on Wednesday evening, the 3d December, by Rev. Simpson Drummond, Mr. C. S.
Greenleaf, to Miss Mary A. Holcombe, all of this District.
    Married on Thursday evening, the 4th December, by Rev. John L. Norman, Mr. Garland
Allen to Miss Mary A. Layton, all of Spartanburg District.
    Married on Thursday evening, the 18th December, by Rev. John H. Ezell, Mr. Miles H.
Ferguson to Miss Lue A. Rogers, all of Spartanburg District.

74

Married on Thursday evening, the 18th December, by John H. Walker, Esq., of this District, Mr. Amos Nix to Mrs. Nancy Sealy, of Union District.

Married on Sunday, the 21st ult., by John H. Walker, Esq., Mr. Benjamin Wells to Miss Nancy Waldrip, all of Spartanburg District.

Married on the 27th ult., by O. P. Richardson, Esq., Mr. E. B. White, to Miss Frances Weatherford, all of Spartanburg District.

Married on the 23rd ult., by Rev. J. G. Landrum, Mr. Wylie Bagwell to Miss Frances Pollard, all of Spartanburg District.

Issue of January 15, 1857

Married in Charleston, on the 25th ult., by the Rev. Dr. Bachman, Capt. Asbury Coward of the King's Mountain Military School (Yorkville, S. C.) to Eliza Corbet, youngest daughter of Mr. John A. Blum.

Married on Wednesday, the 17th December, by Elias Wall, Esq., Mr. William Ballenger to Miss Matilda Seay, all of this District.

Married on Tuesday, the 23rd December last, by William Walker (A. S. H.), Mr. Elias Wall, Esq., of Spartanburg District, to Mrs. Mira McKinney, of Rutherford Co., N. C.

Married on Sunday morning, the 28th December, by E. Wall, Esq., Mr. Jason Blackwell to Miss Nancy Ann Champain.

Married on Sunday evening, the 28th December last, by E. Wall, Esq., Mr. William G. White to Miss Elizabeth Wyatt.

Married on Wednesday, the 7th January, by Rev. Hilliard Haynes, Mr. Thomas J. Gilbert to Miss Caroline, daughter of Woodson Burnett, all of this District.

Married on the 6th inst., at Cashville, Miss Margaret Mahaffe to Mr. John Burns, both of Spartanburg District.

Married on the 11th, Miss C. Davis, to Mr. William Mayfield, also of Spartanburg.

Married on the evening of the 6th inst., by the very Rev. Dr. Lynch, Howard H. Caldwell, Esq., to Agnes, second daughter of Chas. Montague, Esq., all of Columbia.

Died at the residence of A. F. Golding, in Pontotoc Co., Miss., on the 15th September 1856, M. G. Overby of Laurens District, in the 38th year of his age, while on a visit to his relatives.

Issue of January 22, 1857

Married on the 15th inst., by Rev. Jno. G. Landrum, Mr. Wm. J. Wingo of this town to Miss Addie M. Jackson, of Pacolet.

Married on Tuesday the 6th January, by J. N. Covington, Esq., Mr. John Owens to Miss Martha Ann, daughter of James Smith, Esq., all of Rutherford Co., N. C.

Issue of January 29, 1857

Married on the 15th inst., by Rev. B. G. Jones, Mr. James H. Smith and Miss Elizabeth Stewart, all of Greenville District.

Married on Wednesday, the 14th inst., by A. Bonner, Esq., Mr. James Ellison to Miss Cornelia S. Porter, of Spartanburg District.

Married on Tuesday, the 6th inst., by Rev. Jerry Lee, Mr. Lipscomb Wood to Miss Mary E. Austell, of Spartanburg District.

Married on Thursday, the 15th inst., by Rev. William Curtis, Mr. James Wilkins to Miss C. P. Moore, of Spartanburg.

Married on Tuesday, the 23rd ult., Dr. F. W. Littlejohn, Mr. J. Calvin Turner to Miss Christmas J. Nance, of Spartanburg.

Married on Thursday, the 15th ult., by Rev. B. Bonner, Mr. James C. Cyram to Miss Malinda C. Byers, of Spartanburg District.

Married on Thursday, the 15th inst., by Dr. C. Lee, Mr. Mitchell C. McCown to Miss Lavina Tate, of Union District, S. C.

Married on Thursdya, the 15th ult., by Rev. T. Jefferson Campbell, Mr. B. Franklin Blanton to Mrs. Jane C. Newton of Union, S. C.

Issue of February 5, 1857

Married on Sunday evening, January 18, 1857, by Rev. H. M. Haynes, Wm. H. McMillin to Miss Harriet E., daughter of Joseph Finger, all of Fingerville, Spartanburg Dist., S. C.

Departed this life in Grayson Co., Va., on 19th January, William Bobbit, aged 6 years and 7 months, son of George and Sarah L. Bobbitt, formerly of Spartanburg District, S. C.

Died at her residence in Spartanburg District, S. C., Jan. 21, 1857, Jane Buchanan Ross, in the 87th year of her age...born in Mecklenburg Co., N. C. previous to the Revolution, and emigrated to this District in 1821, where she has lived ever since...joined the Baptist Church at Providence in 1840...leaves a son--the only child still living.

Issue of February 12, 1857
    Married at Union C. H. on the 29th ult., by the Rev. R. Y. Russell, Mr. Wm. T. Thomson to Miss Sallie J. Giles, all of Unionville.
    Married on the 4th inst., by the Rev. Wm. Martin, Capt. T. B. Jeter to Miss Anne H. Thomson, all of Unionville.

Issue of February 19, 1857
    Married on Tuesday evening, the 12th of this instant, by Elias Wall, Esq., Mr. John Elder to Miss Elizabeth, daughter of Robert Berry, Esq., all of this District.
    Married in Columbia on Wednesday evening, the 11th inst., by Rev. N. Talley, Rev. John T. Wightman of the South Carolina Methodist Conference to Miss Amelia, daughter of the Rev. H. Spain of Sumter District, S. C.

Issue of March 19, 1857
    Married on the 14th September 1856, by A. E. Smith, Esq., Mr. Waddy Colbert to Miss Lucinda Cash.
    By the same, on the 2d Nov 1856, Mr. Jeter Dewberry to Miss Elizabeth Cash, all of Spartanburg, S. C.
    By the same, on the 26th February 1857, Mr. Alfred Sprouse to Miss Sarah Eastler.
    By the same on 8th May 1857, Mr. Robert Price to Miss Mary Love, all of Spartanburg, S. C.

Issue of March 26, 1857
    Married on the 19th inst., by A. E. Smith, Esq., Mr. Jefferson Turner to Miss R. Tensey Ellis, all of Spartanburg District.

Issue of April 2, 1857
    John Lorin, infant son of Mr. and Mrs. Hiram Mitchell died on Wednesday, the 25th ult., aged 13 months and 15 days.

Issue of April 9, 1857
    Married in Philadelphia (Pa.), on the 14th March ult., by Rev. Dr. Papa., Mr. Lewis Bloomberg of Yorkville, S. C. and Miss Hannah, daughter of B. S. Solms, Esq., of the former place.
    Married on Sunday the 29th ult., by Rev. John Ezell, Mr. Jeremiah Martin, St. to Miss Holly Cash, all of this district.
    Died on Friday, the 3rd inst., in Spartanburg District, Margaret Alice, infant daughter of Hilliard and Martha C. Thomas, aged 4 months and 24 days.

Issue of April 16, 1857
    Married on the 9th inst., by the Rev. Mr. Buist, Mr. William C. Baily of Greenville to Miss Ann Wallace, daughter of Dr. P. M. Wallace, of Spartanburg.

Issue of May 7, 1857
    Died on the 15th ult., near Cashville, at the residence of his son-in-law, Mr. James Brockman, aged 75 years...member of the Baptist Church.

Issue of May 14, 1857
    Married in Yorkville, Tuesday morning, the 5th inst., by Rev. W. W. Carothers, Mr. Samuel W. Melton of the "Enquirer" and Miss Mary Helen Goore, both of this place.
    Married in Laurensville, on the 15th inst., by the Rev. David Wills, Capt. J. D. Garlington and Miss S. E., second daughter of Col. John D. Williams, all of Laurens District.
    Married at Alpine, in Chattanooga Co., Ga., on the 16th inst., by Rev. A. Y. Lockridge, Dr. Robert Y. Rudick of Summerville to Miss Eliza A. Knox, daughter of Capt. Samuel Knox. [The above is probably for Chattooga Co., Ga., there being no Chattanooga County.]

Issue of May 21, 1857
    Married on the 14th inst., by Rev. J. C. McCullough, Dr. Thomas K. Cureton of Lancaster and Miss Mary S., only daughter of Maj. Govan Mills, of this place.
    Died at his residence in Spartanburg District, on Tuesday morning, the 12th inst., Jesse Wakefield, in the 79th year of his age...moved to this state, with his parents from North Carolina and resided in the same place for 63 years.
    Died at Clinton, S. C., J. Henry Kingsmore, of cramp colic, after a short illnes of 5 hours, on the 27th April.
    Departed this life in Spartanburg on the 9th inst., Mrs. Marie A. Duncan, aged 23 years and 4 months.

Issue of May 28, 1857
    Married on Tuesday, the 19th inst., by Rev. C. C. Vaughan, Mr. James Ellis to Miss Mary Jane Green, all of Union District.

Died on Tuesday morning, May 19, at 4 o'clock near Glenn Springs, Mr. George Story, aged 87 years.

Issue of July 2, 1857
    Married on the 18th ult., by Rev. I. D. Durham, William Going to Martha Collins, all of Spartanburg District.
    Departed this life on Friday morning, the 26th inst., at Yorkville, S. C., Mrs. Margaret C. Lester, wife of Rev. A. H. Lester, of the South Carolina Conference, aged 22 years, 11 months and 4 days.

Issue of July 16, 1857
    Married on the 9th inst., by Rev. A. W. Walker, Mr. T. Alonzo Harris of Abbeville to Miss J. E. Deas, eldest daughter of the late Rev. Charles S. Walker.
    Mrs. Mary Hause died in her 44th year on the 9th inst. She left her son and only child (having buried three others) and a husband and sister.

Issue of July 30, 1857
    Luther Wesley Switzer, son of Frederick Switzer, Esq., died at the residence of his father, 23rd July, aged 21, while preparing himself for the study of medicine.

Issue of August 6, 1857
    Married on the 2nd inst., by A. E. Smith, Esq., Mr. Marion Hammet to Miss Maria Cash, all of Spartanburg, S. C.

Issue of August 13, 1857
    Married on the 29th ult., by Rev. Jos. Bochell, Mr. Jas. McCravy of Spartanburg, to Miss Kittie S. Speake, of Newberry.   Laurensville Herald.

Issue of August 20, 1857
    Married on the 12th July, by Rev. J. G. Landrum, Samuel Meredith, Esq., of Laurens, to Mrs. Rebecca Drummond, of Spartanburg District.
    Married on the 28th July, by Rev. Warren Drummond, Dr. Thos S. Wright, to Miss Lou V. Allen, all of this District.
    Died, of Dysentery, on Island Creek, in this District, Jeremiah Martin, on the 5th inst., aged 63 years...member of the Baptist Church...leaves widow and six sons.
    Died suddenly, on Thursday morning, the 13th inst., Mrs. Harriet McKissick, wife of John D. McKissick, Esq., of Union District.

Issue of August 27, 1857
    Married on the 19th inst., by A. E. Smith, Esq., Mr. Robert Shands to Miss Charlotte McAbee, all of Spartanburg.
    Died of Dysentery, on the 10th inst., Mrs. Juliet Lipscomb, wife of Edward Lipscomb, Sen., and daughter of William and Claremont Lancaster. She had just entered her 64th year...connected herself with the Baptist Church in about her 18th year.

Issue of September 3, 1857
    Married on the 30th August last, by A. E. Smith, Esq., Mr. James Swarford to Miss Lucinda Guardener, all of Spartanburg District.
    Married in Carnesville, Ga., on Thurs., the 20th inst., at the house of J. J. M. Bagwell, by the Rev. John A. Aderhold, Washington Polle, Esq., of Carnesville, to Miss Mary E., daughter of David Dumas, Esq., of Alpine, Ga.

Issue of September 10, 1857
    Married on the 1st September, by A. E. Smith, Esq., Mr. Alberry Cash to Miss Mary Turner, all of Spartanburg, S. C.
    Died at the Franklin House, Tuscumbia, Ala., Sunday evening, July 26, 1857, in his 25th[?] year, Samuel M. Green, a native of Spartanburgh, S. C.
    Died, in this city, on the 17th inst., Col. James Brannon, in the 73d year of his age...Captain of Artillery in War of 1812 under General Moore at Charleston, S. C....he was promoted to Colonel at Spartanburg, S. C....served in '25, '26, '27, '28 in S. C. Legislature.... Marietta Georgian & Democrat.

Issue of September 17, 1857
    Married on the 10th inst., by Davis Moore, Esq., at the General Muster of the 37th Regt., S. C. M., Mr. Hugh Sparks to Miss Sallie Gibson.
    Died on the 6th of this inst., at the residence of Dr. F. W. Tucker, in the lower part of this District, Miss Louisa A. Barnett, eldest daughter of Javan and Rachel Barnett, in the 20th year of her age...completed her English education at Spartanburg Female College...she had been for some months engaged in teaching...member of the Baptist Church, converted in the 13th year.

Issue of September 24, 1857
   Married on the 20th August, by Z. Lanford, Esq., Jackson D. Stephens to Miss Rosana
Castleberry, all of this district.

Issue of October 1, 1857
   Departed this life in Lexington, on Saturday, the 5th inst., Mrs. Delilah Shelton,
in the 59th year of her age...a native of South Carolina, but emigrated to this state in
1844, since which time she has lived in Lexington. [eulogy] Lexington (Miss.) Democratic
Advocate, 12th September.

Issue of October 8, 1857
   Married on the 27th ult., by Elias Wall, Esq., Mr. Thomas O. McKelvy to Miss Eliza-
beth Ann Lovelace, all of this District.
   Married on Thursday, October 1, by John H. Walker, Esq., Mr. Samuel S. Johnson, to
Miss Nancy Brown, all of this District.
   Death of our friend and fellow-student F. D. Lytle, who departed this life, October
2, 1857....STUDENT.
   Died at her husband's residence, in this district, near Van Patten's Shoals, Septem-
ber 18, 1857, Mrs. Sarah Ann, wife of N. V. Van Patten, aged 37 years and 6 months....
also her two infant sons died shortly after, one aged 10, the other 12 days...member
of the Baptist Church at Cedar Grove...left a daughter, 5 sons, and a husband. Enoree,
S. C.

Issue of October 15, 1857
   Died at his residence in Spartanburg District, on 13th September, Samuel Gaston, in
the 59th year of his age...left a widow and two children.

Issue of October 22, 1857
   Married on the 8th inst., by Rev. W. H. Lauton, Miss Emma C. Way, only daughter of
Mrs. C. Mallard of St. James, Goose Creek, S. C. to Dr. Thomas C. Poole of St. Matthews,
late of Spartanburg C. H., S. C.
   Died on the 18th August 1857, near Ripley, Miss., Mrs. Elenor Kee Whitten, consort
of Silas R. Whitten, formerly of Greenville District, S. C...member of the Baptist
Church for nearly 50 years.

Issue of November 5, 1857
   Died at his residence in St. Matthews Parish, on the 28th ult., J. M. Dantzler, in
the 53rd year of his age.

Issue of November 12, 1857
   Married by W. H. Bagwell, Esq., on the 24th of May, 1857, Mr. Elijah Hammett, to Miss
Margaret Burnett, both of Spartanburg.
   Married by W. H. Bagwell, Esq., on the 30th October 1857, Mr. Thomas Gillmore to Miss
Nancy Reaves, both of Bivingsville.
   Married in Union District, on the 27th ult., by Rev. Albert A. James, Maj. H. F.
McDowell, of Spartanburg District, to Miss Isabella A., only daughter of J. H. Alexander,
Esq., of the former district.
   Married in Greenville, on Wednesday evening, the 28th ult., by Rev. Whitefoord
Smith, D. D., Mr. W. B. Davis of Prince Williams Parish, and Miss Margaret Ann Smith,
of that place, only daughter of Whitefoord Smith, Sr., Esq.
   Married on Tuesday morning, at the residence of the bride's father, by Rev. W. J.
Scott, Mr. Jas. F. Humphries of Unionville, S. C. to Miss Hattie Joyce of Marietta, Ga.
   Married in Utica, New York, October 22, 1857, by Rev. Dr. P. H. Fowler, Rev. L. W.
Curtis of South Carolina, to Miss Almina D. White, of the former place.
   Married in Union District, S. C. by Rev. J. H. Saye, October 29, 1857, Maj. J. H.
Fant, to Mrs. Sarah J. Thomas.
   Married on the 2d inst., by Rev. C. C. Vaughan, Mr. James Gorden to Miss Frances
Hughes, all of Union District.
   Married in Columbia, on Thursday evening, Nov. 5, by Rev. J. H. Thornwell, Julian A.
Selby, to Miss Alice E. Peers, all of that City.
   Died at her residence in Spartanburg District, on the 29th of October, Julia Ann
Frances, wife of H. P. Darby, and daughter of Elisha and Margaret Hughston, in her 30th
year...left a husband and 6 children...[long eulogy].
   Died at Walhalla, on the 25th of October, John McDowell, infant son of J. Wesley, and
Carrie E. Terry, aged 11 weeks and 12 hrs.
   Died in Panola Co., Miss, on Thursday evening, the 28th ult., in the 78th year of her
age, Mrs. Frances W. Bobo.

Issue of November 19, 1857
   Married at Crawfordsville, on the 15th November 1857, by Rev. Wm. A. Clark, Mr. Thomas

78

Davis to Miss Mary Hawkins; also Mr. James Davis to Miss Sarah Hawkins, all of Crawfordsville.[two brothers married two sisters.]
Married on the 12th inst., by W. H. Bagwell, Esq., Mr. Barham Reaves to Miss Mahaly Thomas, all of Bivingsville, S. C.
Married on September 23rd, by Rev. S. H. Browne, Pinckney H. Kelly to Miss Martha C. Sexton, all of Spartanburg District.

Issue of November 26, 1857
Married by J. B. Tolleson, Esq., on the 18th inst., Mr. Enoch Cantrell to Miss Elizabeth Wall, eldest daughter of Elias Wall, Esq., all of Spartanburg District.
Married on Thursday, the 19th inst., by Rev. A. W. Walker, Mr. Lemuel Burnett to Mrs. Mary Cothran.
Died on the 12th November, in Polk Co., N. C., Mrs. E. G. Foster, formerly of Spartanburg District.

Issue of December 3, 1857
We record with sorrow, the death on Sabbath last ofMrs. Landrum, wife of Rev. J. G. Landrum, pastor of the Baptist Church in Spartanburg.
Married on Tuesday, the 24th ult., by Rev. Washington Baird, Mr. T. R. Jackson of Spartanburg, to Miss Mattie J. Goudelock of Union District, S. C.

Issue of December 10, 1857
Married on the 18th November, by John H. Walker, Esq., Mr. Stephen T. Sexton, to Miss Louise Ann Jane Landrum, all of this District.
Married on the 29th November, by John H. Walker, Esq., Mr. Levi Madison Stone, of Coffee Co., Ala., to Miss Jane Eveline Waldrip, of Spartanburg District.
Died on 29th November, in the 45th year of her age, Mrs. Elizabeth Landrum, wife of John G. Landrum, and daughter of John and Margaret Montgomery...leaves a husband and six children...[long eulogy].

Issue of December 24, 1857
Died at her residence in Spartanburg Village, on Thursday, the 17th December 1857, Mrs. Sally M. Hall, in the 68th year of her age...the eldest daughter of Dr. Jacob R. Brown....[same obituary appeared in Spartanburg Express, issue of same date, see p. 47].

Issue of December 30, 1857
Married in Spartanburg District, on 20th December, by A. Bonner, Esq., Mr. Judge W. Edwards, of Island Creek, to Miss C. Ann Harris of this District.
Married on 22nd December by Rev. Drury Scruggs, the Rev. Thomas Jefferson Campbell, of Limestone Springs, to Miss Jane Simmons of N. C.
Married on the 6th October last, by Elias Wall, Esq., Mr. James M. Cooley to Miss Mira Smith, all of Rutherford County, N. C.
Married on the 17th December, by Elias Wall, Esq., Mr. Elisha Shields to Miss Polly Ann Bishop, all of this District.
Married at Shufordsville, Mississippi, on the evening of 26th November, by Rev. Robert J. Alcorn, Dr. L. C. Nesbitt, formerly of Spartanburg, S. C. to Miss Augusta O'Neal, of Coahoma Co., Miss.
Married on Tuesday, the 22nd inst., by Rev. J. S. Ezell, Mr. C. J. Jarrott to Miss Margaret Hicks, all of Spartanburg.

Issue of January 7, 1858
Married on the 24th December, by the Rev. J. G. Landrum Mr. John T. Cantrell and Miss Hester E. High, all of this District.
Married on the 24th December last, by Rev. Simpson Drummond, Mr. Jesse William Brown to Miss Mary A. Fowler, all of Spartanburg District.
Married on the 30th December, by John H. Walker, Esq., Mr. James C. Pace, to Miss Angeline C. Kelley, all of this District.
Married on the 3rd January, by Elias Wall, Esq., Mr. Abner Cantrell, of Spartanburg District, to Miss Mary Jane, daughter of Ambrose Mills, Esq., of Polk Co., N. C.
Married on 26th December, by Elias Wall, Esq., Mr. Javan Henderson, to Miss Rebecca Hawkins, all of this district.
Married on the 31st ult., by A. Bonner, Esq., Mr. Leonidas Cash to Miss Caledonia Harris, all of this District.
Died in this village, on the 30th December 1857, William Walker (Walker House), in the 65th year of his age...born and raised within six miles of Spartanburg C. H., and has spent his whole life in his native District, except while in the War of 1812. He marched to Sullivan's Island, when only 18. In 1816, he married Harriet Rowland, by whom he had 6 children, 3 of whom survive. In 1829, he moved to this town where he lost his wife. In 1836, he married Mary B. Dean, by whom he had nine children, seven of whom

survive. At the time of his death, Mr. Walker was the oldest citizen of this town...
joined the Baptist Church in 1839.

Issue of January 14, 1858
Married on the 7th of this inst., by W. H. Bagwell, Mr. Simpson Bagwell, to Miss
Elizabeth, eldest daughter of John L. Thompson, all of Spartanburg.
Married on the 30th ult., in Caldwell Co., N. C. by the Rev. Joseph Puett, Dr. W.
Boone Clarke, of Columbus, to Miss Emma, daughter of N. A. Powell, of Caldwell.
Married on Sunday evening, January 10, by Rev. J. G. Landrum, Mr. Edward Miller of
Greenville District, to Miss Sallie Woodruff, of this District.

Issue of January 28, 1858
Married on Thursday, the 21st inst., by the Rev. R. H. Reid, Mr. Jeptha Turner, to
Miss Mary Ann Hadden, all of this District.
Married on the 17th inst., by Elias Wall, Esq., at the house of John Y. McDowell,
Mr. William Forester, to Miss Martha Bullington, all of this District.

Issue of February 4, 1858
Married at Limestone Springs, on the 28th ult., at the residence of the bride's
father, by Rev. T. J. Campbell, Mr. Thomas Edward Gaffney to Miss Christina Lockhart,
daughter of Wm. Lockhart, Esq.

Issue of February 11, 1858
Married on the 31st December last, by Rev. J. M. Runion, Dr. F. A. Miles of Green-
ville District, formerly of Spartanburg District, to Miss Eliza Hagood of Pickens District.
Married on the 7th January by John H. Walker, Esq., Mr. Franklin Rook to Miss Martha
Waldrip, all of this district.
Married on the 14th January, by Rev. Wm. T. Garrow, Mr. Hiram Yarborough to Miss
Martha Layton, all of this district.
Married on the 17th of January by John H. Walker, Esq., Mr. John Jones Johnson to
Miss Eliza Jane Ray, all of Spartanburg District.
Married on the 27th of January, by John H. Walker, Esq., Mr. William H. Rhodes to
Miss Nancy Red, all of this district.
Married on the 30th December last, by John W. Hampton, Esq., Mr. David Edwards to
Miss Arraminta O. Henderson, all of Polk Co., N. C.

Issue of February 18, 1858
We are called upon to record the death of Col. H. H. Thomson, a prominent lawyer and
valuable citizen of Spartanburg, on the night of the 10th inst., in the 53d year of his
age...entered practice of law about 1828. Funeral at the family cemetery, east of this
village.

Issue of February 25, 1858
Thomas L. Young, a member of the Palmetto Regiment, died in Fairfield a fortnight ago.
On Thursday last, the 5th inst., near the residence of Sum Sumner, in this district,
while engaged in placing the rafter in a smoke house, one of them fell upon Andrew
Harrison, killing him instantly. Mr. Harrison leaves a wife and children to mourn the
fatality.

Issue of March 4, 1858
Married on the 23rd February last by Henry White, Esq., Mr. James H. Cunningham to
Miss Margaret Williams, all of this district.
Married on Wednesday evening, the 24th of February, by Rev. Simpson Drummond, Mr.
John S. Perry to Miss Sallie J. Walker, all of Spartanburg District.
Married on the 28th of February last by J. Bankston Davis, Esq., Mr. James McCarter
to Miss Mary Jane Andrews, all of this District.
Death of Col. John A. Easley, Jr. We learn with sincere regret (says the Greenville
Patriot of the 25th ult) that the gentleman expired on Monday last, at his residence
near Pickens Court House. Col. Easley had twice represented the District of Pickens in
the State Legislature.

Issue of March 11, 1858
Married on the 25th February last, by W. H. Bagwell, Esq., Mr. Lecel Lee to Miss Sarah
Emily, daughter of W. W. Bagwell, all of this District.
Married in Charleston, on the 3d inst., by Rev. Mr. Denison, W. T. Russel, M. D. of
Spartanburg to Miss Mary E. Stevens of Spartanburg.

Issue of March 25, 1858
Died of Measles on the 9th inst., the infant daughter of Capt. J. R. and Nancy P.
Switzer, aged about 5 months.

Again, on the 11th inst., the house was visited by the hand of death and Mrs. Nancy
P. Switzer is no more. She was the daughter of Mr. Jared Drummond of Spartanburg.

Issue of April 1, 1858
Married on the 18th inst., by J. H. Tolleson, Esq., Mr. John Kirby to Miss Susan
Constant, all of Spartanburg District.
Died at his residence near Woodruff's in this district, at 11 o'clock on Tuesday
night, the 9th inst., Zechariah Lanford, Esq., in the 54th year of his age. In 1849
he united with the Baptist CHurch at Bethel, and two years after, was ordained as a
deacon. The first of a long line of descendants has been takem from affectionate
parents in their declining years.

Issue of April 15, 1858
Died on the 27th March 1858, at Crowley, Arkansas, Ovey Louisa, infant daughter of
Dr. W. and S. S. Wall, of South Carolina, aged 1 year, 2 months, 27 days.

Issue of April 29, 1858
Married on the 28th inst., by E. Wall, Mr. Marcus Lafayette Davis to Miss Mary Ann
Dunnagan, all of this district.

Issue of May 13, 1858
Died at Cass Co., Ga., on the 27th ultimo, of typhoid fever, Col. Zachariah Edwards,
in the 62nd year of his age...born in Virginia, 21 Feb 1796, but removed to Greenville
District, S. C. when quite small, and then to Spartanburg, where he remained until 1838
...Col. of the 26th Regt, S. C. M....member of the Baptist Church at Bethel...leaves a
widow and children.

Issue of May 20, 1858
Married on the 8th April by Rev. M. C. Barnett, Dr. G. H. King to Miss E. E. Brewton,
all of Spartanburg District.
Married on the 6th of May, by Rev. William Houck, J. W. Sellers to Adreanna, eldest
daughter of Russel H. Zimmerman, all of St. Mathew's Parish.

Issue of May 27, 1858
Married on the 6th inst., by Rev. B. Bonner, Mr. Joseph H. Austell, of Spartanburg
District to Miss Mary Jane Borders, of Cleveland Co., N. C.
Married at Anderson, on the 20th inst., by Rev. Wm. G. Mullinax, John C. Whitefield,
Esq. to Miss Sue Finley, all of that District.
Fell asleep in Jesus, on the 13th May 1858, at her residence in Greenville, S. C.
in the 64th year of her age, Mrs. Margaret Smith, wife of Whitefoord Smith, Esq., and
daughter of the late Robert Shand, all formerly of Charleston...member of the Presbyterian
Church about 45 years.
The friends and acquaintances of Mr. and Mrs. Jame A. Fowler are invited to attend
the funeral of the latter, at the residence of her husband this (Wednesday) afternoon at
4 o'clock.

Issue of June 3, 1858
Departed this life at the residence of her husband, on the 25th of May, 1858, Mrs.
Nancy Fowler, consort of Jas. A. Fowler, in the 25th year of her age...a wife, mother,
and sister...member of the Methodist Church.
Diet at his residence in this district, of typhoid fever, on 3 May, William L. Hobby,
in the 24th year of his age...leaves a widow and infant child. The deceased was the
youngest child of his mother, the son of her old age, the only living son...member of
Bethel (Woodruff's) from which he resided 8 miles.

Issue of June 10, 1858
Married on Thursday evening, the 3d June by John H. Walker, Esq., Dr. Dixon L. Davis,
to Miss Mary Jane Taylor, daughter of Col. Stephen Taylors, decd, all of Spartanburg
District.
Perry D. Gilbert died at his residence in Spartanburg District, on the 24th May, in
the 37th year of his age...member of the Baptist Church.

Issue of June 24, 1858
Married on the 2d inst., by Rev. W. E. Walters, Mr. John W. Robinson of Anderson C. H.
and Miss Rebecca Watt, of Fairfield District.
Died on the 15th inst., M. Elliott, infant daughter of P. & Elizabeth Gossett of
Spartanburg District.

Issue of July 1, 1858
Married on Tuesday night, June 22, by Rev. Charles Taylor, Mr. Lewis Hosse to Miss

Mary Jane Wooten, all of Spartanburg.
    Married at Campobello, S. C., on the morning of the 18th inst., by Jno. Bankston Davis, Esq., Benjamin F. Tucker of Greenville, S. C. to Miss Elizabeth, daughter of Hezekiah Garrett, all of this district.
    Married in New York, on the 16th ult., Col. Thomas R. Agnew, formerly of Columbia, to Miss Maria R. Wells of Spartanburg.
    Died in Winnsboro, Fairfield District, on the 19th ult., Mrs. Mary Ann Carlisle, in the 58th year of her age.
    Died in North Kingstown, Rhode Island, on the 18th ult., William F. Maxwell, in the 81st year of his age...a native of South Carolina.

Issue of July 8, 1858
    Married on the 10th of June, by Rev. J. G. Landrum, O. P.Earle Esq. of this district to Miss Rachel Kate Davis, of Rutherford Co., N. C.
    Married by the same, on the 15th of June, Mr. James A. Webster, to Miss E. Harris, both of Rutherford Co, N. C.
    Col. Thomas W. Waters, died on Sabbath evening last, in the 57th year of his age... He went to Georgia, purchased a plantation, and was preparing for the reception of his family. He received news of the dangerous illness of an infant son, who died on 11th June. Col. Waters was born 8 Mar 1801 and served in the Legislature 1851-52...member of the Baptist Church.

Issue of July 22, 1858
    Married on Thursday evening, the 8th July by John H. Walker, Esq., Mr. Aaron Casey to Miss Frances Casey, all of Spartanburg District.
    Married by the same, Sunday morning, the 11th July,.Mr. William H. Waldrip to Miss Parmelia Caroline Senn, all of this District.
    Married on the 17th inst., near Pacolet Mills, Mr. John Williams to Miss Martha Bell, all of this district.
    Died on the 20th inst., at the residence of his father, in this District, Mr. Frederick Dodd, aged 24 years.

Issue of July 29, 1858
    Married on Tuesday evening, the 20th July by Elias Wall, Esq., Mr. Robert Calvert to Miss Jane Cartee, all of this District.
    Married by the same, on Thursday evening, the 22nd July, Mr. Francis M. Cantrell to Miss Jemima, eldest daughter of John Paris, Esq., all of this District.

Issue of August 5, 1858
    Married in Greenville District, July 27, by Rev. S. S. Gaillard, Mr. Sims F. Clary to Miss Susan Amelia, eldest daughter of Abiel Foster.
    Married on Thursday evening, July 29, by the Rev. J. G. Landrum, Mr. Wm. D. Logan to Miss Emily O., second daughter of Wm. Walker (A. S. H.), all of this District.
    On Sunday morning, the 18th inst., by Rev. Mr. Hill, Mr. Zachariah H. Tate to Miss Mary Ann Y. Goudelock, all of Spartanburg District.
    Departed this life on 22d July, Mrs. Jane H. Kennedy, wife of Rev. J. L. Kennedy, in the 48th year of her age...connected herself in early life with Nazareth Presbyterian Church, then under the pastoral care of Rev. Michael Dickson. Her children (twelve in number) rise up and call her blessed. Pendleton Messenger.

Issue of August 12, 1858
    Married on Thursday evening, the 5th of August, by E. Wall, Esq., Mr. Rial B. Seay, to Mary Malissa, second daughter of Maj. Robert Belcher, all of this District.
    Died in Carnesville, Ga., Tuesday the 27th July ult., of whooping-cough, Willie Monroe, youngest son of John J. M. & Adeline B. Bagwell, aged 2 years, 3 months, and 6 days.

Issue of August 19, 1858
    Married in Unionville on Thursday evening, the 5th August, by Rev. W. W. McSwain, James B. Steedman, Esq., to Miss Carrie V. Dogan, all of Unionville, S. C.
    Married in Baldwin, Florida, July 13th, by the Rev. Mr. Johnson, R. G. Hunt, Esq. to Miss Mary Livingston.

Issue of August 26, 1858
    Married on the 10th August, by Rev. B. Bonner, Mr. James C. Robbs, and Miss Louisa Dillingham, all of Spartanburg District.
    One of the graduates of Cedar Spring Institution died. Mrs. A. A. Templeton, daughter of Jesse Cooper, Esq., of this District, & wife of James C. Templeton (mute also), died at Cedar Spring on the 11th July.

Issue of September 2, 1858
   Married on Sunday morning, the 22nd of August, by Elias Wall, Esq., Mr. John Edgings
to Miss Chaney Seay, all of this District.
   Married on the 22d ultimo, by A. E. Smith, Esq., Mr. Patrick Revier to Miss Catherine
Gardner, all of this District.
   Died at Cedar Spring, Spartanburg District, on the 20th August 1858, Edgar Huguenin
Colcock, eldest son of S. F. Colcock, in the 19th year of his age.

Issue of September 9, 1858
   Married on Thursday, the 2d September, by Rev. J. G. Landrum, Mr. William H. Ray to
Miss Mattie P., daughter of Jas. G. Harris, Esq., all of this town.
   Married on the 21st August last, by Rev. C. S. Beard, Mr. A. C. Gossett and Julia,
daughter of Rev. B. Smith, all of Spartanburg.
   Married on the 25th July last, by Rev. Dr. Cox, Mr. Calvin H. Turner, formerly of
Spartanburg S. C. to Miss Lucy A. Hawkins, all of Bell County, Texas.
   Died in Greenville District, on the 4th inst., Wm. Russell, infant son of Jas. H.
and Anna P. Goss, aged 2 years and 3 months and 2 weeks.
   Died on the 20th August, Mrs. Mary Jane, consort of Dr. Lee L. Smith, aged 19 years,
2 months, and 18 days. educated at Spartanburg Female College. W.C.Kirkland.

Issue of September 16, 1858
   Died suddenly of cholera morbus at the residence of Mr. P. M. Brewton, near Woodruff's,
on Saturday evening, August 1, R. Patillo, second son of George and Elizabeth Hanna, in
the 34th year of his age.
   Departed this life on the 15th of August, Mrs. Julia E. Neville, wife of John C.
Neville, and daughter of S. R. and Anna McFall, in the 25th year of her age.
                                                        Keowee(Pickens) Courier
Issue of September 23, 1858
   Died at his residence near Colter's Ford, on Pacolet, on the 7th of this instant,
James Turner, Esq., in the 48th year of his age...leaves widow and a large number of
children...member and Deacon at Baptist Church at Buck Creek.

Issue of September 30, 1858
   Married by Rev. J. G. Landrum, on the 21st instant, W. S. Moore of Morganton, N. C.
to Margaret C. Montgomery, of this District.
   Married in Spartanburg District, S. C., on the 14th inst., by Eld. A. J. Cansler,
Mr. Thomas Williams, of Polk Co., and Miss M. J. Trammell of Greenville District, S. C.
   Married on the evening of the 28th inst., by J. M. Elford, Esq., Mr. Young Neal
to Mrs. Rebecca Bagwell, all of Spartanburg, District.
   Died near Reidville, on the 21st August 1858, of apoplexy, Jerutha Burnes, wife of
John W. Burnes, and daughter of Joel and Sarah Farmer, aged 39 years, 6 months, 13 days...
a consistent member of the Methodist E. Church for 23 years at Zoar, in Spartanburg Dis-
trict, left a husband, 2 sons and 2 daughters. [long eulogy].

Issue of October 7, 1858
   Married on Sunday morning, the 3rd inst., at Wind Mill Hill, by Jno. Bankston Davis,
Esq., A. T. Reagan to Miss Sophronia Demsy, all of Spartanburg District.
   Married by W. H. Bagwell, on the 30th ult., Mr. John Cowan to Miss Mary Brooks, all
of Spartanburg.
   Married by W. H. Bagwell, Esq., on the 10th June last, Mr. Samuel Elders to Miss
Artimesa Smith, both of Bivingsville.
   Died on the 10th ult., at the lightning's flash, Capt. Joseph Barnett...leaves a wife
and 8 children.

Issue of October 14, 1858
   Married by J. B. Tolleson, Esq., on the 30th of September, Mr. James Parris to Miss
Louisa Wall, second daughter of Elias Wall, Esq., all of Spartanburg District.

Issue of October 21, 1858
   Married on Wednesday evening, the 13th inst., by Rev. J. G. Landrum, Mr. J. Gwinn
Harris to Miss Mary E. Ray, all of Spartanburg.
   Married on the morning of the 20th inst., by Rev. Robert Hett Chapman, Mr. Robert
Hett Chapman Jr., of Asheville, N. C. to Miss Isabella Jane, daughter of Joseph Foster,
Esq., of this town.
   Capt. Silas M. Castlebury died of Typhoid Pneumondia at his residence near Hobbys-
ville, in Spartanburg District, on the 11th inst., in the 45th year of his age...member
and officer of Unity Baptist Church...left and afflicated wife and seven small children
[eulogy].

Issue of November 4, 1858
Married on the 14th October, by A. E. Smith, Esq., Mr. Alexander Gardner to Miss Missaniah Potter, all of Spartanburg.
Married on 26th October, by Rev. P. H. Pickett, at his residence in Chester District, Rev. A. H. Lester, of the South Carolina Conference, to Miss Sue McCollough, of Williamsburg District.

Issue of November 11, 1858
Married on Thursday evening, the 4th November 1858, by Elias Wall, Esq., Mr. Fielding Kimbrell to Miss Nancy, fourth daughter of Rev. Wm. E. Boone of the South Carolina Conference.
Died, at Aiken, S. C., October 29, after a short illness, Rev. Wm. E. Boone, of the South Carolina Conference.

Issue of November 18, 1858
Married on the morning of the 17th inst., by Rev. W. C. Kirkland, Mr. R. H. Patterson of Shelby, N. C., to Miss Mattie, daughter of J. W. Walker, of this place.
Married at the residence of Dr. J. W. Teney in Cleveland Co., N. C., on the 2d inst., by Rev. James D. Hall, Dr. J. L. Neale of Gaston County, to Miss M. Love Stowe of Cedar Springs, Spartanburg District, S. C.
Died in this town on Thursday morning, the 4th inst., Mrs. Catherine F. Judd, wife of David C. Judd, aged 42 years.
Died, on the 20th October 1858, at his residence near Cross Anchor, Spartanburg District, Mr. Land N. Miles, in the 77th year of his age...member óf New Hope Baptist Church and deacan...left a wife and many relations.

Issue of December 2, 1858
Married on Thursday evening, the 25th inst., by Rev. W. M. Wightman, D. D., Mr. Geo. Cofield, of Union, to Miss M. Clementine Moore of Spartanburg.
Died in Spartanburg, on Sabbath, the 28th inst., Mrs. P. Garrett, wife of Mr. Geo. Garrett, in the 60th year of her age.
Died on Sunday, the 14th November, at her home in Spartanburg village, Mrs. Carrie Henry Farrow, wife of James Farrow, and eldest daughter of Maj. James A. Edward Henry, aged 27 years.

Issue of December 16, 1858
Died in Laurensville, on Tuesday, Nov. 30, Laura Henry, eldest daughter of James and Carrie H. Farrow, aged 8 weeks and 2 days.

Issue of January 6, 1859
Married on the 26th December 1858, by A. E. Smith, Esq., Mr. William L. Brown, late of Rockingham Co., N. C. to Miss Susan M. Burgess, of Spartanburg District.
Married on the 22d December, by Rev. M. C. Barnett, Mr. John F. Moss to Miss Frances E. Chapman, all of Spartanburg.
Married by J. B. Tolleson, Esq., on the 26th ult., Mr. Isham F. Kirby to Miss Jane Gossett, all of Spartanburg District.
Married in Columbia, on the 28th ult., by Rev. W. A. Gamewell, Rev. F. Asbury Mood to Miss Sue R. Logan.
Died at his residence on South Tyger in this District, on the 22nd ult., Mr. John Poole, in the 55th year of his age.

Issue of January 13, 1859
Married on the 21st ult., by Rev. John C. Green, at the residence of Nathaniel Morgan, in Greenville District, Mr. Pinckney Burgess of Anderson, to Miss Martha Cunningham, of Spartanburg.
Died at his residence in this district, on the 24th ult., David Brewton, in the 68th year of his age...from his Boyhood, a member of the Baptist Church at Bethel (Woodruff's) ...he accumulated a large estate, which he has left to his widow and children.

Issue of January 20, 1859
Married on the 6th inst., by Rev. M. C. Barnett, Mr. W. W. Lancaster, to Miss Christina, daughter of Thomas and Mary West, all of Spartanburg District.
Married on Sabbath the 16th inst., by J. B. Tolleson, Esq., Mr. William P. Williams, and Miss Nancy Cantrell, all of Spartanburg.
Married in Anderson, on the 4th inst., by Rev. A. Rice, Mr. Isaac Wickliffe of Pickens, to Miss Celestiana Wakefield, of Anderson.
Married in Union District, December 23, by Rev. J. H. Saye, Mr. H. C. Kenner, of Newberry District, to Miss Judith T. S., daughter of Col. J. K. B. Sims.
Married on the 22d December by Rev. J. G. Landrum, Mr. John Ray, to Miss Nancy Long, all of Union District.

84

Married on the 4th inst., by T. J. Sullivan, Esq., Mr. J. N. Terry, formerly of
Laurensville, to Miss Mary Meeks, of Greenville District.
Married on the evening of the 4th inst., by Rev. E. B. Teague, at the residence of A.
G. Stanford, La Grange, Ga., Mr. M. B. Kirby, of Coweta County, Ga., to Miss Hattie N.
Lipscomb, of the former place.
Married on the 22d December by Rev. D. Scruggs, Mr. James L. Scruggs, to Miss Emily
H. Farrow.
By the same on the same evening, Mr. James H. Shands to Miss Rosana J. Finch.
By the same on the 23rd December, Mr. Jas. Epton to Miss Angelina McKelvey.
By the same on the same evening, Mr. Rudicil Cantrell, to Miss Mary Jolly.
By the same, on the 27th December, Mr. Chesterfield Blackwell to Miss Artalissa
Green, all of Spartanburg District.
Married on the 8th inst., by Elias Wall., Esq., Mr. Riley Smith to Miss Adeline
Kimbrell, all of Spartanburg District.
Departed this life, November 10th 1858, Fignola Gabriel, son of Charles and S. E.
Moore aged one year.
Died at Unionville, S. C., on the 6th December, Miss Josepha Cornelia Dogan, aged
20 years, 3 months, and 25 days.

Issue of January 27, 1859
Married on the 13th inst., by W. H. Bagwell, at Bivingsville, Mr. Catha Lockman to
Miss Sarah Thomas, both of Bivingsville.
Married on the 20th inst., by W. H. Bagwell, Mr. John Lee to Miss Cassa Lee, all
of Spartanburg District.
Departed this life on January 12, 1858, at the residence of her father, in the village
of Greenville, S. C., Anna Pe-rry, 3rd daughter of Benjamin Franklin and Elizabeth
Frances Perry, in the 17th year of her age.

Issue of February 3, 1859
Married on the 13th ult., by Rev. A. M. Crietzberg, the Hon. Benjamin Gause to
Miss Susan E., daughter of Robert J. Gregg, Esq., all of Marion district, S. C.
Married at the Greenville Baptist Church on the 20th ult., by Rev. C. H. Lanneau,
Prof. P. C. Edwards to Miss Sophie Bliss Lanneau, all of Greenville, S. C.
Married on the 20th ult., by the Rev. T. J. Earle, Dr. Jno. T. Groves of Cresville,
Ga., to Miss Amanda Lattimer, of Greenville District.

Issue of February 10, 1859
Married on the 18th ult., by Rev. T. J. Earle, Rev. John G. Landrum to Miss Nancy
M. Earle, all of this district.
Married on Wednesday evening, the 2d inst., by Rev. W. C. Kirkland, Mr. J. G. Mabry
to Miss Mary Minerva Tolleson, 3rd daughter of J. B. Tolleson, Esq., all of this district.
Died at Walterboro, on the 26th ult., at 30 minutes past 5 o'clock, Mrs. Eliza
Glover, widow of the late Col. J. H. Glover.
Died at the residence of her father in Spartanburg District, Miss Rilian Pettit,
only daughter of Andrew and Mary Pettit, in the 17th year of her age.
Died on the 10th ult., in the 57th year of his age, Mr. R. W. Vaughan, formerly of
Union District, but for nearly 30 years a resident of Spartanburg District...member
of the Baptist Church 21 years...left an aged widow.

Issue of February 17, 1859
Married on the 10th inst., by W. H. Bagwell, Esq., Mr. C. L. N. Legg, to Miss
Sarah Gilmore, all of Spartanburg District.

Issue of February 24, 1859
Married on the 9th inst., by A. E. Smith, Esq., Mr. William Cooksy to Miss Nancy Ann
Cannon, eldest daughter of Joel Cannon, Esq., decd., all of Spartanburg District.
Married on Thursday evening, the 3rd inst., by the Rev. Mr. Witt, Mr. W. Frank Hanna,
of Spartanburg District, S. C. to Miss Sallie K. Hinds, of Calhoun Co., Ala.
Married on the 15th inst., by Rev. J. H. Thornwell, Mr. W. James L. Max of Abbeville,
to Miss C. Macfie, of Columbia, S. C.
Married in Summerville, Ga., on the 6th January, Mr. John S. Land, formerly of this
town to Miss Sarah A. Russom of Summerville, Ga.
Died of consumption at Ocala, Fla., on the 5th inst., Alvan D. Mason, son of the
late Posey Mason of Spartanburg District. He had gone to Florida to baffle a disease...
left a widowed mother and brothers and sisters.

Issue of March 3, 1859
Married in Abbeville, on the 24th February, by the Rev. John C. Williams, Mr. J.
William Tolleson of Spartanburg, to Miss Sallie Pratt of that district.

Married on Thursday evening, the 24th inst., by the Rev. Tolaver Robertson, Mr. Benjamin Young to Miss Eliza J. A. Hanna, all of this District.

Married on the same evening, by the Rev. Mr. Mauldin, Mr. Frank Griffin of Williamston, S. C. to Miss Hattie E. McCane, of this district.

Married in Laurens on the 15th ult., by Rev. C. B. Stewart, Mr. James W. Goldsmith and Miss Eleanor Woodside, all of that District.

Married on the 17th ult., at the residence of the bride's father, by Rev. C. B. Stewart, Mr. D. C. Stoddard of Laurens, to Miss M. F. Harrison, of Greenville.

Issue of March 10, 1859

Married on the 24th ult., by Rev. B. F. Mauldin, Mr. B. F. Griffin of Williamston, Anderson District, to Miss Hattie C. McLane, of Spartanburg.

[Repeat of marriage of James W. Goldsmith and Eleanor Woodside.]

Married on the 1st ult., by Rev. Dr. Cross, Col. H. W. Garlington and Miss Mary A. Bobo, both of Laurens.

Issue of March 17, 1858

Married on the 10th inst., by Reuben Briant, N. P., Sid. Harvey to Julia Harvey, all of Spartanburg District.

Married on the 8th inst., by Rev. Warren Drummond, Mr. Peter Biter to Miss Mary Ann Ford, 2nd daughter of Allen Ford, all of this district.

Married on the 23d February, by Rev. J. T. Jeter, Mr. J. W. Busley [perhaps an error, meant for Busby?] of Lexington District, to Miss L. A. Jeter of Union.

Nancy Lester, wife of Philip C. Lester, Esq., departed this life at Buena Vista, Greenville District, S. C. in the 65th year of her age, on Saturday , the 5th inst.... leaves a husband and 5 children.

Issue of March 24, 1859

Married at Cherry Grove, St. John's Berkly, S. C. on the 24th February, by the Rev. Roberts Johnson, Mr. Ellison Capers and Miss Charlotte R., third daughter of the late John G. Palmer, Esq., all of Charleston District.

Issue of March 31, 1859

Married on Monday morning, the 28th inst., by Rev. R. Woodruff, Mr. Thos Finch to Miss Eliza Haynes, all of Spartanburg District.

Married on Tuesday, the 23rd inst., by Rev. Jno. S. Ezell, Mr. Wm Vassey to Miss Nancy Logan, all of this District.

Married on the 22d inst., by Rev. A. A. James, Mr. George M. McDowell of Spartanburg District, and Miss Mary Ann Black, of Union District.

Married on the 27th February, by E. Wall, Esq., Mr. Hazel Parris to Miss Nancy Epton, all of this District.

Issue of April 14, 1859

Married on the 24th ult., by Rev. A. Padgett, David Cocherham to Miss Nancy P. Green, all of Polk Co., N. C.

Married by the same, on the 26th ult., K. Harris to Miss S. A. Calvert, all of Spartanburg District.

Issue of April 21, 1859

Married on the 12th inst., in Union District, by W. M. Wightman, D. D. LL. D., Charles Petty, Esq., of the Spartanburg Female College, and Miss Julia D. Davis, of Union District.

Issue of April 28, 1859

Married on Wednesday evening, the 20th inst., by Rev. W. C. Kirkland, Mr. John W. Garrett to Mrs. Clara Trimmier, all of Spartanburg.

Departed this life at Spartanburg Court House, on the 11th April, Miss Cassy Farrow (youngest daughter of Landon Farrow, of Revolutionary memory) in the 60th year of her age...member of the Methodist Episcopal Church from her youth.

Died on 26th March 1859, at 30 minutes past 5 o'clock, at his residence in Marietta, Ga., Col. John Heyward Glover, in the 44th year of his age. He removed from Beaufort District, S. C. in the spring of 1848.

Issue of May 5, 1859

Married on Thuesday evening, April 21, by Rev. D. Humphreys, Mr. William Anderson to Miss R. Lucretia, youngest daughter of Col. John McFall, all of Anderson.

Married on the 12th inst., by Rev. C. B. Stewart, Dr. D. Anderson of Spartanburg, and Miss Nancy Woodside of Greenville District.

Died at the residence of John H. Walker, near Hobbysville, on the 28th April 1859, Mr. John S. Perry, of Cross Anchor, in the 25th year of his age...member of New Hope

Baptist Church...leaves a wife, father, mother and two brothers.

Issue of May 12, 1859

Married on Tuesday evening, the 10th inst., by Rev. R. H. Reid, Mr. Robert Jackson, to Miss Nancy Jane Thompson, all of Spartanburg.

Married at Hendersonville, on the 26th ult., by Rev. R. H. Chapman, D. D., Mr. Andrew Miller to Miss Annie D. Twitty.

Married on Thursday the 5th inst., by W. H. Bagwell, Esq., Mr. Wm Millwood to Miss Mary Allen, all of this district.

Married by the same on Sunday, the 8th inst., Mr. Joseph Lindsey to Miss Susannah M. Humphrey, all of Spartanburg.

Emma Elford Lewis, daughter of Mr. and Mrs. A. F. Lewis born March 13, 1858, and died April 25, 1859. Pendleton Messenger.

Issue of May 19, 1859

Married in Unionville, on Thursday evening, May 5, by Rev. R. J. Boyd, Charles W. Boyd, Esq., to Miss Maria, second daughter of Davis Goudelock, Esq.

Married at Laurens C. H., on Thursday evening, the 28th April, by Rev. C. McLeod, Mr. William F. Beard of Columbia, to Miss Mary E., eldest daughter of Col. J. P. Hoyt, of the former place.

Died on the 7th May, at his residence near Limestone, William Lipscomb Sr., in the 70th year of his age.

Issue of May 26, 1859

Mrs. Essie M., wife of W. H. Whitner, died in this town at the residence of her father Hon. John T. Sloan, on Tuesday evening, the 17th inst., in the 22nd year of her age...funeral preached by Rev. A. A. Morse...remains buried at Stone Church...a member of the Presbyterian Church. Pendleton Messenger.

Died on the 30th April last, in the 73d year of his age, Capt. John Wofford. On Monday he was followed to the grave by Calhoun Lodge, A. F. M. and the Glenn Springs Troop of Cavalry, besides his relatives and friends...an officer in the war of 1812.

Died of pneumonia, in Spartanburg district, Mr. John Trail in the 74th year of his age.

Died on the 12th April, in this district, in the 5th year of her age...Martha Jane; on the 17th of the same month, in the 13th year of his age, Isaac Young; on the 19th May, in the 3d year of her age, Mary--children of John H. and Betsey Ann Cooley.

Died at Anderson C. H., on the 14th inst., Mrs. Missouri Finley, wife of Mr. Daniel Finley, in the 43rd year of her age...a native of Spartanburg District., where she spent most of her life...moved to Anderson village, two years since...left a husband and children.

Died in Waco, Mississippi, on the 2nd April, Dr. B. W. Earle, formerly of S. C., but for 20 years a resident of the former state.

Issue of June 2, 1859

Married on the 19th ult., by Rev. J. G. Landrum, Dr. Robert R. Murphy, to Miss Louisa McDowell, all of this district.

Married on the 30th ult., by A. C. Smith, Esq., Mr. Ellis Cannon to Miss Martha Webster, all of this district.

Issue of June 9, 1859

Married in Milledgeville, Ga., on the 26th May, by Rev. J. M. Curtis, James A. Clendinen, Esq., of Abbeville, Alabama, to Miss Rosa, daughter of Dr. B. A. White.

Departed this life at Pendleton, S. C., on the 30th ultimo, Mrs. Ann E. Shanklin, wife of J. V. Shanklin, Esq., and mother of the late Rev. J. A. Shanklin in the 60th year of her age.

Issue of June 16, 1859

Died on the 4th inst., at her father's residence, Greenville, S. C. Florence Georgianna Jones, daughter of Col. E. P. Jones, in the 20th year of her age.

Issue of June 23, 1859

Married in Ridgeville, on Thursday the 9th inst., by Rev. E. H. Myers, D. D., Mr. Washington M. Cummings to Miss Victoria E., only daughter of Hon. E. and S. C. Brownlee all of St. George's, Colleton, S. C.

Died at the residence of her husband, in Green county, Arkansas, on the 2d May, Mrs. Medora Rudisail, in the 24th year of her age...daughter of Capt. A. P. Bobo, formerly a citizen of Spartanburg. With her husband, left this native state last fall...member of the Baptist Church...left two children and a husband.

Died on the 27th May 1859, at the residence of Dr. J. W. Tracy, Cleveland Co., N. C., Mrs. C. L. Briggs, formerly of Cedar Springs, S. C. in the 27th year of her age.

Issue of June 30, 1859
Married on the 1st May, by Elder Tolaver Robertson, Dr. Saml S. Knight of Pleasant Mound, to Miss Permlia J. Miller of Poolesville, Spartanburg, S. C.

Issue of July 7, 1859
Married on the 28th ult, by Rev. J. S. Ervin, J. A. Fowler, Esq., of Spartanburg, S. C. to Miss M. Bell Cloud, of Fairfield District, S. C.
Married near Templeman's Mill on Sunday morning, the 3d inst., by Rev. Christopher Lee, Mr. William Johnson to Miss Jane Willard, all of this District.
Killed by lightning, on 3d ultimo, near Limeston Springs, S. C., Willie, son of Dr. and Mrs. Wm. B. Nott, aged 16 years and 4 months. The deceased would have finished his academic course with the present year, when he intended to enter South Carolina College.

Issue of July 14, 1859
Z. P. Herndon, formerly of Unionville, died at Glenn Springs, on Tuesday morning last [July 12?].

Issue of July 21, 1859
Married by W. W. Hitch, Esq., at his own house, on Sunday evening, 10th instant, Mr. Pickens Miller to Miss Jane Casey, both of Spartanburg.
Married on the 12th instant, by the Rev. S. J. Hill, Mr. Henry Tate, to Miss Sarah Goudelock, all of Union District.
Elijah Gossett, the subject of this notice, was born in Pittsylvania county, Virginia, in July 1783. He emigrated to Spartanburg District, S. C., when a youth, and settled near Zion Church. In 1808 he professed conversion at a camp-meeting at Fishdam, in Union District, S. C. and joined the M. E. Church at Zion. A few years after, he removed six miles to Lebanon, of which church he continued a faithful member to the day of his death. [long eulogy].
Samuel A. Bobo, died the last day of June, in the 21st year of his age, at his father's residence in Panola Co., Mississippi...eldest son of Sampson Bobo, born in Spartanburg, S. C....received education at Furman University in Greenville...moved in 1857 to the west.
Died at Charlotte, N. C., on the 16th July, Mrs. Elizabeth, wife of C. H. Britton, Esq., in the 41st year of her age.

Issue of July 28, 1859
Died in Spartanburg District, on Thursday, 21st July, Miss Lucy Tanner, in the 78th year of her age...joined Baptist Church at Bethlehem.

Issue of August 4, 1859
Married on Tuesday, 26th July, by Reuben Briant, N. P., Mr. Josephus Mitchell, to Miss Sarah Goforth, all of this district.
Died at Spartanburg, S. C., on Wednesday, the 27th July, Mrs. Elizabeth Ann Cavis, wife of A. T. Cavis, aged 43 years.

Issue of August 11, 1859
Married on Sunday evening, the 24th of July, by J. B. Goudelock, at his office, Mr. Samuel Beam, to Miss Nancy E. Murphy, of Union District.
Married on Monday evening following, by the same, Mr. Lorenzo Cooper, to Miss Mary G. Dillingham, of Spartanburg District.
Died in Green county, Arkansas, on the 17th of July, Mrs. Sarah R. Cothran, widow of the late Jackson Cothran, and daughter of Reuben and Martha Gramling, formerly of Spartanburg. The deceased had been for many years a pious member of the M. E. Church....She has left children....

Issue of August 18, 1859
Mr. Elijah Turner, near Grassy Pond, was killed on Friday last by being thrown from his horse. He was 86 years of age, of considerable wealth.... His daughter, Mrs. Ellis was with him and suffered a broekn thigh.

Issue of August 25, 1859
Married at the residence of the bride's father, on the morning of the 16th inst., by Rev. Albert A. James, Col.W. W. Gaffney of Limestone Springs, to Miss L. Victoria, eldest daughter of Major and Mrs. M. M. Montgomery of Union District, S. C.
Married on the same day by the same, Mr. Matthew S. Lynn of York District, to Mrs. Jane C. Goudelock, of Union District.

Issue of September 1, 1859
Married in Hartwell, Ga., on the 14th ult., by Rev. J. T. W. Vernon, Mr. John W. Haynes, of Spartanburg, S. C. and Miss Samantha F. Neese, of Hartwell, Ga.

Married on the 25th ultimo, by Rev. A. W. Walker, Mr. Geroge Garrett, to Miss Harriet Duggins, all of Spartanburg.

Married in July, by Rev. R. H. Reid, Mr. C. A. Barry, of Spartanburg District and Miss Anna M. Sudderth, of Greenville District.

Married on the 24th ultimo, by Rev. M. C. Barnett, Mr. William Caldwell and Miss Lucinda Tolleson, all of Spartanburg.

Issue of September 8, 1859

Mrs. Sallie Vandike departed this life on Friday, the 26th August, after a protract-ed illness...born 16 March 1794 and joined Nazareth Presbyterian Church at any early age.

Issue of September 15, 1859

Married on Tuesday, Sept. 13, by Reuben Briant, N. P., Mr. James A. Kinnett to Miss Harriet Wyatt, all of Spartanburg.

Married on the 28th of August 1859, by Reuben Briant, N. P., Mr. John Lemaster to Miss Jane Harmon, all of Spartanburg District.

Married on the 13th day June last, by Elias Wall, esq., Mr. Nathan Dyer to Rachel Cantrell, all of this District.

Married on the 2d day of July, by Elias Wall, esq., Mr. Jackson Cantrell, to Miss Mary Belcher, all of this district.

Married on the 12th of September, by Elias Wall, esq., Mr. William A. Johnson, of N. C. to Miss Patsey Piehoof, of Spartanburg District, S. C.

Died at Walhalla, S. C. on the morning of the 6th inst., Mary Ella, infant daughter of J. Wesley and Carrie E. Terry, aged two months and two days.

Issue of September 29, 1859

Married on the 20th instant, by the Rev. S. T. Dill, John Epton, esq., of Spartanburg, to Miss Malinda Stewart, of Greenville.

Married on the 18th instant, by W. H. Foster, esq., Mr. Samuel Piehoof, to Miss Reamoth Hammett, eldest daughter of Mrs. Lucy Hammett, all of Spartanburg District.

With regret we chronicle the death of William B., eldest son of our esteemed friend, Burr J. Ramage, esq., He died at his father's residence in this town, Wednesday, the 7th instant, in his 13th year.... Newberry Rising Sun.

Issue of October 6, 1859

Died on the 28th September last, John Bishop, son of G. W. and Anne Bishop, aged 12 years, 2 months and 19 days.

Issue of October 13, 1859

Married at the residence of E. S. E. Chambers, at Stice's Shoal, Cleveland county, N. C. by Rev. Wm. C. Patterson, Mr. James Heath, of Union County, N. C., to Miss Hester C. Patterson, of Spartanburg, S. C.

At the same time and place, Mr. R. H. Porter, of Lancaster District, S. C. to Miss Laura C. Patterson, of Spartanburg.

Married on the 4th inst., by Reuben Briant, N. P., Mr. William Haynes of Union District, to Miss Mary Reid, of Spartanburg District.

Married on the 9th of October by Reuben Briant, N. P., Mr. J. M. Barnett to Miss Susan J. Rude, all of Spartanburg District.

Issue of October 20, 1859

Married on the 29th ult., by Rev. Rolaver Robertson, Mr. Burwell Bobo, of Spartan-burg to Miss Lou Drummond, of Laurens.

Married on the 28th ult., by Rev. C. B. Stewart, Mr. Harrison White of Spartanburg and Miss Mary R. Simpson, of Laurens.

Died in Panola Co., Mississippi, on Sunday evening, Sept. 11, 1859, Maria Louisa, daughter of Dr. Wm. J. and Margaret L. Bobo, after a short but painful illness. The deceased was a native of Union District, S. C. her father having removed from Cross Keys, in that district, in the winter of 1857. She was a grand daughter, by the mother's side, of the late David Boyce of Newberry district, who was a son of John Boyce, a Revolutionary patriot.

Issue of October 27, 1859

Married on Thursday morning, October 13, by Rev. F. A. Mood, Mr. C. M. McJunkin of the Southern Enterprise, to Miss Anne Robison, 2nd daughter of Mr. E. K. Robison, all of Greenville.

Issue of November 3, 1859

Married on Thursday, the 27th October, by Rev. A. A. James, Mr. Wm. Franklin West to Miss Emily Caroline Mays, all of Spartanburg District, S. C.

Married by W. H. Bagwell, Esq., on Sunday evening, the 30th October, Mr. Hughy Thomas to Miss Martha Bagwell, all of Spartanburg.

Married at Grassy Pond, on the 27th ult., by A. Bonner, Esq., Mr. William E. Turner to Miss Clementine Huskey, all of this District.

Married at Grassy Pond, on the 28th ult., by the same, Mr. J. T. M. D. Helton to Miss Kesiah Jolly, all of this district.

Died at Spartanburg, on Friday morning, October 28, Mary Jane, only daughter of Prof. James H. and Margaret Carlisle, aged 2 years and 4 months.

Issue of November 10, 1859

Married on Thursday, the 3d inst., by Rev. J. H. Landrum, Mr. Louise N. Poole of Spartanburg, and Miss Eva Mazde of Charleston.

Married in St. Petersburg, at the U. S. Minister's residence, on the morning of 1 October, John E. Bacon, Esq., to Rebecca Calhoun, daughter of Hon E. W. Pickens.

Issue of November 17, 1859

Married on the 3d November, by Elias Wall, Esq., Mr. James W. Hambrey of Greenville District, S. C. to Miss Sarah Ann Floyd, of this district.

Married by the same, on the 10th November, Mr. Obadiah Bishop to Miss Abigail Johnson, all of this district.

Married on the 3rd November, by Rev. A. A. James, Mr. Jonathan Weeks of Columbia Co., Fla., to Miss Mary R. Whetstone of Spartanburg District, S. C.

Issue of November 24, 1859

Married by Rev. J. G. Landrum, on the 3d inst., Mr. J. B. Davis of Henderson, N. C. to Miss Hattie H., daughter of W. Walker, A. S. H. of Spartanburg.

Married by W. Walker, A. S. H., Esq., on the 6th inst., Mr. Henry Gilbert, to Miss Carney Kemp, all of this District.

Died in Spartanburg, on the morning, of the 17th inst., at the residence of Maj. W. H. Trimmier, James Vernon Miller, aged 20 years...employee of the Spartan office...member of the Baptist Church.

Issue of December 1, 1859

Married on the evening of the 29th November, by Rev. A. A. James, Mr. David C. Judd, to Miss Eliza A. Attleton, of Springfield, Mass.

Issue of December 8, 1859

We regret to learn that Mrs. Evins, wife of Col.S. N. Evins, and mother of Maj. J. H. Evins, of the Express, died on Monday, the 5th inst.

Married on the 30th ult., by J. B. Tolleson, Esq., Mr. E. L. Higgins, Mr. William Wilkie to Miss Henrietta Epley, all of Spartanburg.

Married on the 4th inst., by the same, Mr. Joseph H. Wooten, of Spartanburg District, S. C. to Miss E. C. Coltfelter, of Greenville District, S. C.

Issue of December 15, 1859

Married by W. H. Bagwell, Esq., on the 18th November last, Mr. James Bagwell to Miss Julia Elders, all of Spartanburg.

Married by the same, onthe 27th November last, Mr. Perry Smith to Miss Julia McCombs, all of Spartanburg.

Married on the 11th inst., by Rev. H. M. Haynes, Maj. W. H. White to Miss Margaret Finger, all of Spartanburg District.

Issue of December 22, 1859

Married on Tuesday evening, the 13th inst., by the Rev. David Wills, Homer L. McGowan Esq., to Miss Jula A. Farrow, all of Laurens.

Issue of January 4, 1860

Married on Sunday morning, Jan. 1, by A. E. Smith, Esq., Mr. Hubbard Cash to Miss Julia Robbins, all of Spartanburg.

Married by John H. Walker, Esq., on the 6th ult., Mr. Anthony Shands to Miss Frances Madillar Landrum, all of Spartanburg District.

Married by the same, on the 27th ult., Mr. Morgan Young Sexton to Miss Sallie C., only daughter of Capt. Asail and Elizabeth Lifflefield, all of this District.

Married on Tuesday, 30th ult., by Wm. Walker, A. S. H., Mr. William Easler, to Miss Talitha Johnson, all of this district.

Married on Thursday, 22d ult., by Rev. A.A. James, Mr. James L. Owen, and Miss Susan Ann Kirby, all of Spartanburg District.

Married on the 25th ult., by Rev. John G. Landrum, Mr. John Camp of Campbell Co., Ga., to Miss Elizabeth, eldest daughter of Charles McClure of Spartanburg District.

Married on the 21st December ultimo, in the Scotch Presbyterian Church, in the city of New York, by the Rev. Dr. Jos. McElroy, the Rev. Dr. A. W. Leland, Professor in the Theological Seminary of Columbia, to Miss Clara A. Blight, of the city of Dresden in Germany.

Died at the residence of her husband on the 5th[?] December, 1859, Mrs. Elizabeth Cunningham Evins, daughter the late Gen. Thomas and Mrs. Martha Moore, and wife of Col. Samuel N. Evins. The deceased was in the sixty-third year of her age, and died after a long illness...for more than forty years she had been an humble and consistent member of Nazareth (Presbyterian) Church...leaves three sons and two daughters...[long eulogy].

Issue of January 12, 1860

Married on Monday, 1 January 1860, by Reuben Briant, N. P., Mr. Jasper Kirby to Miss Jane Harmon, all of Spartanburg, S. C.

Departed this life, on the 7th December last, at her father's residence in Spartanburg District, Miss Adeline Wright, aged 16 years, 2 months and 1 day.

Issue of January 19, 1860

Married on the 22d ult., by Col. W. H. Bagwell, Mr. J. J. Bagwell to Miss Louisa Neighbours, all of Spartanburg.

Married by Col. W. H. Bagwell, on the 15th inst., Wm. J. Reaves to Miss Sarah M. Waldrip, both of Bivingsville.

Issue of January 26, 1860

Married on the 22d December last, by E. Wall, Esq., Mr. F. W. Ray and Miss Mary Jane Ray.

Married on the same day by the same, Mr. Columbus Brannon to Miss Rhody Bishop.

Married on the 9th January 1860, by the same, Mr. T. J. Rollins to Miss Susan Burnett.

Married on the 16th January 1860, by the same, Mr. Sampson Umphries and Miss Missouri Horton.

Issue of February 2, 1860

Married on the 24th ult., by Rev. W. C. Kirkland, Mr. M. T. McKinney to Miss Mary Jane Jackson, all of Spartanburg.

Married on Thursday, the 26th ult., by David Moore, Esq., Col. W. D. Camp to Miss Nancy Lowe, all of Spartanburg District.

Married on the 12th inst., by the Rev. H. W. Haynes, Mr. David McCluer to Miss Martha Bush, all of Spartanburg.

Married on the 10th inst., at Anderson, S. C. by Rev. J. Scott Murray, Henry Morris of Greenville, S. C. and Elizabeth, third daughter of the late Col. Z. Edwards, of Cass County, Ga.

Married on the22d inst., by the Rev. S. M. Green, Dr. W. H. Austin and Miss Mattie, daughter of Mr. M. T. and Mrs. M. A. Hudson, all of Greenville.

Married on Tuesday evening, the 10th instant, at the residence of the bride's father, by Rev. J. Scott Murray, Mr. John Peter Brown, and Miss Julia S., second daughter of Col. J. P. Reed, both of Anderson.

Died on the 25th ult., Henry Lorimer, son of G. and Rachal Ann Hicks, anged 11 years, 4 months, and 20 days.

Died at his residence, near Woodruff's, Spartanburg District, on the 15th ult., Mr. Samuel Pilgram, in the 61st year of his age. Besides a wife and two dear little ones, he leaves a long list of relatives and friends...member of the Baptist Church at Bethel.

Issue of February 16, 1860

Married on the 9th inst., by W. H. Bagwell, Esq., Mr. James Allen of Cleveland Co., N. C. to Miss Lucretia McCombs, of Bivingsville.

Issue of February 23, 1860

Married on the 9th inst., by John C. Caldwell, Esq., Eber Bailey to Miss Amanda Sexton, all of this District.

Died at Spartanburg, on the 10th inst., Recoa Whitner, youngest daughter of Mr. and Mrs. J. B. Tolleson, in the7th year of his age.

Issue of March 1, 1860

Married on the 16th inst., by W. H. Bagwell, Mr. Pinkney Petrel and Miss Nancy Elders, both of Spartanburg.

Died on the 19th inst., at his residence near Limestone Springs, Capt. Robert Lipscomb, who, if he had lived until the 15th of April next, would have been 80 years of age...baptized by the Rev. J. S. Ezell officiating in the absense the Rev. T. Dickson. He advised his wife and daughter not to grieve after him. [long eulogy].

Died on the 9th of this month, Miss Margaret Mason, at the residence of her mother, Mrs. Catherine Mason, in Spartanburg District. Leaves mother, brothers, and sisters. She was but twelve years of age.

Departed this life in Hempstead Co., Arkansas, on the 4th ult., Mr. Theophilus Thorn, aged about 50 years...born in the northern part of Spartanburg District, and resided there till about 9 years ago.

Died on the 19th of September in the same county and state, Mrs. Mahala _____, 2nd daughter of Mr. Thorn, leaving a husband and four children.

Issue of March 8, 1860

Married by Rev. J. G. Landrum, Mr. Pinckney Ramsour and Miss Martha Clark, all of Spartanburg District.

Married on the 26th ult., by the same, Mr. John A. Duncan of Jacksonville, Ala., to Miss Mary Ann Hunter of Spartanburg.

Married on the 21st ult., by Rev. C. Murchison, Maj. George W. Anderson of Laurens, to Miss N. N. Nesbit of Spartanburg.

Issue of March 15, 1860

Married on Sunday evening, the 11th inst., by J. M. Elford, Esq., Robert B. McLean, to Jane Evans, all of Spartanburg District.

Issue of March 22, 1860

Married on the 14th inst., by Rev. J. G. Landrum, Mr. C. B. McMillan and Miss Nancy Catherine Gray, all of Spartanburg.

Married on the 13th inst., by Elias Wall, Esq., Mr. George S. Gilbert and Miss Nancy Cartee.

Issue of March 29, 1860

Married on the 24th of January last, by the Rev. B. Bonner, Mr. John M. Sarratt to Miss Louisa Morgan.

Issue of April 5, 1860

Married on the 13th of March in Gainesville, Arkansas, by Rev. J. G. Glasgow, Dr. Calvin Wall of Greensboro, Ark. to Miss Emma A., daughter of Hon. Jonathan Gentry, formerly of Dresden, Tennessee.

Married on Thursday evening, the 29th ultimo, by A. B. Woodruff, Esq., Mr. Pinckney Bragg to Mrs. Mavel Roebuck, all of Spartanburg District.

Married at Cross Anchor, on the 25th of March, by John H. Walker, Esq., Mr. Benjamin West, of Union District to Miss Permelia E. Campbell, of Laurens District.

Married at the same time & place by the same, William H. Patton of Laurens District to Miss Nancy Casey of Spartanburg District.

Issue of April 12, 1860

Died at his residence at Society Hill, S. C. on the morning of the 2d inst., John D. Witherspoon, Esq., who completed the 82d year of his age on the 17 March last...the oldest member of the Bar of the State of S. C.

Issue of April 26, 1860

Departed this life in Spartanburg District, on the 24th of March, in the 29th year of her age, Mrs. Nancy E. Drummond, wife of Rev. Warren Drummond...married less than 2 years ...member of the Baptist Church at Brushy Creek...corpse conveyed to her father's residence in Greenville District for interment...leaves a husband, an infant son, mother, father, brother and sisters.

Issue of May 3, 1860

Married on Tuesday, the 24th ultimo, at Grassy Pond, by the Rev. Belany Bonner, Mr. Samuel S. Boss and Miss Hardinia Victoria Lipscomb, all of Spartanburg. The incidents of the above event were very marked. Fully five hundred guests graced the occasion....

Married on the 19th ult., by Rev. R. H. Reid, Mr. S Wyatt Miller, of Austin Co., Texas and Miss Elliott E. Drummond, of Spartanburg, S. C.

Married on the 15th ult., by Elias Wall, Esq., Mr. William Garrett to Miss Nancy Cantrell, all of Spartanburg District.

Married on the 20th ult., by A. C. Smith, Esq., Mr. Jefferson Saterfield to Miss Mary Ann Johnston, all of Spartanburg, S. C.

Died, in this village, on the 24th ult., Theodore Lawrence, son of Henry J. and Anne Eliza Mouzon, aged 2 years, 8 months, and 13 days.

Died at Campo Bello, near Pendleton village, on the morning of the 18th ultimo, Colie, eldest son of Archibald G. Campbell, aged 20 years, nine months, and 18 days.

Issue of May 17, 1860

Married in Pickens, on the 19th ult., by Rev. T. L. McBryde, D. D., Dr. J. H. Maxwell to Miss Mary Alexander, of Pendleton.

Departed this life, at his residence in Spartanburg Village, on Saturday, the 12th inst., of Apoplexy, Jefferson Choice, Esq., in the 50th year of his age...born in Greenville District, 29 April 1811, he studied law with his brother Capt. Wm. Choice...buried in our village cemetery...[long eulogy].

Issue of May 24, 1860

Died, near Moultrie, on the 14th inst., Felix, infant son of I. H. and Susan Cantrell, aged 2 years, 2 months, and 28 days.

Issue of May 31, 1860

Married on Tuesday morning, the 22nd inst., at Camp Hill, the residence of Dr. Winsmith, by Rev. C. F. Jones, D. D., Col. John R. Sondley of Newberry to Miss Carrie Smith.

Issue of June 7, 1860

Died on the 28th of April last, at the residence of her husband, in Spartanburg District, Mrs. Mary Gaston, wife of James N. Gaston...born 3 August 1786...member of Nazareth Presbyterian Church.

Issue of June 14, 1860

Married on the ___ ult., by Rev. L. Vaughn, Mr. Leonard Kemp and Miss Sarah Wilson, of Spartanburg. Greenville Enterprise.

Issue of June 28, 1860

Married on Thursday evening, the 14th inst., at the residence of Dr. S. C. Griffin, in Edgefield District, by the Rev. J. J. Brantley, Mr. R. H. Land to Miss Bettie P. Griffin.

Issue of July 5, 1860

Died at Anderson C. H., on Sunday, the 24th ult., Virginia, youngest daughter of J. I. and Mary B. Ash.

Issue of July 12, 1860

Married on the 8th instant, by W. H. Bagwell, Esq., Mr. J. C. Cannon to Miss Elizabeth Fitzgerald.

Departed this life at his residence in the lower part of this district, on the 30th June last, James Alexander, a very old, wealthy, and influential citizen...born in the year 1789, within a very short distance of the place where he died.

Issue of July 19, 1860

Married on Sunday evening, June 17, by the Rev. F. W. Littlejohn, Mr. J. H. Garrison to Mrs. Sallie S. Lipscomb, of Spartanburg District, S. C.

Issue of August 2, 1860

Married on the 26th ult., by Rev. Richard Woodruff, Mr. John Martin to Margaret Susannah Finch, all of this District.

Married on the 29th ult., by the Rev. Lanceford Padget, Mr. Thomas Griffen, Sr., of Rutherford Co., N. C. to Mrs. Martha Thomson of Spartanburg District, S. C.

Married on the 8th of July, by Elias Wall, Esq., Mr. David Pettit, to Miss Louisa Powel, all of this District.

Issue of August 9, 1860

Married at Cedar Spring, August 2, 1860, by Rev. Edwin Cater, Mr. Jas. S. Templeton of Laurens District, to Miss Margaret Jane Hagins of Lancaster District, S. C.

Married on Sunday evening, the 6th inst., by A. E. Smith, Esq., Mr. Hugh Pierce and Miss Sallie Cannon of Spartanburg District.

Capt. Patrick Hoy died at his residence in this district on the 6th July, in the 75th year of his age...a native of Antrim County, Ireland, from whence he emigrated to this state in 1804, about 17 years old. A few years after, he married and settled where he died, having lived there a little over 50 years...member of the Baptist Church 25 years...[long eulogy].

Issue of August 16, 1860

Married at Campobella, on Wednesday evening, the 8th inst., by Jno. Bankston Davis, Esq., Mr. Tandy Kimbrell to Miss Nancy Vernon.

Married at the same place on Thursday evening, the 9th inst., by the same, Mr. Alonzo Wallace, to Miss Axcy Atkins, all of Spartanburg District.

Married by J. B. Tolleson, Esq., on Thursday, the 9th inst., Mr. Leland Wolf and Mrs. _____ Gilbert, all of Spartanburg.

Married on the 9th inst., by W. H. Bagwell, Esq., Mr. William M. Lee and Miss Barbara E. Sloan, all of Spartanburg.

Departed this life at Chick's Springs, on Saturday the 4th August, in the 64th year of her age, Mrs. Nancy P. Farrow, of Charleston, relict of the late Dr. Samuel Farrow.

Issue of August 23, 1860

Married on Thursday evening, the 16th inst., by Rev. Edwin Cater, A. T. Cavis of Spartanburg, and Miss S. A. Hamilton, formerly of Norfolk, Va.

Married on the 9th inst., by Rev. W. M. Haynes, Mr. Alfred Cole to Miss Jane Walker, all of this District.

Married on the 12th inst., by the same, Mr. James C. Blackwood of Spartanburg District, to Miss Mary Deck of Polk Co., N. C.

Issue of August 30, 1860

Departed this life at the residence of her husband, in Greenville District, on Sunday evening, the 12th inst., Mrs. A. E. Bailey, wife of William C. Baily, about 26 years old, leaving an infant daughter three weeks old...member of the Methodist Episcopal Church.

Issue of September 6, 1860

Married by Elias Wall, Esq., on the 26th of August, Mr. Littleberry Gilbert to Miss Jenetta Kimbrel, all of Spartanburg District, S. C.

Died at the residence of his parents, in this village on Wednesday, the 29th August, John David, infant son of Jno. W. and Amanda Maxwell, aged 2 years 10 months, and 5 days.

Issue of September 13, 1860

Married at Limestone Springs, on the 4th inst., by Rev. W. Curtis, LL. D., Mr. L. M. Gentry, Sheriff of Spartanburg District, to Miss Julia A Camp, all of this District.

Married by Rev. Lanceford Padgett, at the residence of George W. Smith, on the 19th of August, Mr. James Smith to Miss Letty Blackwell.

Married by the same, at the residence of Thomas M. Shields, on the 6th September, Mr. James Henderson to Miss Lucinda Steadman, all of Polk Co., N. C.

Died on the 14th ult., in this district, Gabriel B. Styles, in the 63d year of his age, son of a Revolutionary patriot.

Issue of September 27, 1860

Died at the residence of Mrs. M. A. J. Kennedy in Spartanburg, on the 4th inst., Frederica Fanny Temple...She came a stranger among them....

Departed this life at Spartanburg, on the 6th inst., in the 61st year of his age, Mr. Joseph Brown, leaving a wife and 7 children.

Issue of October 4, 1860

Married near Cavin Old Field, on the 14th ultimo, by Rev. Simpson Drummond, Mr. John S. Vise to Miss Eliza Mason, all of this District.

Issue of October 25, 1860

Married in Unionville at the residence of Capt. T. B. Jeter, on the 18th inst., by Rev. Colin Murchison, Dr. P. P. Butler of Spartanburg, to Miss Arsinoe M. Jeter, of Unionville.

Issue of November 1, 1860

Married on the 25th October by Rev. Whitefoord Smith, D. D., Mr. R. R. King of Clarendon District, to Miss Mary E. Bivings of this place.

Married at Granby street Methodist Church, Norfolk, Va., on Wednesday morning, the 24th October by Rev. J. H. Finely, D. D., Mr. John A. Henneman of Spartanburg, S. C. to Miss Louise Rate, of Norfolk.

Married on the 28th October by A. E. Smith, Esq., Mr. Arthur Cash to Miss Kiza Katherine Willis, all of Spartanburg District.

Married on the 2d October by Rev. Wm. Curtis, LL. D., Mr. William S. Lipscomb to Miss Albertine Goudelock, all of Spartanburg District.

Married by the same on the same day, Mr. Davis Jeffries to Lamar Co., Texas to Miss Sallie A. Lipscomb of Spartanburg District.

Issue of November 8, 1860

Married on Tuesday evening, the 31st ult., by Rev. R. H. Reid, Mr. William L. Morgan to Miss Emily Frances Smtih, all of this district.

Married on the 13th[?] ult., by J. B. Sanders, Mr. John M. Smith of Spartanburg, to Miss Artemissa Dodson of Pickens.

Died on the 29th ult., at his residence near Templeman's Mill, Mr. William Hansell, aged about 45 years...jointed the M. E. Church.

Issue of November 15, 1860

Married on Wednesday evening, the 7th November by the Rev. A. W. Walker, Mr. Thomas B. Anderson of Laurens to Miss Fannie M., only daughter of Rev. A. W. & Mrs. L. W. Walker of Spartanburg, S. C.

Married on Tuesday evening, the 6th inst., by the Rev. R. H. Reid, Mr. Simeon Dillard of Greenville to Miss Mary Rebecca, daughter of Denny Anderson, Esq., of Spartanburg.

Married on the 13th inst., by Rev. John G. Landrum, Mr. James O. Harris Jr., and Miss Julia G. Ray, all of this place.

Died at Cavin's Old Field, on Monday, the 5th inst., Mahala Odella, infant daughter of William & Pershea Alexander, aged 1 year 8 months and 23 days.

Issue of November 29, 1860

Married on the 15th inst., by Elias Wall, Esq., Mr. Edmund Manning Bishop, to Miss Avaline Brannon, all of this District.

Married on Tuesday evening, the 6th inst., by the Rev. O. A. Darby, A. S. Douglass, Esq., editor of the Spartanburg Express, to Miss Mary E. Byers of Union District.

Married on the 13th inst., by Rev. M. C. Barnett, Mr. Wm. H. Walker to Miss M. E. Rountree, all of this District.

Married on the 22nd November by Rev. C. S. Beard, Mr. John Harman and Miss Amanda Jane Gossett, all of Spartanburg District.

Died on the 16th inst., Mrs. Thurzy High, consort of Wm. G. High, in the 62nd year of her age...member of the Baptist Church at Mt. Zion nearly 20 years.

Departed this life at the residence of her father in this District, on the 5th inst., Sarah Fleming, who was born 24th February 1828 [eulogy].

Issue of December 13, 1860

Died at Cavin's Old Field, on Monday the 28th inst., Lucinda Texanna, infant daughter of William and Perchea Alexander, aged 5 years and 1 month.

Issue of January 3, 1861

Married in Yorkville, S. C. by Rev. R. T. Russell, Wm. McD. Palmer of this place, to Miss Sallie J. Tomlinson of Yorkville, S. C.

Married on Christmas evening, by the Rev. Mr. Hilliard, Mr. John Mullins to Miss Canzada Bell, all of this District.

Married on the 20th ult., by Rev. R. H. Reid, Col. S. N. Evins to Mrs. N. M. Moore, both of this District.

Married on Tuesday morning, the first inst., by W. H. Bagwell, Esq., Mr. John Reaves to Miss Susan Lindsey, all of this District.

Married on Monday morning, the 24th ult., by the Rev. Mr. Kirkland, Mr. John Martin of Greenville, S. C. to Miss Susan Catharine Stevenson, of this District.

Issue of January 10, 1861

Married by A. E. Smith, Esq., on 20 Dec 1860, Mr. George Sprouse to Miss Mary Huggins, all of Spartanburg, S. C.

On Thursday, the 27th December 1860, by Elias Wall, Esq., Mr. Wi-liam McKinney to Miss Emiline Burnett, all of this District.

Married on Dec. 9, 1860, by R. Briant, N. P., Mr. John Purgoson to Miss Mary Petty, all of this District.

Married on Dec 23, 1860, by R. Briant, Mr. Absalum Kirby to Miss Lucinda Lemaster.

Married on the 27th December by Rev. R. H. Reid, Mr. John M. Thomas to Miss Matilda Jane Smith, all of Spartanburg District.

Issue of January 17, 1861

Died of Consumption, 1 January 1861, Mrs. Anna P., wife of J. H. Goss, in the 30th year of her age...member of the Presbyterian Church of this place...[long eulogy].

Issue of February 7, 1861

Married in the Methodist Church in Edgefield, on the 28th January, by Rev. J. B[?]. Connor, Mr. Wm. K. Blake, President of Spartanburg Female College, to Miss Marina G. Jones, daughter of Lewis Jones, Esq.

Issue of February 21, 1861

Married in this place, on Wednesday evening, the 13th inst., by William Walker, A. S. H., Mr. James P. Sossaman of Cabarrus Co., N. C. to Miss Carrie C. Bryson, of this place.

Married by J. B. Tolleson, Esq., on the 7th ult., Mr. Robert Thomas, of Union Dist., to Miss Elizabeth Dempsey of Spartanburg District.
Married by the same on the 30th ult., Mr. Wm. P. Willis to Miss Sarah E. Dyr, all of Spartanburg District.

Issue of February 28, 1861
Married on the 24th inst., by Elias Wall, Esq., Mr. L. Henry Low, to Miss Judea Cannon, all of Spartanburg District.
Married on the 24th inst., by Elias Wall, Esq., Mr. Cleveland Bonham to Miss Elizabeth Cannon, all of Spartanburg District.

Issue of March 7, 1861
Married by W. H. Bagwell, Esq., March 3, Littleton Bagwell Jr. to Miss Martha Gossett, both of Spartanburg.

Issue of March 21, 1861
Married on Sunday morning, at 10 o'clock, 3d inst., by Rev. Robt. W. Draper, Mr. Geo. W. Poole to widow Fenita White of Calhoun Co., Ala., formerly of Spartanburg.
Married on Tuesday morning last by Rev. Whiteford Smith, D. D., Rev. W. W. Duncan of Virginia, to Miss Medora Rice of Union, S. C.

Issue of March 28, 1861
Married in this District on the 12th inst., by A. Bonner, Esq., Mr. John Price, to Miss Margaret J. Williams.
Married by the same, Mr. Joseph Hammet to Miss G. Goode,
Married on the 12th inst., by the Same, Mr. Orvi Bright to Miss Nancy Cantrell.
Mrs. Catherine Gossett, wife of John Gossett, born March 12, 1801, died at her residence in Spartanburg District, March 13, 1861, aged 60 years and 1 day...member of the Methodist Church.

Issue of April 4, 1861
Married on Wednesday night, the 28th March by Rev. M. C. Barnett, Mr. Elias B. Meaders to Miss Lucinda S. Bearden, all of this District.

Issue of April 25, 1861
Married on the 16th inst., Mr. William R. Neilson of Green Co., Tenn., to Miss M. J. Smith of Union District.
Obituary. Rev. Thomas Frean, born 15 Jan 1793, County of Tipperary, Ireland, and died Sunday last at the residence of his son in law Wilson W. Waldrop in Newberry District, S. C....left Ireland when very young, contemplating a sojourn with relatives in Charleston, S. C. The War of 1812 intervened and he was sent into the interior. During his visit to Newberry, he became acquainted with his wife, Hannah Elmore...became a merchant at Spear's Mill on Brush[sic] River...taught school in Newberry and Spartanburg ...became a Methodist minister, then a Baptist Minister...had charge for several years of the Baptist Churches at Newberry and Rocky Springs...was Surveyor General and Deputy Treasurer...wrote poetry under the nom de plume of "Carolina."...during the latter years of his life he saw his son William H. Frean, his daughter Hannah Belton, wife Hannah Frean and daughter Abigail Caldwell Southerner linger with consumption and die...buried at Friend's grave-yard at Brush [Bush] River.

Issue of May 9, 1861
Married on Sunday, April 21, 1861, by J. Bankston Davis, Esq., Mr. A. J. Reagan to Miss Eliza Bonham, all of Spartanburg.

Issue of May 16, 1861
Married on Tuesday morning, the 14th inst., by Rev. R. H. Reid, Mr. William Means to Miss Margaret Evins.

Issue of May 23, 1861
Died at his residence in this District, of pneumonia, on the 18th inst., J. W. Cooper, in the 74th year of his age...member of the Baptist denomination and a mild Calvinist, attached to the views of Andrew Fuller....buried in the grave yard at Cedar Springs.
Married on Wednesday morning, the 15th inst., by W. F. Parker, D. D., Mr. J. Balys Williamson of Spartanburg, S. C. to Miss L. E. Porter of Liecester[sic], N. C.

Issue of June 6, 1861
Married on Tuesday, the 19th inst., by the Rev. R. H. Reid, Mr. Amos Halmes and Miss E. M. Christopher, both of this district.

Issue of June 16, 1861
       Married on the 28th ult., by Rev. R. H. Reid, Mr. Franklin Smith of Union District,
to Miss Rosa Ann Coan of Spartanburg District.

Issue of June 27, 1861
       Married on Tuesday morning, the 25th inst., by Rev. J. G. Landrum, Dr. W. E. Dean
to Miss Anne E. Camp, all of Spartanburg.
       Married on Sunday the 2nd inst., by C. P. Petty, Esq., Mr. Thompson Humphries to
Miss Nancy Minerva, second daughter of Mr. Joab Bryant, all of Spartanburg District.
       Married at Sardis, Panola Co., Miss., on the 12th inst., at the residence of the
bride's father, by Rev. Mr. Young, Mr. Jonathan Low to Miss Demerious Jones, of this
county.

Issue of July 4, 1861
       Married on the 28th ultimo, by Rev. J. H. Thornwell, Rev. A. F. Smith of Mississippi,
to Miss Carrie M. F. Golding, of this place.

Issue of July 11, 1861
       Died on Thursday, the 27th inst., at the residence of his parents, Lawrence Howard,
infant son of W. H. and M. H. Ray, aged 7 months.

Issue of July 25, 1861
       Died at Spartanburg Court House, S. C., on 4 July 1861, Mr. William Masterman Jr.,
aged 28 years, 8 months, and 7 days...a native of London, England.

Issue of August 22, 1861
       Married on August 11, 1861, by R. Briant, Esq., Mr. Absolum Sparks to Miss Sarah
Petty, all of Spartanburg District.

Issue of September 5, 1861
       Died in Richmond, Va., on the morning the 24th August, at St. Charles Hospital, Mr.
Robert J. Poole of the Cross Anchor Volunteers, 3d Regt. S. C. V....died of typhoid
fever.

Issue of October 3, 1861
       Married on the 29th ult., by Rev. W. T. Farrow, Mr. D. G. Finley to Miss Mary Wilkins,
all of Spartanburg District.
       Obituary. Margaret Freelove and Susan Minnie, youngest child and only daughters of
Robt L. and Mary A. McMillan, died in Spartanburg District--one on 5 July aged 3 years,
3 months and 25 days and the other on 11 July aged 8 months and 12 days.
       Martha McClure, wife of David McClure and daughter of S. & S. Bush, died July 18,
1861, near New Prospect, Spartanburg District...[eulogy]. S. LANCASTER.

Issue of October 24, 1861
       Married by J. B. Tolleson, Esq., on the 21st inst., Mr. Jefferson Varner to Miss
Tabitha Mathis, all of this District.

Issue of November 7, 1861
       Married on the 16th October by William H. Foster, Esq., Mr. Moses Turner to Miss
Nancy Nickols.
       Married on the 29th October by Rev. Hilliard Haynes, Mr. Norman McDowell to Miss
Margaret Chapman.
       Married on the 31st October by Rev. J. G. Landrum, Mr. C. H. McMillen to Miss Mary
Jane Dixon, all of Spartanburg District.
       Married at Summerville, S. C. on Tuesday evening, the 26th October by Rev. Geo.
Howe, D. D., Maj. T. Stobo Farrow of the 13th Regt S. C. V. to Miss Jane F., second
daughter of Col. Richmond S. Beden, of Colleton District, S. C.
       Married on the 6th October by John H. Walker, Esq., Mr. William H. Rhodes to Miss
Mary M. Allen, daughter of Rev. Jesse Allen, all of Spartanburg District.

Issue of January 2, 1862
       Married on the 15th, at the residence of Mr. O. H. Moss by Rev. J. G. Landrum, Miss
Juliet Moss of Spartanburg to Mr. B. F. Montgomery, of Texas.

Issue of February 6, 1862
       Married on the 25th inst., near Limestone Springs by C. P. Petty, Esq.,J. R. Blanton
to Miss Emily Cabaniss, both of Union District.

Issue of February 20, 1862
       Death of Mrs. Eliza Cleveland...late consort of Mr. J. B. Cleveland, departed this

life on Friday evening last [Feb. 14]...born Lincolnton, N. C., 3rd daughter of Dr.
James Bivings, her father being moved into this District about 1832...member of the
Methodist Church 20 years...leaves a husband and 4 children [long eulogy].

Issue of February 27, 1862
    Married on the 2nd February by Rev. Mr. Eaddy in McDowell Co., N. C. at the residence
of Mr. J. W. Patton, Mr. J. C. Moore of McDowell, to Miss A. Amanda Collins of Spartanburg.
    Married on the 2d February, by Reuben Briant, Esq., Mr. Benson Heron to Miss Jane
Mitchell, all of Spartanburg.
    [one death notice--torn]

Issue of March 6, 1862
    Died on the 27th ult., at the residence of his father, Mr. Woodward Allen, near
Cedar Springs, Mr. James Allen, aged 20 years...served full term at Sullivan's Island,
fought in the battle of Manassas Plains...member of Spartan Rifles, Capt. Walker, 5th
Regt. S. C. V.

Issue of March 20, 1862
    Mrs. Elizabeth Leonard, departed this life at her home in Spartanburg District, on
the 4th inst., in the 55th year of her age...in early life united with Nazareth Presbyterian Church until the organization of Antoich church, where she moved her membership...
She has one son and two sons-in-law in the service of the county...left 8 children and
6 grandchildren.

Issue of April 3, 1862
    Died at his lodgings in Richmond, Va., on the 21st February, Col. Thomas P. Butler,
aged 44 years...grandson of Gen. Butler...volunteer during Mexican War, but unlike his
uncle Pierce M. Butler, he denied "a place in that picture"...up to the time of his
death, he was a volunteer in Charleston company...when quite a young man, married Miss
Sarah L. Stone, granddaughter of the late Judge Gantt, who is now the widowed mother of
five children, their oldest son, A. Pickens Butler, not yet 21, is in the Confederate
Army.

Issue of May 15, 1862
    Death of Major J. D. Wright on Wednesday last...Jno. D. Wright departed this life
in Richmond Va., Quartermaster, 5th Regt. S. C. V...A devoted wife and children bemoan
this loss [long eulogy and account of service].

Issue of May 22, 1862
    Died on the 28th ult., near Crawfordsville, Mr. John R. Davis, aged 29 years, a
member of the Brockman Guard, 18th Regt., S. C. V....leaves a wife and infant babe....
His remains lie in the churchyard at Crawfordsville.
    Lt. Col. John M. Dean was killed, 5th April, at Shiloh.

Issue of June 5, 1862
    Married on Sunday morning, the 18th May, by Elias Wall, Esq., Mr. Thomas P. Griffin
to Miss Elizabeth Waldrops.
    Married by the same, on Sunday evening, the 1st June 1862, Mr. Rowland Briant to
Miss Elizabeth Briant, all of this District.

Issue of June 19, 1862
    The list of those killed from our District in the battle of Chicahomony or "The
Seven Pines" is: Martin J. Smith, J. J. Foster, T. W. Martin, George F. Houston, Capt.
J. Q. Carpenter, P. Bonner, R. H. Harris, M. Lipscomb, McDowell, and Wm. H. Bush.
    Captain J. Q. Carpenter from Limestone Springs, a native of Lincolnton, N. C.,
migrated here many years ago, married & here he lived previous to the War with Mexico.

Issue of June 26, 1862
    Died near Hurricane Shoals, on the 9th inst., John Ricmon Turner, infant son of
Jefferson P. and Hortensia Turner, aged 1 year, 9 months, and 14 days.
    Fell asleep in Jesus, on the 24th Many, at the residence of her father, Mr. Charles
W. Seignious, in Charleston, Mrs. Anne Eliza Mouzon, wife of Mr. H. J. Mouzon in the
28th year of her age...Scarcely a month before, laid her infant Charles Henry in the
grave.

Issue of July 17, 1862
    Death of Mr. Thomas C. Duncan...from the Battle of Ft. Sumter, went to Virginia, his
native state...graduated from Wofford College.
    The last of May 1862, George N. Hughston was killed, at the charge of Longstreet's

division...youngest son of Eliasha & Margaret Hughston, who reside at Hobbysville, S. C.

Departed this life on 22 May 1862, Elijah M. Cooper in the 39th year of his age... left a wife and seven children...member of the Baptist Church 13 years, d in Virginia of pneumonia in the Confederate service.

Died of fever in camp, on the coast, on the 1st inst., Robert Bullington, son of Wm and Mrs. Bullington...a member of Bethlehem Baptist Church.

A. Y. Wright, orderly sergeant of Capt. Todd's Co., 3rd S. C. V. died last January.

W. A. Woodruff, a private in Capt. Kennedy's Co., same regt, died of pneumonia.

Capt. Seaborn Mitchell Lanford, died on the 29th ult., at Richmond, 1st orderly sgt. of Capt. Kennedy's Co.

Issue of July 24, 1862

Samuel Wildes Miller, eldest son of Dr. J. P. and Mrs. A. Miller & grandson of the late Sheriff Samuel Miller, was born 20 May 1839 and feel in the great battle near Richmond, 30 June 1862...volunteered as a private in the "Spartan Rifles," Capt. J. Walker, 5th Regt. S. C. V., Col. Jenkins commanding...connected himself with the Presbyterian Church at Columbia...began study of law with his relative E. J. Arthur...[long account of his war service].

At the residence of Mrs. Greaner, Richmond, Va., Felix Walker died July 8, from Lock Jaw, resulting from a wound in the battle of Seven Pines.

Issue of July 31, 1862

Bethuel Phelps Hopkins, who fell in the battle before Richmond, was born in Springfield, Massachusetts, but for three years before his demise, a resident of Spartanburg... His mother and brothers, who reside in New York City, wrote to him to desert his southern home and return north, but he refused...member of Co. A., Capt. J. W. Goss (of Union), Palmetto Sharp Shooters...member of the Episcopal Church.

Death of Sgt. James Thomas Holt, aged about 19 years, member of Capt. J. Walkers Co. for 12 months, 5th Regt., S. C. V....member of the Methodist Episcopal Church...died 30th of last month.

Mr. Thomas Hammett died near Richmond, July 23 of Typhoid Fever, son of Mr. C. B. Hammett.

Issue of August 7, 1862

Death of Maj. Govan Mills...died at his mountain residence on Tuesday last. This evening (Thursday) at 4 P. M., interment will be at the family burying ground near our village.

Death of Dr. James J. Thornwell at Charlotte, N. C. 1 Aug at 12 m., in the 50th year...born 9 Dec 1812 in Marlboro District...in 1834, admitted to the pulpit of the Presbyterian Church and in 1835 became pastor at the Presbyterian Church in Lancasterville...[long obituary].

Died today about 3 P. M., aged 11 or 12 years[!], Martha second daughter of George Robuck, decd, & since marriage, Mrs. M. C. Bragg. Aug. 2, 1862.

Issue of August 14, 1862

J. Randolph Bush fell on 27 June before Richmond, son of Isaiah Bush from the vicinity of New Prospect, volunteered from Georgia.

Tribute of Respect to C. P. Petty, decd, from Limestone Springs Baptist Church.

Tribute of Respect to Pvt. Enoch Thomas, by Co. H., 1st Regt. S. C. V.

Mrs. Amanda H. McBride, daughter of Mr. Marcus & Elizabeth Kirby, departed this life 20 June 1862, aged 21 years, 7 months and 3 days. Her husband is a member of Capt. A. K. Smith's Co. Her babe William Adda, soon followed her mother to the tomb. She died 2 July, aged 2 years, 11 months and 16 days...member of the Methodist Church since 1858.

Died on 1 July at Adams' Run, Mr. James Thompson, aged 21 years...member of Capt. Sloans Co., Holcombe's Legion...buried at Oak Grove Church yard.

Issue of August 28, 1862

In Memoriam. Norman Bomar, son of Gen. A. C. Bomar. Norman was the first born, left early motherless, scarcely old enough to remember her whose maiden name he bears...died in the 21st year of his age...member of the Baptist Church at Mt. Zion, died July 26, 1862.

Zachariah Edward Bomar, son of Booker Bomar, fell in battle, Tuesday July 1...a resident of Mississippi some months before his enlistment.

Died near Richmond, Va., on the 29th June, William McDonald Patrick, aged 24 years, 1 month and 3 days...volunteer in Capt. McCorkle's Co., 12th Regt., S. C. V., wounded at battle of Gaines Hill.

Died Sunday, July 1, in the battle before Richmond, Cpl. J. D. C. Abernathy, Cross Anchor Volunteers, Co. D., 3d Regt, S. C. V.

Died at her father's residence in Spartanburg Distr., Elvira West, daughter of Isaac L. West, in her 19th year...joined the Baptist Church in 1860, died July 17, 1862.

Died in Spartanburg on the 21st inst., Clara Isabel, infant daughter of Mr. and Mrs. R. H. Chapman Jr., aged 1 year, 1 months and 20 days.

Died at Cedar Springs, Aug. 14, 1862, Horace, youngest son of Rev. N. P. and M. L. Walker, aged 3 years and 22 days...the widowed mother is called upon to bow to the hand of Provdence again.

Died at the residence of Mr. Wyatt Lipscomb, on 1 Aug inst., Mr. T. T. Wilkens, aged 29 years 6 months and 6 days...member of Capt. Boyd's Co., 16th Regt, S. C. V., left a wife, children and a widowed mother [eulogy].

Issue of September 4, 1862

Departed this life near Richmond, 1 August 1862, Mr. William W. Crocker, aged 19 years...member of Capt. A. K. Smith's Co., S. C. V. ...buried in Laurel Hill Church yard six miles east of Richmond.

John Miller died at his residence in this District on 20 August 1861[sic] in the 75th year of his age...member of Nazareth Church for 40 years.

Waddy Thompson, son of Henry and Eliza Thompson, of Spartanburg, S. C. born July 19, 1845, died June 30, 1862 from effects of the battle near Richmond June 29...remains buried in the village cemetery of Spartanburg, S. C.

West Bennet, son of James and Delila Bennett, departed this life May 26, 1862, in the 22d year of his age, member of 22d Regt, S. C. V....in his 21st year, joined the Baptist Church...an affectionate husband, and a tender father.

Berryman Bennett, son of James and Delila Bennett, departed this life May 29, 1862, in the 29th year of his age...member of 22d Regt, S. C. V....member of the Baptist Church.

Thursday morning, the 14th inst., Samuel James, eldest son of Mr. D. A. Chamblin, of this district, died aged 20 years...member of Capt. Brockman's Co., 13th Regt. S. C. V. (Col. Edwards). Woodruff's, August 16, 1862.

Married on the 31 August 1862, by J. B. Tolleson, at the house of the bride's father, Mr. John Gossett to Miss Mary Ann Sellars, all of this District.

Issue of September 11, 1862

Death of Dr. Jno. C. Oeland. Died of consumption at his residence in Spartanburg District, 7th August last. The deceased was a gentlemen of fine education. A native of this District, graduated from S. C. College in 1848 with honor. Professor of Reidsville Institution of this District. [eulogy].

Issue of September 25, 1862

Died of wounds received in the battlefield near Manassas, on Saturday, the 30th ult., Jas. G. Harris, Jr., aged 26 years the first of June last, b. June 1, 1839. Orderly Sergeant of Morgan Rifles under Capt. Jno. E. Bomar, Holcombe Legion. In Oct. 1854 joined the Baptist Church of this place, clerk of Mr. Landrum's church.

Sgt. Horace A. McSwain, son of Rev. W. A. McSwain of the S. C. Conference of the M. E. Church, South was born Dec. 9, 1843, commenced a literary course in Wofford College, Oct. 1858...member of Spartan rifles, Palmetto Sharp Shooters (S. C. V.) originally 1st Regt...fell mortally wounded 30th August 1862.

J. Belton Tolleson, son of Lt. Col. J. B. Tolleson, died of wounds received 30th August 1862 at the battle of Manassas...on the 13th inst., member of Capt. Bishops Co., Holcombe Legion.

Issue of October 16, 1862

Married on the 12th inst., in Spartanburg, S. C., by Rev. W. C. Kirkland, Mr. A. J. Nickerson to Miss Sophia C. Koch, all of Charleston, S. C.

Killed at the Battle of Manassas, 30th August, Francis Marian[sic] Wilder aged 24 years on 8 September last...member of Capt. Tucker's Co., 18th Regt. S. C. V....member of the Baptist Church at Cedar Shoals.

Capt. Henry Julius Smith, of Col. D., Hampton Legion, was wounded in the battle of Sharpsburg, buried at Shepherdstown, Va., Sunday 28th September...son of Whitefoord Smith, Esq., of Greenville & youngest surviving brother of the Rev. Dr. Whitefoord Smith of Wofford College...born in Charleston, S. C., October 4, 1832, and moved with his family to Greenvile in 1846...member of the Presbyterian Church.

Departed this life about 1 August at "Wayside Hospital" in this place, James A. Vehorn, son of John Vehorn, aged about 20 years...member of the Army of the Potomac.

Corp. T. Monroe Miles, son of Maj. W. H. and Rebecca Miles of this District, enlisted in Capt. F. M. Rucker's Co., 18th Regt S. C. V., killed in Manassas Plains, Aug 30, 1862.

Issue of October 30, 1862

William Leonidas Speack, a member of Co. F, 5th Alabama Regiment, fell in the battle of Gaines Mill, 27 June 1862 and died in an Alabama hospital 4 July following... son of the Rev. Henry Speack, of the N. C. Conference, M. E. Church.

Issue of November 13, 1862
Died at Warrenton, Virginia, on 26 Sept 1862, Sergt. W. R. Kendrick of Spartanburg District, S. C., member of Capt. Brockman's Co., Col. Edwards Regt...he was 19 years old on 6 September before his death...wounded at Manassas 29 Aug 1862...member of the Methodist Church at Zoah[sic].

Issue of November 20, 1862
Tribute of Respect to Capt. J. M. Martin, Sergeant J. H. Windle, T. T. Wilkens, and S. A. Shuford, by Spartan Lodge 70, A. F. M.

Issue of December 11, 1862
Brother Joseph P. Smith died November 5, 1862...born in Anson Co., N. C., but for some years past a resident of Spartanburg...member of the M. E. Church.

Sgt. Rufus J. Kennedy, son of Rev. John L. Kennedy, of Williamston, Anderson Dist., S. C. and member of Co. D, Capt.'H. Julius Smith, Hampton Legion, fell at Sharpsburg.

James Palmer, son of Jno. S. Palmer of Santee, Charleston District...entered the Sophomore Class of Wofford College in January 1857, in his 16th year...in 1860 went to Virginia University to study medicine...died at Manassas.

In Memoriam. Whitefoord Andrew Smith, only son of Rev. Dr. Whitefoord and Eliza C. Smith, was born in Wilmington, N. C. where his father was station on 23 July 1844....

Married in this place on Tuesday, the 18th ult., by Rev. A. Toomer Porter, H. Simton Ball to Rosana, daughter of the late Jonathan Lucas, all of Charleston.

Married on the 9th November, by Elias Wall, Esq., Mr. Noah Wolfe to Miss Lucinda Gilbert.

Married on the 23d November, by Elias Wall, Esq., Mr. L. D. Demsy to Miss Lucinda Sosbee.

Issue of December 18, 1862
Jesse W. Dye, aged 20 years, 6 months, and 17 days, son of Mr. William Dye, died of small pox near Richmond, about 1 December...[account of service given].

Issue of January 29, 1863
Tribute of Respect to James Wethersford and Mathew Cole who fell at Kinston, Sunday, Dec. 14, 1862, by Co. I, Holcombe Legion.

Married in the Baptist Church in this town, on Thursday evening, 25th December 1862, by Rev. Whitefoord Smith, D. D., Miss Lizzie E. M. Dean, eldest daughter of the late Maj. H. J. Dean of Spartanburg, to Dr. C. E. Fleming, Surgeon, C. S. A., formerly of Columbia.

Married in Greenville, S. C. on the 30th December 1862, by Rev. T. J. Earle, Capt. R. L. Bowden, 13th Regt, S. C. V. to Miss Mary C. Fleck.

Issue of February 12, 1863
Sergeant W. B. Wofford died at Richmond, the 26th ult., from a wound received at Fredericksburg...member of Capt. Young's Co K, 3d S. C. Regiment.

Issue of February 19, 1863
Tribute of Respect to Andrew T. Bowie by "Calhoun Literary Society," Wofford College.

Death of Lt. Henry K. Stevens of Confederate State Navy. Although in youth a resident of Florida, he was associated with South Carolina...killed 18th ultimo aboard the Steamer "Cotton"...born in State of Connecticut.

Died of consumption on the evening of the 8th inst., in Spartanburg Village, Mrs. Lou E. Williamson, wife of J. B. Williamson, and daughter of the late R. W. Porter, formerly of Asheville, N. C., inthe 3rd year of her age.

Issue of February 26, 1863
Hon. Edmund Rhett departed this life in our village, on Sabbath morning, the 15th inst....remains were carried to Columbia and interred.

Issue of March 12, 1863
Another Soldier Gone. Died on the 19th January, at his home in this district, John M. Griffin...member of Capt. Crockman's Co., 13th Regt, S. C. V....leaves a wife and three children.

Died at Richmond Va., on the 7th February 1863, Robert Daniel, in the 28th year of his age from a wound received at Fredericksburg...left a wife and two small children... member of the Baptist Church.

Issue of March 19, 1863
Married on the 8th March 1863, by R. Briant, Esq., Mr. John Harvey to Miss Joanna Reid, all of Spartanburg District.

Issue of March 26, 1863
    Married on the 1st March, by Wm. Moore, Esq., Dr. L. L. Smith to Miss Georgiana
Shipley.

Issue of April 2, 1863
    Married on Sunday, the 20th March, at the Methodist Episcopal Church, by Rev. Dr.
Whitefoord Smith, Lt. Edward J. Dean of 22d S. C. Regiment, to Miss Justina Walton,
eldest daughter of Peter Shand and Mary D. Smith, all of Spartanburg.

Issue of May 7, 1863
    Death of Col. A. Simpkins on Wednesday, the 29th ult., Editor of Edgefield Adver-
tiser and Senator in the State Legislature.
    William H. Barnett, son of Rev. M. C. and Nazareth Barnett of Cedar Spring, died a
Chimberago Hospital, on 7th April 1863 of typhoid fever, in the 24th year of his age...
at the opening of the war, he was in Georgia, teaching school [long account of service].

Issue of May 14, 1863
    Lt. E. J. Calbert, Co. C, 22d Regt. S. C. V., was a native of Spartanburg District,
killed at the battle of Boonsboro, Maryland, 14 September 1862...leaves a wife and
several children.
    Died on the 29th ult., at the residence of Mr. D. G. Harris, Mrs. Sallie Lies, aged
72 years...member of the Baptist Church at Cedar Springs 21 years.

Issue of June 4, 1863
    Wm. H. Lancaster, son of Rufus and N. C. Lancaster of Rich Hill, Spartanburg Dist.,
died at the General Hospital in Richmond, on the 26th January 1863 of wounds received
in the battle of Fredericksburg...in the 22nd year of his age...[long account of service
and eulogy].

Issue of June 11, 1863
    Died on Saturday, the 23d ult., at the residence of her parents, Ammie, infant daugh-
ter of W. H. and M. H. Ray, aged 4 months and 2 weeks.

Issue of June 18, 1863
    Married at the residence of Leonard Chapin, Esq., in Spartanburg District, on Wed.
evening, June 10, by Rev. A. M. Shipp, D. D., President of Wofford College, F. G. de
Fontaine, and Georgia W. Moore, of Charleston, S. C., daughter of Rev. G. W. Moore, of
the S. C. Conference.

Issue of June 25, 1863
    Col. Oliver E. Edwards died on Sunday morning last in Goldsboro, N. C. from wounds
received at the battle of Chancellorsville...body to be returned to this town.

Issue of July 2, 1863
    Married on Thursday, the 18th ult., by John Epton, Esq., Mr. Thomas Cooksey to Miss
Martha Patterson, all of this District.

Issue of July 9, 1863
    Death of John C. Holt, Co. K, Palmetto Sharp Shooters, Capt. John H. Blassingame...
the deceased was a native of this District and descendant of Mr. and Mrs. Hugh Holt of
our town...died of wounds received the 22d June by the accidental discharge of his gun
at Weldon, N. C....lived a brief time in Georgia, aged 22 years and 4 months...leaves
father, mother, and brothers and sisters.

Issue of July 30, 1863
    Killed at Gettysburg, Pa., Co. I, 13th S. C. V.: Andrew Kirby, Perry L. Smith,
Thomas Willis, James Bagwell, Eliphus R. Harmon.

Issue of August 6, 1863
    Died near Friendship Church in this District, 15 June 1863, Mrs. Elizabeth M. Smith,
wife of Richard B. Smith, and daughter of Randolph and Mary Vaughan, in the 33d year of
her age...the only immediate relations lefts are her husband and mother.
    Departed this life in Spartanburg District, 21 June 1863, Mrs. Frances C. Hoy,
consort of Maj. William Hoy and daughter of Mr. and Mrs. Alfred Dean. The next day her
infant followed her to the grave.

Issue of August 20, 1863
    In Memoriam. Privates S. J. Nesbit, A. S. Harvey, and Aaron Arnold of Capt.
Thos. Y. Simons Co., Charleston Battalion.

102

Issue of September 3, 1863
    A List of Killed and Wounded of Co. C., Holcombe Legion, since the war began to
August 1863. [gives name, type of wound, and battle in which wound was received.]

Issue of September 17, 1863
    Died on Tuesday morning, Sept. 8, 1863, Augustus Ramage, son of James H. and Alta
Wilson, aged 5 year, 8 months and 4 days.

Issue of October 1, 1863
    John W. White, son of Robert and Mary White was a native of Spartanburg District,
born February 27, 1832...in Oct. 1856, connected himself with the Baptist Church at
Cedar Springs...in 1857 he married Miss Mary Cooper, daughter of the late James W. and
Mary Cooper...13th Regt, Col. Edwards, Lt. in Capt. A. K. Smith's Co...died July 21...
[eulogy].

Issue of October 8, 1863
    Tribute of Respect to Lt. John R. Ford, who was killed at Gettysburg, July 1, 1863,
by "Rutherford Volunteers" Co. G., 16th N. C. Troops.

Issue of November 12, 1863
    Tribute of Respect to M. T. McKinny.
    Died at home, 15th September last, Mrs. Susan Walker, wife of the late Absalom
Walker, of this District, in the 76th year of her age...her death was produced from a
fractured arm...member of the Baptist Church about 15 years[sic]...first united herself
to Padget's Creek Church in Union District, until 1829 when she moved to the vicinity
of Cedar Spring Church & united with that church until the day of her death. [She was
the mother of William "Singing Billy" Walker, A. S. H., and daughter of Frederick Sr.
and Mary Greer Jackson.]
    Tribute of Respect to Lt. James B. Gardner (d. 9 Sept 1863); Pvt. W. G. Hawkins,
Pvt. N. Edwards; Pvt. Cannon Smith; Co. G. Charleston Battalion, Oct. 22, 1863.

Issue of November 26, 1863
    Died at Weldon, N. C., June 18, 1863, C. Columbus Bishop, in the 28th year of her
age...Co. D, Palmetto Sharp Shooters, Capt. Alfred Foster.

Issue of December 17, 1863
    Died of Typhoid Fever at Camp Hospital, near Lookout Mountain, Oct. 19, 1863, aged
21 years and 2 days, Maynard Cooper Layton of Spartanburg, S. C....born in Charleston
District, removed to Spartanburg in his 16th year & entered Wofford College...[eulogy].

Issue of January 28, 1864
    Married, January 10, 1864, by R. Briant, N. P., Mr. Adolphus Kirby to Miss Jane
Kirby, all of Spartanburg District.
    Death of Mrs. Jane Snoddy, 90 years of age...raised in this District and in early
life joined Nazareth Church...she was about 8 years of age at the time of the Revolution
and lost her father in that struggle, he being shot on Tiger.

Issue of February 4, 1864
    Married on the 19th ult., by Rev. J. J. Brantley, D. D., Mr. B. H. Lovelace, former-
ly of Spartanburg to Miss Sallie A. Dalrymple of Newberry, S. C.

Issue of February 11, 1864
    Richard Hix, Esq., died at his residence on Broad River about 10 days since...member
of the Baptist Church and belonged to the firm of Hicks and Simmons, merchants, Island
Ford. [See obituary in issue of February 25.]
    Married on the 3d inst., at her father's residence by Rev. J. G. Landrum, Mr. J. E.
Goodgion to Miss Kate C., daughter of Dr. W. G. Bennett, all of Spartanburg.
    Married on the 19th ult., by R. Bryant, N. P., Mr. Thomas J. Fowler of Union to Miss
Orpha Kennett of Spartanburg.

Issue of February 25, 1864
    Married on the 23d inst., by Rev. R. H. Reid, Lt. Crawford S. Thompson, 2d S. C.
Cavalry, to Miss Lizzie Morgan, eldest daughter of Samuel Morgan, Esq., all of this
District.
    Departed this life, on 29 January inst., at his residence on Island Ford, N. C.,
Capt. Richard H. Hicks, aged 49 years, 3 months and 2 days...leaves a wife, seven sons,
and one daughter...in 1838 commenced the mercantile business...in 1851, joined the
Baptist Church at Camp Creek...his eldest son just off to join the army.

Issue of March 10, 1864

Married on the 2d February last near Cross Anchor by John H. Walker, Esq., Mr.
Robert W. Bobo of C. S. A., 13th Regt. S. C. V., to Miss Laura A. Taylor, only daughter
of M. Taylor.

Issue of March 24, 1864
Mr. Oliver Clark died at his home in this District on the 8th instant, in the 66th
year of his age...member of the Presbyterian Church.
Departed this life on 3 February 1864, at the Confederate Hospital in Charleston,
S. C.(buried at Nazareth Church, Spartanburg District), Mr. John Alexander Brice,-eldest
son of D. M. and Mrs. M. C. Brice...member of Capt. Lord's Co., Charleston Battalion,
in the 19th year of his age.

Issue of April 14, 1864
Death of Judge J. N. Whitner occurred at his home in Anderson, on Thursday, the
31st ult....elder in the Presbyterian Church.
Sgt. James Rountree was wounded at Chickamauga, Sept. 20, 1863, and died at McClaws
Division Hospital, Sept. 24, aged 26 years...member of Blackstock Volunteers, now Co.
K, 3rd S. C. Regiment...joined the Baptist Church at age 19.

Issue of April 21, 1864
Married by R. Briant, Esq., at his own house, April 10, 1864, Mr. Charles Littlejohn to Miss Amanda Littlejohn.

Issue of May 5, 1864
Married on Sunday morning last, by Elias Wall, Esq., Mr. Charles Shilds to Miss
Emily Bishop, all of this District.
Died of a congestive chill near Richmond, Va., March 26, 1864, Elias B. Meadors,
son of Benjamin and Catherine Meadors, aged 27 years 8 months and 24 days. The fourth
and last one of the brothers which have all died immediately after going to Virginia...
member of Co. K, 1st Regt., Engineers...attached himself to Philadelphia Baptist Church
Nov. 15, 1860 [Pauline, S. C.]...an affectionate husband and kind father.

Issue of May 12, 1864
Married on Tuesday evening the 3d inst., by Rev. Washington Johnson at the residence
of the bride's father, Pvt. John T. Moman, of Washington Co., Kentucky, of Gen. Morgan's
command, to Miss Elizabeth J., fourth daughter of Mr. and Mrs. Matthew Moore, of Spartanburg District.

Issue of May 26, 1864
Capt. R. B. Seay died on the 15th inst., in battle field, a Lt. of Capt. Wm. Clark-
sons Co., 27th Regt, S. C. V.

Issue of June 2, 1864
Lt. James P. Lockwood was wounded at Spottsylvania Court House, on the 12th and died
at Gordonsville, on the 24th inst., 21 years old last October... acct of service.]
Married on the 19th inst., by J. B. Tolleson, Esq., at the bride's residence, Mr.
William A. Albrite of Virginia, to Miss Eliza Ann Miller, of Spartanburg District, S. C.
Died on the 25 April last, Mrs. Cassander Barnett, widow of J. B. Barnett, in the
63d year of her age...member of the Baptist Church for 40 years...the corpse was interred
in the grave yard at Bethel Church.

Issue of June 9, 1864
Married by R. Briant, N. P. on 25 May 1864, Mr. John Pucket to Miss Martha Ann
McBride, at the brides mothers.

Issue of June 30, 1864
Married at the brides residence on Thursday a. m., the 23d inst., by Reubin Bryant,
Esq., Mr. A. Reid, formerly of Greenville District, for three years a member of Earles
Battery, S. C. Coast, to Miss Altemira L. Petty.

Issue of July 7, 1864
Married on the 29 June 1864, by Rev. Jerry Lee, Mr. B. F. Hammett to Miss P. Willis,
only daughter of Wm. Willis, all of this District.
George Washington Bomar, son of Booker Bomar, departed this life on 7 March, in the
17th year of his age...a member of the Baptist Church. Also, James Vernon Bomar, son
of Booker Bomar, died on the 12th inst., in the 12th year of his age. Also, Eliza
Adella Hunter, daughter of Booker Bomar, died on the 19th inst., in the 3d year of her
age.

Issue of July 14, 1864
In Memoriam of Lt. Robert A. Snoddy who was killed 16 November 1864 near Knoxville, Tenn...born and raised in Spartanburg District, son of Capt. John Snoddy, decd...in the 24 year of his age.

Married by W. H. Bagwell, on the 24th June, G. W. C. Gossett to Miss Sarah McAbee, late of Spartanburg.

Married on the 12th inst., by J. C. Caldwell, Esq., Mr. W. A. Bryce to Miss Celia Jane Hawkins, all of this District.

Issue of July 21, 1864
Married on the 15th inst., by J. M. Elford, Esq., at Spartanburg Court House, Mr. B. F. Williams to Mrs. Missouri Humphreys, all of this District.

Issue of July 28, 1864
Married on the 19th inst., by Rev. Washington Johnson, Mr. W. W. Ralf to Miss Sallie Wakefield.

Married on the 24th inst., by J. C. Caldwell, Esq., W. A. Dobbins to Miss Levina Davis, all of this District.

In Memoriam...by Morgan Lodge, No. 19, I. O. O. F....J. D. Wright, died in Richmond, May 1852[sic]; Henry Theile killed at Seven Pines, 31 May 1862; J. H. Windell, Sgt. of Co. C. Holcombe Legion, died 1863; J. Belton Tolleson, died at Manassas, Nov. 1862; O. E. Edwards, died June 1863, at Goldsboro, N. C.; M. B. A. Legg, died at Charleston, Oct. 1863; J. M. Bost, Capt. Co. C., Holcombe Legion, died Stony Creek,Virginia, June 1864.

Issue of August 4, 1864
Departed this life on 11 July 1864, Margaret Barbara, infant daughter of Gen. J. W. Miller, aged 2 months and 4 days.

Tribute of Respect to W. P. Robuck, J. A. Compton, J. H. Wofford,W. Y. Wofford, (brothers), G. Simmons, and J. W. Bishop, Co. K., 3d S. C. Regiment.

Issue of August 11, 1864
Died of fever, 16 July last at Washington, N. C. Pvt. John Morris Padget of this District...aged 18 years, 50th N. C. Regiment, Capt. J. F. Eaves Co....buried at Providence Church, Rutherford Co., N. C.

Issue of August 18, 1864
John Pearson, Co. E. 14th S. C. V., fell in the Wilderness a few months ago.

Corp. J. N. Zimmerman, died in the battle of Spottsylvania C. H., May 12, 1864... Co. I, 13th R. C. Regiment.

Issue of August 25, 1864
In Memoriam. John Easterling Walker, oldest son of Rev. Charles Walker (S. C. Conference), born Oct. 13, 1842, killed near Petersburg, July 2, 1864...[eulogy].

Issue of September 8, 1864
In Memoriam, Andrew Soule Durant, who died at Jackson Hospital, Richmond, Va., 2 July 1864, in the 19th year of his age...3rd son of Rev. H. H. Durant of the S. C. Conference.

Married on the 4th inst., at Bivingsville, by W. H. Bagwell, Esq., Mr. G. W. Bates to Miss Elizabeth Harper.

Married by the same, Mr. Marcus M. Turner, to Miss Amanda Smith [no date].

Issue of September 22, 1864
Dr. James Jordan Vernon died on Sunday last at his residence in our town...graduated from Medical College at Philadelphia...member of the Presbyterian Church...in his 58th year. [see obituary, issue of October 13, 1864].

Married on the 20th inst., by J. M. Elford, Esq., Mr. Samuel Sumner to Miss Elizabeth Halford, all of Spartanburg District.

Issue of September 29, 1864
In Memoriam, Sgt. Lemuel Moorman, Co. C. 13th S. C. Regiment, killed at the battle of White Ravern, 16 August last...in the 23d year of his age...member of the Methodist Church...at the same time were killed Charles Baker and Howard S. Bobo.

Issue of October 13, 1864
Dr. James Jordan Vernon, born in North Tyger River, Spartanburg District, died 18th September 1864, in the 58th year of his age...descendant of one of the oldest families in our district. His grandfather Jordan, for whom he was named, was Judge of the county court...[full column obituary].

Married on the 9th inst., by J. M. Elford, Esq., Mr. W. Simpson Kirby to Miss Permelia Nolan, all of Spartanburg District.

Issue of October 27, 1864
    Death of Smith Patterson, son of Mrs. Leverton of our town...member of Co. K, Palmetto Sharp Shooters.

Issue of November 3, 1864
    Died at the residence of her mother in Spartanburg District, 8 October 1864, Platha Ann M. Dodd, 3rd daughter of William and Eliza Dodd.

Issue of November 10, 1864
    John W. Owens, killed on the 7th inst near Petersburg...associated with us in the printing office.
    Lt. Richard F. Ballenger fell at the battle of the Wilderness, Virginia, May 6, 1864 aged 26 years...second son of Wm. Ballenger, of Spartanburg District.

Issue of November 24, 1864
    Mr. Richard M. Smith of the lower part of this district, was murdered by a slave on Saturday morning last.

Issue of December 1, 1864
    Married by Rev. D. Scruggs, on 22 October, Mr. Wm. Ramsey to Miss Rebecca Greer, all of Spartanburg District.
    Married by the same on the 24th November, Mr. Isaac D. Milland of Rutherfordton, N. C. and Mrs. Lucenda Champion of Spartanburg, S. C.
    Tribute of Respect by Calhoun Lodge, No. 81, A. F. M. to J. W. Bobo, J. W. White, G. W. James, Wm. P. Lee, J. H. Mitchell and Wm. Bearden.

[No issues extant from 1865.]

ADDENDUM:
  Issue of April 17, 1851
    Mrs. Susanna Murphy, wife of Sion Murphy, of Union District, S. C., was found dead on the morning of the 12th inst., aged about 71 years.

THE CONSERVATIST

Issue of February 2, 1858 [Volume 1, #1]
    Married on the 24th December by Rev. Charles H. Bernheim, Dr. William T. McFall to
Miss Mary Ann, daughter of Jacob Singley, all of Newberry, S. C.

Issue of March 2, 1858
    Dr. E. L. Gunter, died at his residence on the evening of the 25th inst., left a fam-
ily and realtions.
    Mr. Ivy Dansby followed Dr. Gunter to the grave a short time intervening between
their deaths. Mr. Dansby was the father in law of A. E. Stoddard, who died a few weeks
ago.

Issue of March 9, 1858
    Obituary. Dr. E. L. Gunter died February 26 last, aged 31 years.

Issue of March 16, 1858
    Married on the 11th inst., by Josiah Stewart, Esq., Mr. Josephus Thomas, of Newberry,
to Miss Nancy Vines of Edgefield.

Issue of March 23, 1858
    Sudden Death. Dr. Adams, a drover from Kentucky, stopped at Carter's Hill, took ill
and died.

Issue of April 6, 1858
    Married on Thursday, April 1, by Rev. T. S. Boinst, Mr. William Buzzard, to Miss Cor-
nelia McCollum,all of this District.

Issue of May 4, 1858
    Married on Tuesday evening, the 27th ult., at the Baptist Church, by Rev. John J.
Brantly, J. M. Ward to Miss Helen O'Neal, all of this place.

Issue of June 1, 1858
    Married on the 18th ult. by the Rev. Mr. McLeod, Mr. Duffie Metts to Miss Sallie
Hargrove, all of this District.
    Married on the 26th ult., by the Rev. W. B. Johnston, Dr. John C. Caldwell of Newberry
C. H., to Miss E. D. Owen of Abbeville District.

Issue of June 15, 1858
    Obituary: Mrs. Fannie R. Hatton, daughter of Maxamillion and Sarah Sheppard, born
Newberry District, 2 Sept 1834, d. 20 April 1858...married to Capt. John W. Hatton, 12
October 1854, and moved to Sevier Co., Arkansas, where she lived until her death...joined
the Methodist Episcopal Church. [eulogy].

Issue of August 17, 1858
    Married on the 12th inst., at the res. of S. P. Kinard, by the Rev. C. McLeod, Andrew
Jackson Harris to Miss Laura E. Gauntt, all of Newberry.

Issue of August 31, 1858
    Obituary: Mrs. Ellen Gunter died on the 21st inst., leaving two children (the youngest
but a few days old)..[eulogy].

Issue of September 21, 1858
    Neville Pope, fourth son of the late Thomas H. Pope and Mrs. Harriet N. Pope of this
town, died on Sunday night last of congestive fever...14 or 15 years old.
    Married on the 16th inst., by the Rev. A. H. Lester, Mr. Russell W. Wiles of Orangeburg,
S. C. to Miss Sallie J. Hornsby of Richland District.

Issue of October 12, 1858
    Married on the 30th of September by Dr. J. D. Durham, Rev. John R. Proffitt, of East
Tennessee, to Miss Mary Calhoun, of Abbeville District.

Issue of October 26, 1858
    Died at Sherman Hill, Mississippi, July 14, 1858, Myla E. Eichelberger, daughter of
Wade S. and Fannie V. Eichelberger, aged 11 months and 27 days.
    Died on the 7th inst. at his residence in this district, Dr. D. C. Graham, in the 35th
year of his age.

Issue of November 2, 1858
    Married on Thursday evening, the 28th October, at the residence of Dr. T. B. Rutherford,

in Newberry District, by Rev. W. A. McSwain, Mr. Richard V. Gist of Union, to Miss Vinnie
Rutherford of Newberry.
Married on the 28th ult., by Rev. C. McLeod, Mr. P. H. Duckett to Miss Kate Brown,all
of this place.
Died in St. Helena Parish, La., on the morning of the 23rd of October, Micajah Harris,
in the 31st year of his age...born 15 April 1828, made a handsome fortune in California.
In 1856, returned to Newberry for a short visit...went to New Orleans and became a leading
member of Smith, Harris & Co.

Issue of November 16, 1858
Married on the 11th inst., by Rev. Mr. McCleod[sic], Mr. J. D. Hornsby to Miss Mary
Ann Blats, all of this place.

Issue of December 7, 1858
Married at Marrietta, Ga., on the 1st inst., by Rev. W. H. Roberts, Dr. D. R. Sartor
to Miss Mary Eleanor Dunn.

Issue of December 14, 1858
Married on the 2nd inst., by Burr J. Ramage, Esq., Mr. J. Mathis to Miss Martha A. M.,
daughter of Henry and Mrs. Caroline Summer, all of this District.

Issue of December 21, 1858
Married on the 16th inst., by Rev. J. L. Murphy, Mr. Joseph S. Reid to Miss C. D. Boyd,
all of this District.
Married on the 15th inst., by Rev. J. J. Brantly, Dr. R. S. Whaley to Miss Ann Moon,
all of this place.
Married by Rev. S. Bauknight, on the 9th inst., Mr. Wm Jennings, to Miss Mary, daughter
of Jesse Wise, all of Newberry District.
Died on the 12th inst., at the residence of Col. Sitgreaves, in this District, his wife
Mrs. Elizabeth Sitgreaves.

NEWBERRY SENTINEL

Issue of September 1, 1852
Died. Mrs. Phebe C. Williams, wife of Col. John C. Williams, at White Plains, Laurens
District, on the 28th July...native of Laurens District...educated at Salem, N. C.

Issue of October 11, 1854
Married on the 4th inst, by Rev. W. B. Telford, Mr. G. D. Smith of Newberry, to Miss
Susan M. Bragg of Salem, Alabama.

108

THE RISING SUN

<u>Issue of March 10, 1858</u>

Married on the 11th ult., by Rev. M. M. Boyd, Mr. William Henry to Miss Sophia Boozer, both of Newberry.

Married on the 27th ult., by Rev. T. Raysor, Mr. S. H. Tillery to Miss N. E. Lark, all of Newberry District.

Married on the 23rd of February, by Henry White, Esq., Mr. James H. Cunningham to Miss Margaret Williams, all of Spartanburg.

Married on Wednesday evening, the 24th of February, by Rev. Simpson Drummond, Mr. John S. Perry to Miss Sallie J. Walker, all of Spartanburgh District.

Married on the 25th of Feburary by Henry White, Esq., Mr. William Owens to Mary Pack, all of Spartanburg District.

Married on the 28th February by J. Bankston Davis, Esq., Mr. James McCarter to Miss Mary Jane Andrews, all of Spartanburg District.

Married on the 18th ult., by Rev. J. G. Landrum, Mr. Theron E. Montgomery and Miss Sarah, third daughter of Maj. William Ballinger, all of Spartanburg District.

Married on Thursday, the 25th of Feburary by Rev. D. Efird, Mr. D. Miller to Miss Mary Ann Stoudemire, all of Lexington District.

Married on the 25th February, by Rev. Joseph Filbert, Mr. E. F. Power to Miss J. C. Biles, all of Abbeville District.

Married on the 24th ult., by Rev. A. Rice, of Anderson, Dr. J. W. Thomas and Miss Mary M. Cheatham, both of Abbeville District.

Married on the 3rd inst., by D. W. Hawthorn, Esq., at the residence of Jas. Wier, Mr. Lorenzo Dow Wright to Miss Lucinda Burnett, all of Abbeville District.

Married on the 25th February by Rev. C. B. Betts, Mr. John T. Huey, of Abbeville District, to Miss Mary C. Bell of Fairfield District, S. C.

Married on the 23rd ultimo, at the residence of Joel S. Barnett, Esq., by Rev. J. G. Richards, Mr. Reece W. Workman to Miss Martha A. Barnett, all of Yorkville, S. C.

<u>Issue of March 17, 1858</u>

Married in the neighborhood of Mount Bethel, in Newberry District, on the 25th ult., by Rev. H. L. Murphy, Mr. Ossian Adams Rutherford and Miss Harriet Caldwell, eldest daughter of Joseph Caldwell, Esq.

Married on the 4th inst., by D. L. Wicker, Esq., Mr. George M. Boyd to Miss Mary Jane Thompson, all of Newberry District, S. C.

Married at Aberdeen Mississippi, on Thursday, the 18th ult., by Rev. Bishop Payne, Miss Celestia A., daughter of Gen. E. Strong of Aberdeen, and Dr. Burwell A. Duncan of Greenville, S. C.

Married on Thursday evening, the 4th inst., by Hon. Clark Aldridge, Mr. John G. Butler, formerly of Newberry District, S. C. and Miss Nancy H., daughter of Alfred Peterson, Esq., all of Russel Co., Ala.

Married on the 25th February last, by W. H. Bagwell, Esq., Mr. Lecel Lee to Miss Sarah Emily, daughter of W. W. Bagwell, all of Spartanburg District, S. C.

Married in Charleston, on the 3rd inst., by Rev. Mr. Denson, W. T. Russell, M. D. of Spartanburg, to Miss Mary E. Stevens of Charleston.

Married on Sunday, the 28th February, by A. Todd, Esq., Mr. Wm. H. Leverett to Miss Barbara Whitman, both of Anderson District.

Married by D. W. Hawthorn, Esq., on the 3rd inst., Miss Lucinda Burnette to Mr. L. D. Wright, all of Abbeville District.

Married on the 25th February by Rev. John Trapp, Mr. Porter _____ Brooklin, N. Y., _____, daughter of Capt. James Dorn of Edgefield District. [torn].

Married on the 2d inst., by Rev. A. J. Cauthen, in Lancaster District, E. A. Young of Camden and Miss Jane E. McDow of the former place.

Married on Wednesday evening, at the residence of her father, by Rev. T. Robertson, Mr. B. F. Brown to Miss Mary Knight, all of Laurens District.

Died at the residence of her mother, in the town of Newberry, on the 9th inst., Miss Jane Brown, daughter of Mrs. Rosa Brown...member of the Lutheran Church at Betheden.

<u>Issue of March 24, 1858</u>

Married on the 11th inst. by H. T. Thompson, Esq., Mr. Elijah Howard, and Miss Cornelia Batson, both of Greenville District.

Married on Thursday evening, the 11th inst., by Rev. J. M. H. Adams, Mr. J. M. Henderson of Mecklenburg County, N. C. and Miss Leonora Simril of Yorkville.

Married in Yorkville on the 23rd ult., by the Rev. J. M. H. Adams, Rev. William B. Corbett and Miss Lizzie, daughter of Col. I. D. Witherspoon.

Married at Elmwood Cottage on the 11th inst., by the Rev. Mr. Pickett, Dr. LaFaytte [sic] B. Wever, to Miss Mecca H. Miles, daughter of L. J. and M. S. Miles, all of Edgefield District.

Married on the 4th of March, by Rev. W. S. Black, Mr. W. R. Forsyth and Miss Polly Newton, all of Anderson District.

Death has again visited the house and family of J. B. Wilson of this District, and the wife of his youth has been called hence. Last summer, they lost one by one, three lovely daughters. Mrs. Wilson died on Sunday morning, the 14th inst., in the 43rd year of her age...member of the Methodist Church and a professor of religion.

Issue of March 31, 1858

Married on the 18th inst., by Prof. P. C. Edward, Mr. Thomas Wildman of Salford, Manchester, England, to Miss M. A. Murphy of Greenville C. H., S.C.

Married on the 18th inst., by Rev. G. W. Mullinax, Mr. William B. Gaines of Pickens District, to Miss Lucy A. M., daughter of Col. H. Hammond of Anderson District.

Married on Thursday, the 18th inst., by Rev. B. L. Beall, William W. Ross, Esq., and Mrs. Martha Boyd of Fishing Creek--near Lewisville.

Married on Tuesday, the 16th inst., by J. C. Humphries, Esq., Dr. Isaac Welch and Miss Louisa Dallas, all of Chester District.

Married on the 23rd inst., by Rev. T. Robertson, Mr. Robert Bryson to Miss Louisa Davis, all of Laurens.

Married on the 25th inst., by Rev. Y. Hawkins, Mr. Harrison Cannon to Miss Rosa, second daughter of Jacob Singley, all of Newberry District, S. C.

Died at his residence in Newberry District, S. C., on the 7th inst., Mr. Henry Metts, in the 76th year of his age...[eulogy].

Issue of April 7, 1858

Married on the 25th inst., by the Rev. A. Efird, Mr. David Crout of Lexington Dist., to Miss Lucinda E. Moore, of Newberry District.

Married on Thursday, the 1st April, by Rev. T. S. Boinest, Mr. Williamson Buzzard to Miss Cornelia McCollum, all of this District.

Married in Sumter, S. C., on the 18the January, by Amos Nettles, Esq., Mr. William S. Thames, to Miss Angelica Irean[sic], daughter of Mr. and Mrs. Jarrot Canty of Clarendon District, S. C.

Married on the 11th of February, by Rev. S. C. DeSchamps, Mr. John B. Gaymon to Miss Sarah, daughter of John Barwick, Esq., all of Clarendon, S. C.

Married on the 25th inst., by John C. Whitfield, Esq., Mr. Abner Hutchins of Pickens District, to Mrs. Nancy Johnson.

Married on Thursday, the 25th inst., by Rev. W. B. Boyd, Mr. Samuel Austin to Miss Mary Reed, all of Laurens.

Married on the 24th inst., by Rev. R. H. Reid, Dr. C. A. Saxon of Laurens, to Miss Martha A., daughter of Dr. Pinckney Miller, of Spartanburg District.

Married on the 18th inst., by J. B. Tolleson, Esq., Mr. John Kirby to Miss Susan Constant, all of Spartanburg District.

Issue of April 21, 1858

Married on Thursday, the 15th inst., by the Rev. W. A. McSwain, Mr. R. S. Bradley, to Miss Emeline Hatton, all of Laurens District.

Married on Thursday morning, the 15th inst., by the Rev. Mr. Montgomery, Gen. W. A. Hunt to Miss Susan McCaughrin, all of this place.

Married on Sunday the 5th inst., by M. B. Whittle, Esq., Mr. Abraham Powell, and Miss Henrietta Mitchell, all of Edgefield District.

Married on Tuesday evening, the 6th inst., by Rev. Edward Reed, Mr. Charles Douglas of Lownesboro, Ala., Miss Emma A., daughter of Mrs. Nancy Blocker, of Edgefield District.

Married on the 31st ult., by Wm S. Pickens, Esq., Mr. Isaiah Ford to Miss Emily Moore all of Anderson District.

Married on Tuesday evening at Trinity Church [Episcopal], Columbia, by the Rev. J. M. Pringle, Hugh S. Thompson, Esq., to Miss Lizzie A., second daughter of Col. T. B. Clarkson, all of Columbia.

Married in March last, by M. P. Evins, Esq., Capt. Dempsey Armstrong, to Miss Mary Mahaffy, all of Laurens District.

Issue of April 28, 1858

John H. Monroe died on the 6th inst., in the 29th year of his age.

Issue of May 5, 1858

Married on Lowndesville, on the 14th inst., by Rev. C. Murchison, Mr. J. W. Huckabee, to Miss Annie Mosely, all of Abbeville District.

Married on Tuesday evening, the 27th ult., at the Baptist Church by Rev. John J. Brantley, J. M. Ward to Miss Helen O'Neall Pope, all of this place.

Married on Thursday evening, the 22d inst., by Rev. Mr. Willis, Mr. James H. Arnold of Laurens District to Miss M. Pauline Ware of Greenville District.

110

Married on the 15th inst., by Rev. J. R. Meynardie, Thomas McCully, Esq., of Chesterville, S. C. to Miss Sallie A. M., daughter of Adam T. Walker, Esq., of Chester District, S. C.

Married on the 14th inst., by Rev. John Trapp, Mr. Wm. L. Stepens[sic], and Mrs. Zeline Smyly, all of Lexington District.

Married on the 18th inst., by John Quattlebum, Esq., Mr. Joseph Parkman and Mrs. Martha May, all of Edgefield District.

Married in Lexington District, on the 25th inst., by the Rev. A. Efird, Mr. William Hook to Miss Rebecca Roof, 2nd daughter of Mr. John Roof.

Issue of May 12, 1858

Married on Tuesday morning, the 4th inst., at 10 o'clock, by Rev. Thos. Raysor, Mr. Jno. Cannon, to Miss Sallie Lake, all of Newberry District.

Married on Thursday, the 22d inst., by Rev. Robt. McLees, Mr. W. H. Eddy to Miss Susan E. Hunter, all of Newberry District.

Married on the 29th inst., by Rev. D. L. Watley, Mr. H. A. Gray and Miss Martha Bryan, daughter of R. D. Bryan, Esq., all of Edgefield District.

Married on the 26th April, [by] M. M. Padgett, Esq., Mr. G. M. Spearman to Mrs. Eleanor Crowder, all of Edgefield District.

Married on the 29th April, by the Rev. A. Efird, Mr. Conford S. Sox, to Miss Sarah Ellen Baughman, all of Lexington District.

Issue of May 19, 1858

Married on Thursday, the 6th inst., by M. B. Whittle, Esq., Mr. William A. Jones to Miss Mealian Padgett, all of Edgefield.

Married on Tuesday evening, May 4, by Rev. Richard Furman, Mr. Thomas D. Long to Miss Susan Perry, both of Greenville.

Married on Tuesday evening, May 4, by Mr. Hawthron of Fairfield, to Miss Susan Foster, daughter of R. S. C. Foster, Esq., of Greenville. [groom's name not given].

Married on Sunday, the 2d inst., in Chester, by Wm. H. Anderson, Esq., Mr. George W. Lowe and Miss Margaret, daughter of J. A. Estes, Esq.

Married on the 13th inst., by the Rev. J. Hawkins, Dr. J. E. Brenan, to Miss Francis Cates, all of this District.

Died on Wednesday, the 12th inst., Mrs. Sophia Singley, aged 74 years.

Issue of May 26, 1858

Married on the 13th inst., by Rev. T.olaver Robertson, Mr. Achilis Dendy to Miss Mary Powel, all of Laurens.

Married on the 22d April, by the same, the Rev. Wm. B. Boyd, to Mrs. Lucinda Pain, all of Laurens.

Married at the residence of John S. Lorton, Esq., in Pendleton, on the 29th ult., by Rev. A. W. Ross, Mr. J. W. Livingston of Abbeville, to Miss Clara Kilpatrick, of the former place.

Issue of June 2, 1858

Married on the 25th ult., by Rev. James Peterson, Mr. Elihu Toland, of Tylersville, S. C., to Miss Linda Lowery of Edgefield.

Married on Sunday, the 16th ult., by M. M. Padgett, Esq., Mr. A. B. Watson and Miss Ellen Orender, eldest daughter of Mr. Isaac Orender, all of Edgefield District.

Married on the 18th ult., by Rev. J. G. Richardson, Mr. Daniel C. Williams, and Miss Mary, daughter of the late Wm May, Esq., all of York District.

Married on the 18th of May, by Rev. C. McLeod, Mr. McDuffie Metts to Miss Sallie C. Hargrove.

Married on the 26th ult., by Rev. Benjamin Johnson, Dr. John C. Caldwell of this place, to Miss Elleanor D. Owen, of Abbeville.

Issue of June 9, 1858

Married on the 23rd May, by Rev. E. Gaughman, Mr. J. Smith to Miss Mary, daughter of George Smith, all of Lexington District.

Married on the 27th May, by Rev. A. Efird, Mr. S. P. Wingard, Esq., Sheriff of Lexington District, to Miss Mary Ann Maria, daughter of Jacob Wingard, Esq., of Lexington.

Issue of June 16, 1858
Married on the 27th May by Rev. R. J. Edwards, Mr. Hammond T. Shuler, to Miss Colistia M. Wolfe, all of Orangeburg.
Married on the 4th of May, by Rev. Mr. Richbourg, Mr. Joseph Hammond to Miss Selina Smith, of Sumpter [sic], S. C.
Married on Sunday evening, the 13th inst., by Rev. Thos. Raysor, Dr. Bonds and Miss Ann Ruff, all of Newberry.
Obituary of Mrs. Fannie R. Hatton. [same as in issue of June 15, 1858, Conservatist].

Issue of June 23, 1858
Died in this village on the 14th inst., Ann P. Daughter of B. M. & E. V. Blease, aged 1 year and 11 days.

Issue of July 7, 1858
Married on the 5th July by Rev. A. D. Montgomery, the Rev. Robert McLees to Miss Susan E. Werts, daughter of the late William Werts, all of Newberry, S. C.

Issue of July 14, 1858
Died at his father's residence in this District, on 10 July, Walter Harrison Hentz, in his 20th year...member of St. Matthew's Evangelical Lutheran Church.

Issue of July 28, 1858
Married on Wednesday, the 21st inst, at the Morgan House, by the Rev. Mr. McCleod, Miss W. J. White of Vermont to Dr. L. L. Pollock, of South Carolina.

Issue of August 18, 1858
Died on the 3d inst., at Clinton, Louisiana, after an illness of some weeks, Mr. Thos. B. Harris...formerly a native of this district, but for the last few years had been residing in Louisiana.

Issue of September 1, 1858
Died on the afternoon of the 27th August 1858, Caroline Rebecca, infant daughter of Thomas W. and Sarah R. Boozer, aged three years and five days.

Issue of September 8, 1858
Departed this life, at his residence in the town of Newberry, Jacob Sligh Buzzard, aged 37 years...born 2 September 1821, died 2 September 1858.

Issue of September 29, 1858
Married on the 23rd September by Rev. M. M. Boyd, Dr. David A. Cannon to Miss Mary C. Herbert, all of this district.

Issue of October 6, 1858
Died in Edgefield District, S. C., on the morning of the 27th ult., James Cameron, Esq., leaving a widow and five children, three sons and two daughter...aged 60 years wanting 13 days.

Issue of October 27, 1858
Married on the 23rd inst., by Rev. Mr. Blakely, of Mississippi, Mr. T. D. Feaster of Alston, S. C. to Miss Mary Cribbison of Philadelphia, Pa.

Issue of November 3, 1858
Married on the 26th October, by the Rev. H. Herlong, Mr. M. Mitchell, of Edgefield and Miss Susan P. Scurry, of Newberry.
Married on the 27th October by the Rev. J. I. Bonner, Mr. John McMorries, of this District, to Miss Lizzy Hawthorn, of Abbeville District.
Married on the 28th October, by Rev. W. A. McSwain, Mr. Richard V. Gist of Union, to Miss Lavinia Rutherford of this District.
Married on the 28th ult., by Rev. C. McLeod, Mr. Patrick H. Duckett to Miss Kate Brown, of this district.
Died on the 20th October at his residence in this District, Mr. J. Reeder Sr., in the 83rd year of his age of Typhoid Fever.

Issue of November 17, 1858
Married on the 11th inst., by the Rev. Mr. McCleod, Mr. J. D. Hornsby to Miss Mary Ann Bista, all of this place.

Issue of December 8, 1858
Married on the 1st inst., by the Rev. W. H. Roberts, Dr. D. R. Sartor of Newberry District, to Miss Mary Eleanor Dunn of Marietta, Ga.

112

Married on Tuesday, December 2, by the Rev. C. Bernheim, Mr. C. B. Counts to Miss Eugenia Chapman, all of the Dutch Fork.

Died at Asheville, N. C., on the 20th ult., Mrs. Sallie E. Smith, consort of W. M. Smith, in the 22d year of her age...leaving two small children and a husband.

Issue of December 22, 1858

Married on the evening of the 16th, by the Rev. H. L. Murphy, Mr. J. S. Reid to Miss Dallas Boyd, all of this place.

Married on the 15th by the Rev. J. J. Brantly, Dr. R. Whaley to Miss Ann Moore, all of this place.

Issue of January 19, 1859

Married by James N. Crosson, Esq., on the 11th inst., near Mount Bethel, Mr. Jacob Wicker to Miss Polly McCullough, all of Newberry District.

Issue of January 26, 1859

Died in Newberry District, S. C., on Thursday night, the 20th inst., Mrs. Mary Boozer, wife of Adam Boozer, decd., in the 63rd year of her age...member of the Presbyterian Church at Smyrna.

Issue of February 2, 1859

Died at the residence of his grand mother, Mrs. Kincaid, Fairfield District, S. C., on the morning of the 12th of January, the anniversary of his bith, aged 17 years, Edward Kirkpatrick Anderson, second son and third child of E. A. Anderson, decd., of Charleston...returned from the Citadel, 29 July last, to his widowed mother, and died of consumption.

Issue of February 9, 1859

Married on Thursday the 3rd, by the Rev. H. L. Murphy, Mr. Jos. Caldwell to Miss Angelina, eldest daughter of Captain Turnipseed, all of this District.

Married in Glebe St. Church, Charleston, on the 2nd inst., by the Rev. J. L. Girardeau, Mr. R. L. McCaughrin of Newberry, to Miss Anna P., daughter of J. L. Kirkpatrick, D. D., of the former places.

Issue of February 23, 1859

Married on Wednesday, the 16th by the Rev. J. J. Brantly, Mr. E. H. Christian, to Miss Rebecca Sterling, all of this place.

Issue of March 16, 1859

Married on the 17th of February, by the Rev. Mr. Roland, Mr. John G. Morgan, of Newberry, to Miss Martha C. Love, of Clinton, Ga.

Dr. George M. Eichelberger, was next to the oldest son of George and Mahala Eichelberger, born Lexington District, S. C. 17 August 1829. The first elements of his education he received at the neighborhood school of St. John's, Broad River, and went to Lexington C. H. Academy. He entered South Carolina College in 1849 and graduated with honor in 1849...[mentions studied in Paris, Vienna, Philadelphia]...taking M. D. degree 31 March 1855. His father and brother purchased land in Scott County, Mississippi.... He died 28 February 1859 in Pilatka, Fla. Buried at family burial ground on Broad River ...funeral was at J. C. Hope's on 6 March. Rev. J. Moser officiated.

Issue of March 23, 1859

Married on the 17th inst., by Lewis Culbreath, Esq., Mr. Leonard Reams of Edgefield to Miss Julia F. Thomas, of Newberry.

Died at her residence in Fairfield District, S. C., on the 5th inst., Mrs. Elizabeth Kincaid, in the 69th year of her age.

Issue of April 6, 1859

Married on the 16th ult., at Inora, the residence of Albert Miot, Esq., Columbia Co., Fla., by the Rev. Basil Lanneau, Mr. Joseph David Miot of Columbia, to Miss Pamela E. Moore, of Newberry, S. C.

Issue of May 4, 1859

Married on Thursday, the 28th April, by Rev. Mr. McLeod, Mr. W. F. Beard of Helena, Newberry District, to Miss M. E. Hoit, of Laurens.

Mrs. Nannie E. Tillery was born Newberry District, Dec. 14, 1832, and died April 1, 1859...left husband, father, mother, sister and three brothers.

Issue of May 18, 1859

Married on the 10th ultimo, by the Rev. H. L. Murphy, Mr. D. M. H. Langston of Clinton to Miss L. E. Cannon of Glymphville, Newberry District, S. C.

Issue of June 8, 1859
Died in Newberry District, S. C. on the 16th of May, Harriet Narcissa, infant daughter of Dr. C. H. and M. Sondley, aged 11 months and 10 days.

Issue of June 15, 1859
Married on Thursday last [June 9], by 'Squire Knotts, Miss Letitia Domas to Mr. Daniel Montgomery.

Issue of June 22, 1859
We regret to chronicle the death of one of our apprentices Marcus Henry Barger...he has been with us for three years.

Issue of July 6, 1859
Deceased on the 11th of June, at the residence of her husband in Newberry District, Mrs. W. K. Knight...member of the Lutheran Church...left two children, one a year and 3 months old and an infant of three months. The infant has died; it survived her but two weeks.

Issue of July 13, 1859
Capt. Robert Cunningham died at his residence, Rosemont, Laurens District, on the 7th inst., in the 73d year of his age. His name is associated with the War of 1812.

Issue of July 20, 1859
Death of Col. Z. A. Herndon...died at Glenn Springs, on the 12th inst., in the 68th year of his age...he had but a short time removed from Union to Columbia.
Mrs. Hannah Frean, wife of Rev. Thomas Frean, of the City of Columbia, died at the house of her husband, on Wednesday, the 29th of June last, daughter of Mathias Elmore and wife Rebecca Kelly. born 25 Oct 1795, died in the 64th year...born and riased near Friends' Meeting House on Bush River. Her remains were conveyed to Friends Burying Ground and placed near the children who were buried in '55 and '58. She was the mother of 8 children, two now survive...the youngest child William H., died of measles....She left her husband, Rev. Thomas Frean, two daughters Bridget Honora Waldrup, wife of Wilson W. Waldrup, of Newberry District, and Abigail, the wife of John P. Southern, Esq., of Columbia, and three grandchildren; Thomas Frean Harmon; Sarah, wife of Middleton M. Kinard, of Newberry and Sarah Belton of Columbia.
Departed this life at Vaughansville, Newberry District, July 7, 1859, Mrs. Mary T. Vaughan, wife of the Rev. J. C. Vaughan, in the 47th year of her age. The disease which terminated her existence was cancer...for many years a member of the Baptist Church.

Issue of July 27, 1859
Died July 19th, 1859, Martha A., consort of Thomas F. Paysinger, daughter of the late Michael Werts, in the 18th year of her age...joined the Evan. Lutheran Church in 1857...funeral discourse delivered in Mt. Zion Baptist Church.

Issue of August 10, 1859
Married on Sunday, the 7th inst., at the residence ofMr. D. T. Vaughan, Esq., Newberry District, by the Rev. I.C. Vaughan, Dr. Calvin C. Higgins, of Laurens District, to Miss Mary E. Crawford of Edgefield Village.

Issue of August 31, 1859
Departed this life, August 8, 1859, at the residence of Col. S. St. George Rogers, Ocala, Marion Co., Fla., Mrs. Rachel Johnson, consort of James h. Johnson, Esq...married to Mr. Johnson in January last...member of the Lutheran Church...left a son Freddie, a child by a former marriage.

Issue of September 7, 1859
Died on the 12th inst., Rachel Welch, infant daughter of James H. and Rachel N. Johnson, aged 4 days.
Died in this District, Aug. 22, 1859, Pettis Ward Wilson, son of Jas. B. Wilson, aged 6 years and 9 months and 1 day.

Issue of September 14, 1859
William B., eldest son of Burr J. Ramage, Esq., died at his father's residence in this town, on Wednesday, the 7th inst., in the 13th year of his age.
Abbie Southern, infant daughter of Thomas F. and Mary Harman, died on the 6th inst., aged 1 year, 3 months, and 20 days.

Issue of September 28, 1859
Married on Wednesday evening, the 7th inst., by Rev. W. P. Counts, at Capt. H. Dickert's, Mr. W. Long to Miss Sarah Dickert, all of Newberry District.

Married on the 13th inst., by Rev. Tolaver Robertson, Mr. Henry L. Fuller of Newberry, to Miss Jennie Casey, of Laurens.

Died on Tuesday, the 13th inst., of Croup, James M. infant son of C. W. and Virginia Lindsay, aged 2 years and nearly 6 months.

Issue of October 12, 1859

Died on the 15th inst., at the residence of her father, Mr. Hopkins Williams, in Newberry District, Mrs. Bettie Caldwell, wife of Maj. S. T. H. Williams, in the 26th year of her age...member of the Presbyterian Church at Laurens C. H.

Issue of October 19, 1859

Ebenezer L. Moore, principal over the St. Matthews Academy in this district over 5 years, died at the residence of J. H. Suber, in the 28th year of his age...left behind a father, mother, brothers and sisters [long eulogy].

Died on Thursday, the 13th inst., at his residence in Laurens District, John Suber, in the 63d year of his age [long eulogy].

Issue of November 9, 1859

Married on the 3d inst., at the residence of Mr. Mark Hawkins, in this District, by the Rev. A. Efird, of Lexington District, Mr. A. P. Dominick to Miss E. L. Shealey, of this District.

Married on Wednesday, the 28th ult., by Rev. Mr. Boyns, Mr. Wm. Koon to Miss A. E. C. Riddle, all of Lexington District.

Issue of November 16, 1859

Married on the 10th, by Rev. H. L. Murphy, Dr. Thompson Wilson to Miss Lydia Johnson, all of this District.

Issue of November 23, 1859

Married in Newberry District, on Wednesday the 16th inst., by Rev. M. A. McKibben, Mr. Junius J. Neville, of Charleston, S. C. to Miss Malvina J. Sharpe, of Anderson, S. C.

Married on the 17th inst., at the residence of Mr. James Caldwell, by the Rev. Robert McLees, Mr. Lemuel H. M. Boozer to Miss Rosannah E. Wilson, all of Newberry, S. C.

Died in Newberry District, on Wednesday last [Nov. 16], of Croup, Dorothy Eustacia Antoinette, daughter of Thomas and Dorothy Chalmers, aged 3 years, 4 months, 17 days.

Issue of November 30, 1859

Died at the residence of his father in law, Jacob S. Long, in this district, on the 22d inst., at 10 minutes past 1 o'clock a. m., Dr. J. L. Hall, only son and child of Matthew and Polly Hall, in the 27th year of his age...left father, mother, wife and one child...member of Seceder Church.

Issue of December 7, 1859

Departed this life on the 19th ult., Mrs. Christian Dickert, consort of George A. Dickert, aged 38 years, 4 months, and 25 days...lefts 5 sons, 2 daughters, and a husband ...member of the Lutheran Church.

Issue of December 21, 1859

Married on the 13th December by Rev. T. Hawkins, Mr. John Calvin Swittenberg of Trenton, Miss., and Miss Harriet Kinard of Pomaria, S. C.

By the same, on the 14th December, DR. James McH. Ruff and Miss Elvira Lavinia Suber, all of Newberry, S. C.

Died at his residence in this District, on the 13th inst., after an illness of 51 days, Col. John Glen, aged 84 years and 11 days.

Issue of February 1, 1860

Departed this life on the 28th ultimo, in the 15th month of her age, Sallie Allene, youngest child of Thomas F. and Caroline Greneker.

Issue of February 8, 1860

Married in Columbia, on Thursday the 2d inst., by Rev. J. J. Brantly, D. D., P. A. Eichelberger Esq., of Newberry, to Miss Margaret Hobbs of Edgefield District.

Dr. John Edwards Bobo departed this life on Saturday morning, the 4th inst., at 11 o'clock at his residence after 10 days illness of Pneumonia.

Issue of February 15, 1860

Married on the 9th inst., by Burr J. Ramage, Wm. P. Harriss to Miss Mary, daughter of Mr. John Levingston, all of this district.

Issue of February 22, 1860

Robert Caldwell died at his residence, four miles north of Newberry, on the night of the 17th inst...born 8 September 1781 (the day of the battle of Eutaw), he was therefore in his 79th year of his age...lived all his life in the Black Jack region of Newberry... belonged to the Reformed Presbyterian Church.

Married on the 9th inst., by Rev. Daniel Efird, Mr. Wilson Dickert of Newberry to Miss Elizabeth Epting of Lexington.

Married by Rev. A. B. Stephens, on the 14th inst., in Orange Parish, at the residence of the bride, Mr. Jno. L. Carroll of Central House, Columbia, and Mrs. Sarah E. Culler.

Issue of February 29, 1860

Married on the 21st inst., by Rev. N. M. Boyd, Mr. Robert Whitesides of Yorkville, to Miss Mary Schumpert of Newberry.

Issue of March 7, 1860

Married on the 28th February by Rev. D. Efird, Mr. Richard Epting of Lexington, to Miss Mary A. Setzler of Newberry.

Married on the 22d ultimo by the Rev. A. D. Montgomery, Mr. Henry D. Boozer of Newberry, to Miss L. W. Anderson of Waterloo, Laurens District, S. C.

Issue of March 21, 1860

Married on the 8th of March by Henry Metts, Mr. Solomon Dowel to Miss Nancy Rister, all of Lexington District.

Died in Newberry, at the residence of Dr. P. B. Ruff, the father of the decd., on the 15th inst., Mrs. Mary A. Kinard, consort of John M. Kinard, Dsq....born March 31, 1839, joined the M. E. Church in 1854, and was converted to God in 1858 [long eulogy].

Issue of April 4, 1860

Married on the 22d March, by Rev. M. M. Boyd, Mr. James Waldrop to Miss Elliott Sterling, all of Newberry.

Married on the 29th of March, by Rev. M. M. Boyd, Dr. J. W. Spearman to Miss S. A. Stephens, all of Newberry.

Issue of April 18, 1860

Died at his father's residence in this District, on the 9th ultimo, Hosea Anderson Johnson, son of David V. and Sarah Johnston, in the 17th year of his age...experienced converting grave at a revival at Bush River Church last September.

Issue of April 25, 1860

Maria Elizabeth Pasinger was born Jan. 3, 1755, and died April 15, 1860, aged 95 years, 3 months, and 12 days...had eight children, 4 of whom are deceased...at the day of her death she had 49 grandchildren and 125 great- grandchildren.

J. W. B. Long departed this life 20th March 1860, at the residence of his uncle in Newberry District, S. C., aged 17 years, 5 months, and 10 days...was baptised at Bethel Baptist Church, Newberry District, by Elder A. W. Asbill, 30 July 1857. Saluda Mills, S. C. March 24.

Issue of May 2, 1860

Died on the 6th ultimo, at the residence of Dr. W. J. Bobo, in Panola Co., Miss., James Law Brown, M. C. only surviving son of Samuel and Margaret Brown, born March 1826 at Long Lane, the family residence in Newberry District, S. C....married first to Miss Rebecca, daughter of Dr. G. W. Glenn, who died Nov. 1853, and by whom he left two surviving children, Richard and Glenn. His second marriage with Miss Anne, eldest daughter of Dr. W. J. Bobo, of Union District, S. C., occurred in May 1855. By this marriage he leaves a son and a daughter...a sister, Mrs. Dr. T. B. Kennerly, of Newberry District, S. C....in 1854 connected himself with the Presbyterian Church at Newberry C. H. [eulogy] Panola Co., Miss., March 12, 1860.

Issue of May 9, 1860

Married on the 6th inst., by Rev. J. L. Smithdeal, Mr. Levi Amick to Miss Sarah Stockman, all of Newberry District.

Issue of May 16, 1860

Died after an illness of four days of Palsy, Mrs. Catherine Taylor, wife of J. B. Taylor of this place, aged 46 years, 9 months, and 8 days [date of death not given].

Issue of May 23, 1860

Married on the 17th inst., by Rev. J. J. Brantley, James M. Baxter, Esq., to Miss Fannie C. Nance, daughter of Drayton Nance, decd, all of Newberry.

Issue of May 30, 1860

Died at his residence in Laurens District, of typhoid dysentery, on the 26th inst., Mr. George Metts, in the 69th year of his age...consistent member and elder of Liberty Hill Evangelical Lutheran Church...buried at Shady Grove, in Laurens, funeral preached by Rev. Jacob Hawkins.

Issue of June 6, 1860

Married on the 8th of May, by E. P. Lake, Esq., Mr. J. Rolison to Miss Helen Burnham, all of Newberry District.

Died of apoplexy, on the evening of the 26th inst., at the residence of his uncle, Thos. F. Harmon, in Newberry District, Thomas Harmon, son of William P. and Sarah Harman ...about 11 years of age.

Issue of June 20, 1860

Married on Thursday evening, the 14th inst., at the residence of Dr. R. D. Griffin, in Edgefield District, by the Rev. J. J. Brantly, Mr. R. H. Land to Miss Bettie R. Griffin.

Issue of June 27, 1860

Departed this life at the residence of her father, Mr. Landon Waters, on the 9th inst., after a protracted illness, Mrs. S. M. Smith, of Newberry village, consort of Mr. Geo. D. Smith, in the 31st year of her age...leaves three daughters and a husband [long eulogy].

Issue of July 4, 1860

Departed this life, at the residence of her brother, Jas. Y. Harris, Miss Eleanora Francis Harriss, in the 20th year of her age...member of the Lutheran Church [date of death not given].

Issue of July 11, 1860

Married on Sunday evening, the 8th inst., by C. W. Montgomerty, Esq., Mr. Sullivan Herbert to Miss Nelly Bone, of Newberry.

Lavinia A. E., wife of Col. R. C. Maffett, and daughter of N. G. & E. Gallman is no more...leaves one daughter 4 years old...died July 5, at 3 o'clock in the 25th year of her age.

Issue of July 18, 1860

James Witherspoon Wardlaw, an accomplished gentleman and ripe scholar, died in Columbia recently.

Issue of August 1, 1860

Died of a congestive chill, on the morning of the 18th inst., at the residence of her aunt in Laurens District, Virginia C. Watts, daughter of Braxton and Harriet Watts, in the 18th year of her age...left a mother and six sisters...[eulogy].

Issue of August 22, 1860

Died in Newberry District, August 15, 1860, of Tabes Mesenteria, Jacob Abram Suber, the only child of Jacob and Hannah T. Suber, aged 2 years, 4 months, and 1 day.

Issue of September 5, 1860

Married on the 23rd of August, by Rev. J. L. Smithdeal, Mr. R. Calvin Boozer to Miss Rhoda Lester, all of this district.

Died on September 1, in Newberry District, Mr. Jacob Suber, in the 50th year of his age...an efficient elder in St. Matthews Ev. Lutheran Church.

Issue of September 19, 1860

Died in Ocala, Fla., Sept. 1, 1860, Thomas P., son of Daniel & S. A. Cappleman, aged 11 years, 7 months, and 22 days.

Issue of September 26, 1860

Married on the 1st instant, by Rev. J. H. Bailey, Mr. John B. Simpson, and Miss Elizabeth Cook, daughter of John Cook, Esq., all of this District.

Married on the 3rd instant, by Rev. J. H. Bailey, David W. Boozer to Miss Rebecca Hawkins, daughter of Mark Hawkins, of this district.

Married in this town by 'Squire C. W. Montgomery, Mr. Charles Clem of Newberry, to Mrs. Caroline Haw, of Greenwood.

Issue of October 17, 1860

Married on the 11th inst., by E. P. Lake, Esq., Mr. W. H. Knight to Mrs. Laura E. Gore, all of this District.

Departed this life on the morning of the 4th inst., in Newberry, Beulah Relief, youngest daughter of Mrs. Elizabeth A: Rice of Charleston...just attained her 12th year.

Issue of November 7, 1860
Married by Rev. M. M. Boyd, on the 18th of October, Mr. Thomas H. Adams, to Miss Eliza F. Kelly, all of Newberry.
By the same, on the 1st inst., Mr. John D. Taylor, to Miss Eve E. Coulter, all of Newberry.

Issue of November 14, 1860
Married by Rev. Wm. Hill, on the 1st inst., the Rev. J. C. Vaughan of Newberry District, to Mrs. Ursula Smith of Laurens District. The said Mrs. Smith was married by J. C. Vaughan to Wm. R. Smith on 9 October 1850 and baptised by the same 22 Oct·1853.
Died in Newberry District, on the 8th November, 1860, Joel Thomas, infant son of W. T. and Mary R. Wright, aged 12 days.
Died at the residence of her mother near Pomaria, Mrs. M. M. Elizabeth Folk, wife of Levi Folk, Esq., daughter of the late Col. Wm. Counts, aged 29 years and 24 days...six weeks ago returned from her home, in Macon Co., Ga., to visit and was taken sick...[long eulogy].

Issue of November 28, 1860
Married on the 19th inst., by Rev. J. M. C. Breaker, W. H. Jones of Newberry, to Miss M. J. Pope of Columbia, S. C.
Married by Rev. J. L. Smithdeal on the 20th inst., Mr. S. Olander Hartman to Miss S. Jane, daughter of David Rikard, all of this Distict.
Died on the 13th inst., at the residence of Capt. Jacob Wheeler, of Newberry District, Mr. Stephen Bowers, in the 93d year of his age...a member of the Ev. Lutheran Church. J. L. Smithdeal.

Issue of December 5, 1860
Married on the 29th inst., by Rev. J. L. Smithdeal, Mr. Henry S. Boozer of Frog Level, Newberry District, S. C. to Miss Mary J. Young, of Newberry District, S. C.

Issue of December 12, 1860
Died at his residence in Newberry District on the 4th of December, Mr. Charles L. Sligh, in the 51st year of his age.

Issue of December 19, 1860
Married by Rev. Robert McLees, on Wednesday evening, the 12th December, at the home of the bride's mother, Mr. Leonidas K. Glasgow, of Newberry, to Miss Susan H. Hillhouse, of Newberry.
Died in Mushulaville, Miss., on the morning of the 4th November, 1860, Mrs. Margaret consort of M. M. Higgins, aged 49 years...born and raised in Edgefield District, from the time of her marriage until November 1856, when she her husband, and most of their children moved to Noxubee Co., Miss, where she remained until her death...member of the M. E. Church 14 years.

Issue of December 26, 1860
Married on the 19th inst., by Rev. Dr. Brown, Col. T. P. Slider (bachelor of the Sun) to Miss Ellen Ring, of Newberry.
Married on the 5th inst., by Rev. M. M. Boyd, Mr. Langdon Moore to Miss Rachel A. Counts, all of Newberry.
Married Dec. ____, at Helena, by Rev. Mr. May(fi)eld, Mr. A. Skillman of Winsboro, to Miss Mary Davis of Newberry.

Issue of January 8, 1861
Married near Pomaria, on the 26th ult., by Rev. Dr. Efird, Mr. John Wm. Summer to Miss Elvina Epting.
Married on the 20th ultimo near Pomaria, Mr. John Summers and Miss Sarah Hipp, both of Newberry District.
Married on the 27th ult., Mr. Nathan Hipp and Miss ___ Jones, both of this District.
Married on the 27th December, by Rev. M. M. Boyd, Rev. Wm. B. Currie of S. C. Conference, to Miss Martha Glymph of Newberry.
Married on the 23d ult., by Rev. S. Dunwoody, Mr. J. A. Enlow to Miss E. C. Enlow, all of this District.
Died at his residence in Newberry District, December 5, 1860, Lemuel Glymph, aged 65 years 11 months...member of the M. E. Church 30 years, class leader of New Hope Church, Newberry circuit.

Issue of January 16, 1861

Friends and acquaintances of Mr. Thos. F. Greneker & Mrs. Mary C. Greneker are invited to attend the funeral services of the latter at the Methodist Church, this afternoon (Wed.) at 3 o'clock.

Married on the 8th inst., by Rev. J. J. Brantley, Mr. J. B. Hodges of Edgefield, to Miss Sallie Brown of Newberry.

Mrs. Lou C. Floyd, wife of J. N. B. Floyd and daughter of Moses and Evaline M. Anderson, died January 4, 1861, leaving a little babe, brother and two sisters.

Issue of January 23, 1861

Married on the 10th inst., by Rev. T. S. Boinest, Mr. D. F. Rikard to Miss T. C. Barre, both of Newberry.

Departed this life on the morning of the 14th inst., Mrs. Mary Caroline Greneker, in the 26th year of her age...leaves a husband, an only daughter, a sister and a brother [long eulogy].

Issue of January 30, 1861

Married by Rev. Robert McLees, on the 24th inst., at the house of the bride's father, Mr. John H. Copeland to Miss Martha T. Phiney, all of Laurens, S. C.

Died in the town of Coala, Fla., on the 9th January 1861, Mrs. Sarah A. Cappleman, wife of Daniel B. Cappleman, Sheriff of this county, in the 38th year of her age...born in Newberry District, where she lived until the removal of her husband to Florida... jointed the Presbyterian Church at about 14 years of age.

Issue of February 13, 1861

Mary Anna Walker, daughter of H. H. and Mrs. L. C. Kinard, born Dec. 11, 1853, died Jan. 8, 1861.

Married on the 8th ult., by R. W. Clary, Mr. William Kelly to Miss M. E. Geans, all of Newberry.

Issue of February 27, 1861

Married on the 14th inst., by Rev. M. M. Boyd, Mr. Samuel Wood to Miss Glymph, all of Newberry.

Issue of March 13, 1861

Married on the 28th ult., at the bride's father's near Pomaria, Mr. W. W. Koon to Miss Mary Feagle, both of Newberry district.

Departed this life on the evening of the 7th inst., Susan Emma, youngest daughter of Solomon P. and Susan Kinard, aged 2 years and 1 month.

RISING SUN [apparently a new series]

Issue of May 11, 1864

Death of Col. James Drayton Nance...of 3rd Regt, SCV was killed in a recent battle in Virginia [eulogy].

Issue of March 10, 1865

Married on the 14th ult., by Rev. Prof. J. P. Smeltzer, Mr. Samuel Sieg to Miss Amanda Elizabeth Epting, all of Newberry District.

Married on the 2d ult., by Rev. H. L. Murphy, Dr. W. A. Williams to Miss Sallie C. Montgomery, all of Newberry, S. C.

THE LEXINGTON TELEGRAPH

Issue of 11 March 1856
Departed this life at his residence in this District, Capt. Martin Caughman, aged 58 years, 4 months, and 20 days...consistent member of the E. L. [Evangelical Lutheran] Church 48 years or more...left a wife and 11 children.

S. C. TEMPERANCE STANDARD

Issue of July 1, 1854 [Volume 1, #1]
Mr. John Frey was killed in Columbia on Tuesday last (accidental death).

Issue of July 29, 1854
Departed this life at the residence of his father in Lexington Dist., on the 14th inst., of bilious fever, John Q. A. Seay, aged 24 years...member of the Lutheran Church.

Issue of November 18, 1854
Brother Thomas J. Warren, Editor of the Camden Journal, and Miss Maria Louisa, daughter of Robert A. Maxwell, Esq., of Pendleton, S. C. were married on the 6th inst.

Issue of March 10, 1855
Married on Thursday, the 1st inst., by Rev. Jesse Lowman, Mr. James Bouknight of Florida, to Miss Maria Smith of Lexington Dist.
Married on the 18th February, at the residence of Samuel Metz, by Squire Levi Metz, Mr. Noah Metz to Miss Sarah Metz, all of Red STreak, Lexington Dist.
Died at his residence in Lexington Dist., on Monday, 5 February 1855, William Geiger, Sen., aged 81 years, 6 months, 10 days.
Died at his residence in Lexington Dist., on the 14th February 1855, Mr. Abraham King, aged 58 years, 11 months, 16 days.

Issue of April 7, 1855
Married on the 20th inst., by J. I. Chaney, Esq., Mr. Lewis Barrs and Miss Barbara E. Williams, all of this District.
Died at her residence in Lexington Dist., on 24th March 1855, Mrs. Sophia Leaphart, aged 66 years, 1 month and 17 days.

Issue of January 13, 1855
Married on the 27th December by Francis Kennada, Esq., Mr. Marshal Gunter to Miss Eliza Gault, all of Lexington Dist.
Married on the 28th December by Mr. Samson Duffy, Mr. John K. Boatwright, of Lexington Dist., to Miss Ellendar, daughter of Richard Gregory of Edgefield District.
Married on the 27th inst., by Rev. J. H. Bailey, Mr. Jesse Dooly to Miss Sarah Ann Wilson, all of this District.
Married on Sunday, the 24th December, in Edgefield Disrict, by Rev. Henry Dunton, Mr. John Brown to Miss Martha Breare, both from England.
Married on Thursday the 23rd December, by Rev. William Berly, Mr. Luther Smith to Miss Mary Harman, both of this District.
Married on 30th November, by Rev. J. H. Bailey, Mr. Emmanuel Lybrand, to Miss Cornelia Hook.
Married on the 26th inst., by Rev. J. H. Bailey, Mr. James Shull to Miss Elizabeth Roff, all of this District.

THE LEXINGTON FLAG

Issue of March 12, 1857 [Volume 1, #5]
Died in Edgefield Dist., on the 3d inst., Mrs. Elizabeth Shealy, aged 56 years, 4 months, 29 days.

Issue of April 23, 1857
Died on Wednesday, the 15th inst., near Lexington Village, Joseph Wingard, aged 44 years and 16 days.
Died near Broad River, in the upper part of this District, on Saturday monrning, the 18th inst., Adam Stuck, son of Michael Stuck, aged 37 years, 4 months and 28 days.

Issue of September 10, 1857
Married in this District, on the 6th inst., by W. E. Sawyer, Mr. Willis Burnet, formerly of Edgefield District, to Miss Marrina Jones.

Issue of September 17, 1857
Married on the 10th inst.,by Rev. Mr. Bradly, A. D. Bates, Esq., to Miss Georgana Mitchell, all of Edgefield District.

Issue of October 29, 1857
Married in this District, on the 11th inst., by Rev. D. Efird, Mr. G. W. Summer to Miss Martha, daughter of George Epting.
Married on the 9th inst., by Rev. L. Eichelberger, D. D., Mr. Godfrey Gable to Miss Martha Louise Sharp, all of Lexington.
Married on the 4th inst., by Rev. D. Efird, Mr. John Shealy to Miss Catherine Dehart, all of this District.

Issue of February 25, 1858
Died January 22d in Barnwell District, S. C., Mr. J. S. DeGaffarelly, late editor of the "Lexington Telegraph"...in his 34th year...member of Methodist Episcopal Church... leaves a wife and 3 small children.

Issue of March 4, 1858
Married on Thursday, the 25th February, by Rev. D. Efird, Mr. D. Miller to Miss Mary Ann M. Stoudemire, all of Lexington District.
Died in this District, Mrs. Mary Barbara Holtawanger, widow of Mr. John G. Holtawanger, aged 94 years, 4 months and 7 days...burial service by Rev. D. Efird.

Issue of April 22, 1858
Married on the 18th inst., by Rev. A. Efird, Mr. J. J. Francklow to Miss Barbara Rickard.

Issue of August 19, 1858
Married on the 10th August, by Rev. J. Austin, Dr. J. R. Haltiwanger, to Emily S. Morgan, all of Springfield, Ga.
Married on Saturday, the 16th inst., near Clark's mills, Mr. Felix Poole, to Miss Marina Ricard, by James Clark, Esq.

Issue of September 30, 1859
Died on the 14th inst., of croup, Oscar Sylranus, infant son of Mr. Godfrey and Mrs. Serena Younginer, aged 1 year,4 months and 6 days.

Issue of June 16, 1859
Married on the 26th May last, by Rev. S. Bouknight, Rev. E. Caughman to Edgefield to Mrs. Nancy Mayers of Lexington.

Issue of August 4, 1859
Married on the 26th ult., by David Counts, Esq., Mr. G. W. Freshley to Miss Salinda Buzzard, all of Lexington.
Married on the 28th ult., by Rev. A. Efird, Mr. T. Harman, to Miss Lucy Robert, all of Lexington.

Issue of August 18, 1859
Died in this place, on the 7th August, in the 23d year of his age, Jno. W. Lee, Jr. son of J. W. and Mary Lee of Lexington [long eulogy].

Issue of December 15, 1859
Married on the 1st inst., by J. Keisler, Esq., Mr. Geo. Halman, Jr. to Miss E. C. Boland, all of this District.
Married on the 7th inst., by Rev. S. Bouknight, Capt. James Dudley of Leesville to Miss Nancy Fulmer of Edgefield.
Married on the 8th inst., by Rev. A. Efird, Mr. Wm Clapp, to Miss Margaret Baughman.
Married on the 1st inst., by Rev. E. Caughman, Mr. L. E. Lott to Miss Julia Yonce, all of Edgefield.

Issue of May 10, 1860
Married on the 29th April, by Rev. Wm. B. Curfie, Mr. Jacob Quattlebaum to Miss Zenovia A. Steedman, all of Lexington.

Issue of September 13, 1860
Died September 1, 1860, at her Brother's in Frog Level, S. C., Miss Caroline Spruse, in the bloom of youth...member of Colony Church, under the pastoral care of Rev. J. H. Bailey.

Died in this District, on Thursday the 6th inst., Mr. Paul C. Chapman, aged 27 years and some months...leaves a wife, a child and a sister.

Married by the Rev. J. L. Smithdeal, Aug 23, 1860, Mr. R. Calvin Boozer, to Miss Rhoda Lester, all of Newberry District, S. C.

Married on the 6th inst., by Rev. W. Werts, Mr. Samuel Shealy to Miss Susan Derrick, all of Edgefield.

LEXINGTON TELEGRAPH

Issue of November 3, 1853

Married on the 27th October, at the residence of Uriah Bauch, by Rev. Prof. Berly, Mr. W. M. Cook to Miss S. J. McNure, all of Lexington.

Issue of April 8, 1856

Departed this life in Emanuel Co., Ga., on 7th March 1856, Miss Rebecca E. Ward, aged 12 years, 1 month, and 22 days...born in Barnwell District, and resided there till she was 10 when her father moved to Georgia...her mother departed this life, when she was quite an infant...leaves father, sister, and stepmother.

Issue of June 8, 1846 [contd.]
Married on the 28th ult., by John Whitmore, Esq., Mr. Miles BEnnet to Miss Nancy Montgomery, all of this District.
Married in Greenville District, on Thursday the 21st inst., by Rev. Jonathan Deuese, Mr. Spartan Berry to Miss Jane Brown, formerly of Laurens District.
Married in Greenville District on Thursday, the 28th by Rev. Jonathan Deuese, Dr. Berry ____[torn] to Miss Eliza Donalson, all of the same place.

Issue of June 15, 1846
Married on Thursday evening, the 28th ult., by Rev. Silas Knight, Capt. Walter Stewart to Miss ____ Garrett, daughter of Mr. John Garrett, all of Laurens District.
Married in Spartanburgh District, on the 11th inst., by Rev. Tolivar Robinson, Dr. B. F. Nichols of Orangeburgh District, to Miss Eliza, daughter of Willis Dickie, Esq., of the former place.
Died in this village, on Tuesday the 9th inst., Capt. William Cornwell, in the 42d year of his age, a native of Springfield, Massachusetts, but for 19 years a resident of this place...in the cabinet making business.

Issue of June 29, 1846
Died on the 20th inst., at the residence of Mr. Jesse Fuller, her son-in-law in Laurens District, Mrs. Elizabeth Canant, widow of Maj. Hardy Canant, in the 95th year of her age...member of the Presbyterian Church.
Died at White Plains, Laurens District, on the 15th inst., after a short illness, Keturah Caroline, daughter of Col. J. D. and Phoebe C. Williams, in the 5th year of her age.
Died on the 25th inst., at the residence of Willis Benham, Esq., in Laurens District, Willis Benham Howard, infant son of J. J. & L. H. Howard, aged 3 weeks.

Issue of July 13, 1846
Married on the 25th inst., by Rev. J. W. McCall, Mr. W. B. McElroy to Miss Mary Alexander, all of Greenville District.

Issue of July 27, 1846
Lamentable Catastrophe. Dr. N. V. Bailey, the senior proprietor & editor of this paper, departed this life on the night of the 20th inst., about 12 o'clock, in the 24th year of his age...came to his death by a fall from his buggy...member of the Protestant Episcopal Church...[long obituary].
Died of typhoid fever at Huntsville, Laurens District, on the morning of the 4th inst., Mr. David Martin, in the 52d year of his age...born in Fairfield District, S. C. from which place he moved to this District. [eulogy].

Issue of August 10, 1846
Died on Monday 27 July last, at her residence near Waterloo, Laurens District, Mrs. Mary Finley, relict of Paul Finely, decd, in the 89th year of her age...[long eulogy].
Departed this life on the 29th ult., in the 70th year of her age, Mrs. Rebecca Kennedy, consort of the Reverand and venerable John B. Kennedy, and daughter of the late Dr. George Ross, Sr. [long eulogy].

Issue of August 24, 1846
Departed this life on the 6th inst., 8 miles NE of Laurens, Mrs. Nancy Hitch, wife of W. W. Hitch, Esq., in the 45th year of her age...member of the Presbyterian Church... leaves husband, 3 daughters, and 3 sons.

Issue of August 31, 1846
Married on Thursday evening, the 28th inst., by Rev. Mr. J. L. Young, R. B. Leak, Esqr., to Miss Mary Jane, eldest daughter of James Copeland, Esq., all of this District.

Issue of September 7, 1846
Married on Thursday, August 6, by the Rev. J. L. Young, Mr. Robert A. Henry to Miss Jane Todd, all of this District.
Married by the same, on the 3d inst., Mr. Nathan Rodd to Miss Sarah E., daughter of James F. Blakely, all of this District.
Died at her residence in Spartanburg District, on the 22d ult., Mrs. Christina N. Foster, wife of Maj. Calvin Foster...leaves a husband and two infants...member of the Presbyterian Church.

Issue of September 21, 1846
Married on the 10th inst., by Rev. Silas Knight, Mr. Wiley Hughes to Miss Nancy Delong.
Married on the same day, by the same, Mr. William H. Franks to Miss Minima Power.
Married on the same day by the Rev. Tolaver Robertson, Elford L. Knight to Miss Sally

Power, all of Laurens District.
    Married on the 13th inst., by Jesse Cooper, Esq., Mr. John Waldrop of Alabama, to
Miss Elizabeth Farrow, of Spartanburg District.

Issue of September 28, 1846
    Married in this village on Tuesday evening last, by Rev. S. B. Lewers, Mr. F. Nance
to Miss Susan L. Burnside. Also at the same time and place, Mr. James C. Young to Miss
Sarah Watts, all of this place. [Marriages were on 22 Sept.]
    Married in Spartanburg District, on thursday evening, the 24th inst., by Rev. S. B.
Lewers, Mr. Thomas P. Park of Laurens to Miss Mary Ferguson.

Issue of October 5, 1846
    Married on Laurens District, on the 23rd ult., by W. W. Hitch, Esq., Mr. Jesse Sparks
to Miss Nancy McKitrick, all of Laurens.
    Married on the 16th ult., by Rev. S. B. Lewers, Dr. N. Henry to Miss Rosiana Renwick,
all of Newberry District.

Issue of November 9, 1846
    Died on Saturday the 10th October, Adam J. Stoddard in the 26th year of his age...a
teacher of our youth...his aged father & sisters were standing by his bed....

Issue of December 7, 1846
    Married on Tuesday the 1st inst., by Rev. S. B. Lewers, Mr. Robert McLintock to Miss
Isabella Hunter.
    Married on the same day, by Dr. D. F. Hadden, Mr. R. F. M. Cowan, to Miss Mary Thomp-
son, all of Laurens District.

Issue of December 28, 1846
    Married on the 8th inst., by Rev. Mr. Holtom, Maj. A. C. Garlington of this place,
to Miss S. L. Moon of Newberry District.
    Married on the same evening by Rev. S. B. Lewers, Dr. D. L. Anderson to Miss M. E.
Nickels of this District.
    Married on the 26th ult., by Jas. Clardy, Esq., Dr. W. Clardy to Miss Sarah, daughter
of Ira Arnold, all of Laurens District.
    Married on the 22nd inst., by Rev. Silas Knight, Mr. Washington Fillaland of Georgia,
to Miss Sarah Ann Brock of Laurens.
    Married on the 26th ult., by Rev. Elbert Lindsey, Mr. James Meador of Laurens to Miss
Mary S. McKitrick of Newberry.

Issue of January 21, 1853
    Married on the 13th inst., by Rev. D. F. Hadden, Mr. A. Coleman to Miss Matilda
Thompson, all of Laurens.
    Married on the 20th inst., by the Rev. Tolaver Robinson, Mr. John Boyd to Miss Jane
Henderson, all of this District.
    Died on the 24th ult., in this District, Mr. Jefferson James, in the 26th year of his
age, at his father's residence, leaving a wife and one child....

Issue of January 28, 1853
    Died in this District, on the 22d inst., after a short illness, Mrs. L. M. Luke,
consort of J. Y. Luke, in the 20th year of her age...attached herself to the Baptist
Church in 1849.
    Died on the 8th ult., of Typhoid Fever, at his residence in this District, William
R. Fowler, leaving a wife and 4 small children...member of Mt. Pleasant Baptist Church.
    Married on Thursday, the 27th inst., by Rev. A. P. Norris, Dr. H. R. Godman of Col-
umbia, to Miss E. Ward of Edgefield District.
    Married on the 23d of last month, by Rev. S. Sprewel, Capt. Benjamin Hitt to Miss
Sarah Austin, all of Laurens.
    Married on the 13th inst., by Rev. S. Sprewel, Mr. James W. Chandler to Miss Emmeliza
Teague, all of Laurens.
    Married on the 13th inst., by Rev. Jesse Motes, Mr. Y. J. H. Pitts to Miss Martha A.,
daughter of Rachel and Ephraim Pitts.

Issue of February 4, 1853
    Died at the residence of her father, Allen Barksdale, Esq., near this place, on
Thursday the 27th ult., Miss Mary Barksdale, in the 33d year of her age...a few months
ago the aged parents were with with profound grief at the death of a son who had left
the parental roof to seek his fortune in the distant West.

Issue of February 11, 1853
    Married on December 22, by Wm. B. Boyd, Austin Workman to Margaret Liles.

124

Issue of February 11, 1853 [contd.]
Married on December 23, by the same, John Day to Miss Martha, daughter of Henry O'Neal, Esq.
Married on January 11, by the same, Lafayette Turner to Catherine Coats.
Married on January 27, by the same, James Cheek of Laurens, to Miss Elizabeth, daughter of Maj. Nesbit of Greenville.
Married on January 30 by the same, J. Clark to Martha Clark.

Issue of February 18, 1853
Married on the 3d February by Rev. McWhorter, W. H. Sheldon of Spartanburg, to Margaret S. Glenn of Pickens, daughter of A. W. and J. Glenn.

Issue of February 25, 1853
Married at Greensboro, N. C. on the 30th December last, by Rev. E. W. Caruthers, J. H. Baker of this place, to Miss Martha C. Young, daughter of the late Col. Mathew Young.
Married on the 10th inst.,by Rev. Tolaver Robertson, Mr. Wiley Fowler to Miss Nancy Mary Riddle.
Married at the same time by the same, Mr. Thomas Martin to Miss Elizabeth Riddle., all of Laurens District.
Married on the 10th inst., by Rev. Silas Knight, Fleming DeLong to Miss Margaret DeLong, all of this District.
Died in this place on the 18th inst., Mr. Robert H. McClintock, in the 25th year of his age...had entered upon his last term in the Medical College of a neighboring State... associated himself with the Luther Church in 1851...[eulogy].

Issue of April 22, 1853
Married on the 20th March in Oktibbeeha[sic], Mississippi, by Elder S. W. Woolard, Mr. J. H. Abercrombie to Miss Mary A. Coater, of Laurens District, S. C.
Died at her residence Nov. 8, 1852, Mrs. Levinia Parmelia Lindsey, consort of T. F. Lindsey of Choctaw Co., Mississippi, and daughter of Benjamin and Rebecca Martin of Laurens District, S. C....born July 4, 1820, professed religion in the 13th year of her age and was baptized into the fellowship of the Baptist Church...leaves six children.
Departed this life near Looxahoma, DeSoto Co., Mississippi, 25 March 1853, Miss Sarah A. Brownlee, a native of Laurens District...member of the Methodist Church...leaves an aged and infirm mother...but six weeks had elapsed since the death of a son[of her mother].

Issue of May 13, 1853
Died of Paralysis of the lungs, at her residence near Scuffletown, Friday the 13th inst., Mrs. Sarah, wife of Samuel McIntyre, leaving a husband and five step-children... a few days previous her husband left to visit Mississippi and Georgia.

Issue of June 3, 1853
Died at his residence four miles from Laurensville, on the 6th of April, Col. Robert Milam in the 49th year of his age...commander of the 10th Regt. of S. C. Cavalry.

Issue of June 24, 1853
Married on the 14th, by the Rev. J. C. Vaughan, Mr. John Dean of Newberry District, to Miss Emily Coleman of Laurens District.
Died on the morning of the 18th inst., of colitis, Mary Henrieeta, only child of William H. and Elizabeth Pool, aged 3 years, 1 month and 2 days.

Issue of July 1, 1853
Departed this life on the 8th ult., at the residence of her father, in the upper part of this District, Mary C., daughter of William & Abigail Ellison, in the 9th year of her age.

Issue of July 8, 1853
Departed this life on the 4th May 1853, John M. youngest son of Reubin G. and Caroline Ball, aged 3 years, 8 months, and 11 days.
Departed this life in Looxahoma, Mississippi, 20 June 1853, Caroline Rhett, only daughter of Samuel and R. J. Lewers, aged 1 year 10 months and 1 day.

Issue of July 15, 1853
Married on the 7th inst., by Rev. R. Rabb, Mr. Samuel Avery to Miss Sarah Parker.
Died at the residence of Raply Owens, 6 July, LaFayette C. Cheshire, aged 30 years.
Died in Newberry Village, on Tuesday the 21st June, Mr. Robert Thompson, aged 36 years, 2 months, and 21 days...born of Abraham and Nancy Thompson in Laurens District...member of the A. R. P. Church at Head Spring...moved to Newberry District in 1846 and married Miss Eliza K. Davis in 1848...he was desirous to have his wife and children baptized....

Died on Sunday morning, the 3rd inst., Mrs. Elizabeth, consort of Hargrove Miller, aged 38 years, 9 months, 24 days...leaves a husband, two daughters and one son.

Died near Cokesbury, Abbeville District, Tuesday the 28th June, John Harrison, son of J. K. and Laurens L. Vance, aged 2 years and 24 days.

Issue of July 29, 1853

Died on the 14th inst., near Greenwood, S. C. in the 5th year of his age, Rosa, daughter of Jas. & Hariet Baily.

Issue of August 5, 1853

Married on the 28th July, by Rev. W. McCall, J. R. Childress to Miss Ann, daughter of William and Hannah Dial, all of Laurens District.

Departed this life on the 23d ult., near Laurens C. H., in the 20th year of her age, Miss Sarah L. Martin, daughter of Harbert and Margaret Martin...became member of the Baptist Church at Chesnut Ridge in 1849...In her last illness, called her father, mother, brothers, and sisters....

Issue of August 12, 1853

Married on the 4th inst., by Wm Power, Esq., Mr. Lewis R. Burns to Miss Mahany, daughter of Abner and Mahany Putnam.

Died in this village, on the 11th inst., Ida Florence, daughter of Richard and Harriet Denton, aged 3 months and 17 days.

Issue of August 19, 1853

Died at the residence of Mr. S. L. Davis, on the 31st July, in the 5th year of her age, Nancy E., eldest daughter of Robert, lately deceased, and E. K. Thompson.

Issue of September 9, 1853

Died on the 9th of July, of consumption, at the house of his brother, James A. Hill, near New Albany, Pontotoc Co., Mississippi, Mr. Robert P. Hill, aged 35 years, 6 months and 29 days...born and raised in Laurens District, S. C., emigrated to the place of his decease a few years ago....His remains were deposited by the side of his mother in the graveyeard at Cherry Creek Church...left one brother.

Died on the 20th ult., at the residence of Davis Williams, near Martin's Depot [now Joanna, S. C.], in this District, Miss Jane Busby, aged about 78 years...member of the Baptist Church about 40 years.

Issue of September 30, 1853

Died at his residence in this District, on Thursday, the 22d inst., John Felts, aged 69 years, 7 months and 3 days, leaving a disconsolate wife and two dutiful children... for at least 20 years, a member of the Baptist Church.

Died on the 20th ult., in Laurens District, Mr. William L. Duval, in the 33d year of his age...for 10 years, a member of the Baptist Church at Union.

Issue of October 21, 1853

Died on the 11th inst., Mr. John F. R. Saxon in the 27th year of his age. The deceased has left an affectionate wife and a large circle of relatives to lament....

Died on the 9th inst., in this District, Mrs. Maria E. Jones, wife of Maj. W. J. M. Jones, and daughter of Dr. W. T. Jones, in the 30th year of her age...in early life joined the M. E. Church...she has left a husband and child, father, brothers and sisters, and a large connexion[sic]....

Died on the 8th inst., Mrs. Martha A. Ramage, in the 27th year of her age. She was the daughter of Thomas and Elizabeth Blakely of Duncan's Creek, and has left an affectionate husband and tender child...a member of Bethany Church....

Departed this life at his residence near Cross Hill, on the 26th September, Mr. James Lowe, born in 1800 and married at an early period...joined the Baptist Church in 1832.

Died at his residence in Greenville District, John McDowel Terry, in the 58th year of his age...member of the M. E. Church.

Married on the 4th inst., by Rev. E. Lindsay, Woodbury H. Farrow to Mrs. Mary A. Rook, all of Newberry.

Married on the 7th inst., by the Rev. Jesse Motes, Mr. R. H. Goodman, to Miss E. Austen, all of Laurens District.

Issue of October 28, 1853

Married on the 19th inst., by Rev. E. Lindsay, Maj. John Johnson to Miss Margaret Dalrimple, all of Laurens District.

Married on the 25th inst., by Rev. Samuel Leard, Dr. J. C. Paslay to Miss Mary Smith, all of Cokesbury.

Died at his residence in DeSoto Co., Miss., on Sunday, the 19th June last, Drury G. Boyce, in the 34th year of his age...formerly a citizen of Laurens District, S. C. But a short time before the sad misfortune, his family and friends had to mourn the loss of a lovely and only living son, Samuel Downs Boyce, in the 9th year of his age. Thus, in the space of a month or two, his wife and three daughters have been bereft of a husband and son, father and brother...[eulogy].

Issue of November 4, 1853
Married on the 20th ult., by W. D. Watts, Esq., Mr. Young E. Wood to Miss Elizabeth J. Taylor, all of Laurens District.

Married on the 2d ult., by Rev. M. Donally, Mr. L. Martin to Miss C. E. Henderson.

Departed this life on the 22d ult., in Newberry District, Mrs. Lewra B. Watson, daughter of John and Mary Reeder, and consort of James E. Watson, in the 21st year of his age... member of the Baptist Church at Bush River...left a husband and one child.

Died on the 22d ult., Mary Cornelia, daughter of Dr. John F. and Mary Dorroh, aged 2 years, 7 months, and 11 days.

Issue of November 11, 1853
Married on Thursday, the 27th ult., by Rev. C. S. Walker, Mr. A. E. Stoddard to Miss Mary A. Dansby, all of the town of Newberry.

Died on the 9th October, Mary Eliza, only daughter of John F. and Martha E. Saxon, aged 18 months.

Issue of November 18, 1853
Married on the 6th inst., in Merriwether Co., Ga., by James F. A. Peebles, Esq., John Milam, formerly of Laurens District, S. C. to Miss Irene C. Evans.

Departed this life on the morning of the 25th October, Laura Anne Carmichael, first born child of Dr. Patrick and Mary Todd of Lexington District, aged 22 years...funeral conducted by Rev. J. H. Bailey.

Died at his residence in this District, on the 7th inst,, James Y. Rodgers, in the 45th year of his age, leaving a wife and four children...member of the Baptist Church.

Issue of November 25, 1853
Married on the 17th inst., by W. H. Langston, Esq., Mr. Wm Sims of Georgia, to Miss Eliza Wallace of this District.

Married at the residence of Mr. John Ferguson, by W. D. Watts, Esq., Mr. Wilkerson Milam to Miss Belinda Taylor, all of Laurens District.

Departed this life, Mrs. Mary McClintock Murrell, in the 33d year of her age...entered her marriage relation 18 months age...Her husband set out to make a home in the "Great West" intending to return for his partner...left an infant....

Died in this village on Saturday morning last, Maj. W. J. Blakely, in the 30th year of his age.

Died on the 17th inst., at Richland, Holmes Co., Miss., E. B. Green...the 31st year of his age...born in Laurens District, moved to Mississippi in March, 1848

Died in Oktibeha Co., Miss, on the 30th ult., Mrs. Mary A., wife of James H. Abercrombie, in the 40th year of her age...daughter of Joseph and Sarah Cooper, born in Abbeville District, resided in Laurens District 10 years previous to her removal to Miss. ...member of Pleasant Grove M. E. Church in this district...a devoted wife and kind stepmother.

Issue of December 16, 1853
Married in Trinity Church, Columbia, on the 13th inst., by Rev. P. J. Shand, Mr. John Waties, of Stateburg, Sumter District, to Miss Fannie C., daughter of Dr. Parker, of this place. Carolinian.

Died on the 21st of October at the residence of her daughter in Greenville District, Mrs. Sarah Graydon in the 84th year of her age, and her 30th year in the membership of the Baptist Church.

Issue of June 1, 1849 [in private hands; found at the last minute!]
Married in this District on the 22nd ult., by Rev. E. Lindsay, Maj. A. P. Martin to Miss K. G. Gary.

Married in Fairfield District, on the 24th ult., Col. Elias Earle, of Greenville, to Miss Mary Cloud.

Married in Abbeville District, on the 20th ult., by the Rev. J. C. Vaughan, John Stribling, Esq. of Newberry to Miss Frances Childes.

Married at Eufaula, Ala., on the 10th ult., Tennent Lomax, Esq., editor of the "Eufaula Democrat," and formerly of Abbeville District, to Miss Sophia H. Shorter.

Married in Abbeville District, on the 26th ult., by Rev. T. L. McBryde, Mr. James Carlisle to Miss Mary Jane Manning.

Married in Abbeville District, on the 17th ult., by Rev. B. Corley, Mr. William D. Calhoun to Miss Eleanor Jones.

Married at Earle's Furnace, Cass Co., Ga., on the 10th ult., by Rev. John W. Lewis, Col. E. M. Fields, of Canton, to Miss Cornelia M. Harrison, formerly of Greenville, S. C.

Married in Pickens District, on the 15th ult., Andrew J. Dorsey to Miss Nancy Isabella Colhoun.

Married in Pickens District, on the 17th ult,, William M. Gassaway to Miss Jane McWorter.

Married in Caswell County, N. C. Major Thomas T. Slade, of Lincolnton to Miss Emeline H. Cobb.

Died in this District, on the 12th ult., Mr. Howard Pinson, aged about 73 years.

Died in this District, on the 30th ult., Julia E. Q., infant daughter of R. & J. W. Brown.

Died in Anderson District, on the 12th ult., Miss Sarah Ann Robinson, aged 27 years.

Hoyt, J. P., Col. 86
  Mary E. 86
Huckabee, G. W., Rev. 72
  J. W. 109
Huckaby, Richard 6
Hudgens, John, Col. 42
  John Henderson 42
  Sally 36
  W. L. 39
Hudson, D. R. 49
  Joshua H. 62
  J. W. 53
  M. A., Mrs. 90
  Martha T., Mrs. 53
  Mattie 90
  M. T. 90
  N. S., Mrs. 49
  Sarah Rebecca 49
  Z. P. 7
Huey, John T. 108
Huff, Thomas 60
Huggins, H. H., Dr. 62
  Mary 94
Hughes, Frances 77
  Hesekiah 52
  H. R. 4
  Wiley 122
  William T. 52
Hughey, Harlan 70
  Harlin 70
  Rebecca 70(2)
Hughston, Eliasha 98
  Elisha 77
  George N. 97
  Margaret, Mrs. 77, 98
Hughy, Ann 16
Huiet, Ann, Mrs. 46
  John, Col. 46
  E. Statira 46
Humbert, J. G., Rev. 11, 73
  J. H., Rev. 10, 11
Humphrey, Susannah M. 86
Humphreys, D., Rev. 8(2), 55,
  85
Humphries, D., Rev. 7, 15
  James F. 77
  J. C. 109
  Missouri, Mrs. 104
  Stephen 61
  Thompson S. 1, 96
Humphris, Susanna 56
Hunt, Jane 73
  R. G. 81
  W. A., Gen. 109
Hunter, Elizabeth 20
  Henry M. 21
  I. E. 29   Isabella 123
  John 35
  John, Judge 22
  M. A., Dr. 6
  Margaret 26
  Mary Ann 91
  Mary Ann Elizabeth 21
  Mathew 26
  M. H. 34
  M. M., Dr. 2
  N. A. 9
  Nancy, Mrs. 35
  R. C., Dr. 24
  Robert 27
  Susan, Mrs. 27
  Susan E. 110
  William 39, 73
Hurt, Isham 73
Huskey, Clementine 89
  Mary 56
Hutchins, Abner 109
Hutchinson, A. S. 17
  Isabella, Mrs. 17
  Martha Minerva 17
Hyde, E. F., Rev. 3, 4, 9,
  56
Irby, James H., Jr. 34

Irby, Cont.
  Samuel H. 4
  William, Capt. 15
Irivn, Dolphus 72
Irvin, Rev. Mr. 40
  C. M., Rev. 27
  William 56
Jacks   , Isaac 13
  Thomas S., Dr. 5
Jackson, Addie M. 74
  C. H. 69
  Foster 60
  Frederick 64
  Frederick Sr. 102
  Mary Greer, 102
  Mary Jane 90
  Polly(?) 13
  Polly, Mrs. 26
  Robert 86
  Samuel 26
  Susannah 64
  T. R. 46, 78
  William 13
Jacobs, Rev. Mr. 50
James, A. A., Rev. 46, 47, 60,
  70, 85, 88, 89(3)
  Albert A., Rev. 77, 87
  Benjamin 10
  Elias 72
  G. W. 105
  James M. 71
  Jefferson 123
Jamison, Henry 64
  Shadrach 5
Jaratt, G. W. 17
Jarrott, C. J. 78
Jason, John 7
Jefferies, James 64
  John, Capt. 64
  Nancy Elmira, Mrs. 70
  Rachel 64
Jeffries, Davis 93
  James, Col. 55
  Permelia Ann 55
Jenkins, Col. 98
  M. J., Capt. 24
Jennings, John, Rev. 59
  M. Louisa 59
  Sarah Ann 27
  William 107
Jeter, Antoinette 33
  · Arsinoe M. 93
  Camillus, Rev. 62
  J. T. Rev. 85
  L. A. 85
  T. B., Capt. 75, 93
Johns, John 49
  Martha E. 49
Johnson, Rev. Mr. 81
  Abigail 89
  A. M., Lieut. 43
  Andrew 36
  Benjamin 20
  Benjamin, Rev. 110
  Bettie G. 25
  Burris 17
  David V. 115
  Henry 6
  Hosea Anderson 115
  J. 13
  James Edwin 20
  James H. 113(2)
  Job 24
  John 13, 71
  John, Maj. 125
  John Jones 79
  Lydia 114
  Margaret S. 42
  Mark M., Dr. 25
  Martha A., Mrs. 17
  Mary 34
  Mary, Mrs. 20
  Mary T. 12

Johnson, Cont.
  Nancy, Mrs. 109
  N. L., Mrs. 36
  Rachel, Mrs. 113
  Rachel N. 113
  Rachel Welch 113
  Rebecca 13
  Roberts, Rev. 85
  Samuel S. 46, 77
  Sarah 115
  Talitha 89
  Thomas C. 10
  Washington, Rev. 103, 104
  William 87
  William A. 88
  William James 17
Johnston, James 4
  Mary Ann 48, 91
  M. S. 28
  W. B., Rev. 106
Jolly, Kesiah 89
  Mary 84
Jones, Dr. 65
  ___ 117
  Abner Sr. 21
  Amy, Mrs. 9
  Benjamin F., Jr. 35
  B. F. 20
  B. G., Rev. 75
  B. S., Col. 37
  Carra, Mrs. 69
  C. F., Rev. (D.D.) 48, 92
  Cornelia 7
  Demerious 96
  E. 27
  Eleanor 126
  Elizabeth, Mrs. 30
  Eliza L. 24
  Ellen 4
  Emily, Mrs. 7
  E. P., Col. 86
  Georgianna 86
  James A. 4
  J. M., Mrs. 23
  J. N. 23
  John H. 42
  Joseph 30
  Lewis 94
  Maria E., Mrs. 125
  Marrina 119
  Marina G. 51, 94
  Martha 27
  Nancy, Mrs. 11
  Richard 1
  Roland 23
  Sarah Ann 23
  Sarah Ann, Mrs. 35
  S. B., Rev. 36, 37
  Simpson, Rev. 26
  T. F., Gen. 7
  Thomas 15
  T. R. 30
  W. H. 117
  William A. 110
  W. J. M., Col. 24
  W. J. M., Maj. 125
  W. T., Dr. 125
Jordan, ___ 104
  Daniel 4
Joy, John R. 18
  Margaret Ann 18
  Sarah A. 18
Joyce, E. E. 71
  Hattie 77
Judd, Catherine F., Mrs. 83
  David C. 83, 89
Junior, Andy 6
Keisler, J. 120
Keith, Eliza 4
Kellar, Wilson 15, 58
Keller, David 23
Kelley, Angeline C. 78
Kelly, Eliza F. 117

www.ingramcontent.com/pod-product-compliance
Lightning Source LLC
Chambersburg PA
CBHW072136020426
42334CB00018B/1822